JUDICIAL REVIEW
IN PERSPECTIVE

JUDICIAL
REVIEW
IN PERSPECTIVE

Lee Bridges
George Meszaros
Maurice Sunkin

Cavendish
Publishing
Limited

Published in Great Britain 1995 by Cavendish Publishing Limited, The Glass House, Wharton Street, London WC1X 9PX.

Telephone: 0171-278 8000 Facsimile: 0171-278 8080

First published by Public Law Project

© Public Law Project and Sunkin, M 1995

Second Edition   1995

British Library Cataloguing in Publication Data. A catalogue record for this book is available from the British Library.

ISBN 1-85941-203-3

Printed and bound in Great Britain

Foreword

by Mr Justice Brooke
Chairman of the Law Commission

I was delighted to be asked to write a short Foreword to this new edition of *Judicial Review in Perspective*. As its authors say, attitudes towards judicial review have traditionally been based on the experience of those of us who are involved in it: there has not been much imput from the detailed and painstaking investigations in which they are such specialists. This new edition of their book illustrates vividly the problems they have identified over certain aspects of people's access to judicial review. It also illuminates the uneven spread of the relevant skills in lawyers' offices around the country.

The first edition cast light on some of the weaknesses in the system in the late 1980s: for example, the inconsistencies between judges in the way they were granting leave. Chapter 4 of this new edition throws up a series of worrying new questions. Why, for instance, did only 2% of legal aid applicants in a three-month period come from that great expanse of England between Leeds and Bradford in the south and Newcastle in the north? Or why do 20% of appeals against legal aid refusals take over three months to hear? The publication of this new evidence poses as many uncomfortable questions for the solicitors' profession and the legal aid authorities as the earlier research should have posed for the judiciary.

In this book reference is made, not always in ecstatic terms, to the Law Commission's recent report on Judicial Review. Our recommendations were made as part of a balanced package, and we did not expect to please everybody all the time. The authors will be pleased to know that our idea of a smaller cadre of judges to hear leave applications is already dead. And I have always been relaxed about the use of the expression 'serious issue' (a term which works well in private law): we had no intention of moving the goalposts, but we do need an expression to weed out the utterly trivial as well as the application that is not properly arguable.

Today the prospective waiting time in Part II of the Crown Office List is down from 23 months to 5: a huge judicial success story. In contrast, there is now evidence that in a sample of applications for leave between January and September 1994 80% of the 186 applications by litigants in person were refused: another set of variables to tease out in the author's next project?

Henry Brooke
3 August 1995

Preface

In 1991 the Lord Chancellor announced that the Law Commission would undertake a comprehensive review of the procedures and remedies available through judicial review.[1] Coinciding with this announcement, the Public Law Project, in collaboration with Maurice Sunkin of the University of Essex, launched a major empirical study of access to and the use of judicial review. The research was supported by a generous grant from the Nuffield Foundation.

The first findings of the research were published by the Public Law Project in 1993[2] relating to an analysis of applications for judicial review made in the three year period, 1987–1989 and in the first quarter of 1991. The aim of this earlier publication had been to present as comprehensive a picture as possible on the volume and nature of applications for judicial review and of the subsequent processing and judicial determination of those applications, in order to assist both the Law Commission and its consultees.[3]

This second revised and expanded edition of *Judicial Review in Perspective* up-dates the original report. In particular, we are now able to present the results of further analysis of our original data on the progress of leave applications considered by individual judges through to their final outcome and new data on legal aid applications to take judicial review proceedings.

Since publication of the original study the Law Commission has issued its final report and recommendations on reform of the judicial review procedure,[4] and these are now being considered by the Government. Although we do not agree with all the Law Commission's conclusions, we are pleased that our research was of value to its enquiry. We now take the opportunity to comment, where appropriate, on some of the Law Commission's proposals in the light of our findings.

As well as its use by the Law Commission, the original report has been cited in Parliamentary enquiries, in the law reports, and in the academic literature on judicial review. It is pleasing to see that there is a growing demand for empirical information on judicial review to be used for policy-making and for teaching and analytical purposes in

---

1   Cmnd 1556 Law Commission *Fifth Programme of Law Reform*, London, HMSO, 1991.

2   M Sunkin, L Bridges and G Mészáros, *Judicial Review in Perspective: An Investigation of Trends in the Use and Operation of the Judicial Review Procedure in England and Wales*, Public Law Project, 1993.

3   Law Commission Consultation Paper No 126, *Administrative Law: Judicial Review and Statutory Appeals*, London, HMSO, 1993.

4   Law Commission Report No 226, *Administrative Law: Judicial Review and Statutory Appeals*, HMSO, 1994.

universities. We are grateful to Cavendish Publishing for giving us the opportunity to make our research accessible to a much wider audience.

We wish to extend our thanks to the Nuffield Foundation and to its Deputy Director, Pat Thomas, for their support for our research. Also, our research on judicial review applications would not have been possible without the co-operation and assistance of Lynne Knapman and her staff in the Crown Office, who have always been ready to accommodate our many demands and put up with our intrusion into their work. We would also like to thank Roger Venne of the Lord Chancellor's Department for his assistance in obtaining access for the research to the Crown Office; Jack Beatson of the Law Commission for his invaluable support for and comments on our research; Anthony Barker of the Department of Government at the University of Essex for advice on coding classifications; Jerry Reid of Computing Services at the University of Essex for his guidance and continuous 'trouble-shooting' in our computer analysis of the data; and the staff of the Department of Law at the University of Essex for their support throughout the research. Maurice Sunkin is particularly grateful to the Department for allowing him study leave during the Spring term 1995, thereby enabling much of the writing of this edition to be undertaken. He would also like to mention the sad loss of his dear mother during the night of 2nd and 3rd of November 1995; she would have loved this book whatever the quality of its content.

Richard Green, Colin Stutt and Terry Coles of the Legal Aid Board Head Office in London all gave valuable advice and assistance in setting up the research on legal aid and judicial review, and this part of our study could not have been completed without the very considerable help of the staff in all thirteen Legal Aid Area offices throughout the country. The legal aid data were collected by Lynda Hiscock, who left the project shortly after finishing this work, and we would extend our thanks to her for completing this laborious task with the greatest efficiency and good humour.

The staff and management committee of the Public Law Project have supported the research throughout. Responsibility for the research findings and conclusions drawn in the report is solely that of the authors, and these do not necessarily represent the views of the Public Law Project.

LB
GM
MS
November 1995

Contents

Chapter 1

Introduction

Judicial review is the principal means by which the courts in this country exercise supervision over the conduct of central and local government and other public authorities.[1] Since undergoing substantial reform in 1977, the procedures for judicial review have been widely seen by legal commentators as having 'transformed the face of administrative law' and led to a 'torrent' of cases against public bodies being brought before the courts.[2] In 1984 the then Lord Justice Donaldson opened his judgment in *Parr v Wyre BC* with the following remark:

> The citizenry of this country ought to appreciate better that the Divisional Court ... provides a means of obtaining speedy assistance if they think they are oppressed by authority or that they are failing to receive the assistance which Parliament has required authorities to afford them.[3]

This statement reflected a view widely held among judicial and legal observers that use of judicial review should be encouraged and that access to the procedure was not problematical. The then Lord Justice Woolf reflected these views when, in his influential Hamlyn Lectures of 1989, he stated that:

> ... the simplified procedure and the length of hearings normally keep the cost [of judicial review] within reasonable bounds. There is therefore little risk of those who are moderately well off not being able to afford the costs of an application for judicial review.[4]

More recently, the main cause of judicial anxiety has not been any perceived lack of access to judicial review but rather the substantially increased numbers using the process and the resulting delays and workload pressures on judges and administrators in the Crown Office in London. Lord Justice Woolf in 1991 again reflected the mood of the time when he compared judicial review to a motorway where the:

---

1   The procedure is governed by the Supreme Court Act 1981, s 31 and RSC Order 53.

2   Justice-All Souls, *Administrative Justice: Some Necessary Reforms*, (1988) Oxford University Press, pp 1–2.

3   *Parr v Wyre BC* [1982] HLR 71, at 80.

4   Rt Hon Sir Harry Woolf *Protection of the Public: A New Challenge*, (1990) London: Sweet and Maxwell, p 101.

... tailback, or backlogs, are becoming more and more disturbing. The use of judicial review has grown and is continuing to grow at a pace with which the present structure cannot cope.[5]

He went on to report delays of 21 months to two years in judicial review cases coming on for hearing and a situation where for every case disposed of two more were entering the lists. Since then, the Law Commission has reported considerable improvements in the time taken to process judicial review cases, although the need to keep the caseload within manageable proportions continues to be a major impetus behind proposals for reform.[6]

In general, attitudes toward judicial review have been based on judicial and practitioner experience of the process rather than on any detailed investigation of access to and use of the procedure. Writing in 1984, Harlow and Rawlings commented:

Doctrine and case-analysis we possess; research into *who* litigates, how *often*, and in respect of *which* governmental activities, has been singularly lacking.[7]

Early work in this field was carried out by Sunkin, whose initial analysis published in 1987[8] was based on data collected from Crown Office records on civil applications for judicial review over the 1981-1986 period. From this analysis, Sunkin drew the conclusion that, despite the overall increase in the number of judicial review applications in this period:

Judicial review has provided a facility primarily used by applicants in a very limited range of subject areas against a correspondingly narrow band of public agencies ... It appears to have played a minimal role in the redress of grievances and has provided the community with a partial and limited check against government illegality.[9]

Following his initial study, Sunkin was able to extend his data collection to cover the 1987-89 period, and a preliminary discussion of his findings relating to this period was published in 1992.[10] Sunkin and

---

5   H Woolf, Administrative Law Bar Association Annual Lecture, 4 November 1991.

6   Law Commission Report No 226, *Administrative Law: Judicial Review and Statutory Appeals*, London: HMSO, 1994.

7   C Harlow and R Rawlings (1984) *Law and Administration*, London: Weidenfeld and Nicolson, p 257.

8   M Sunkin, 'What is Happening to Applications for Judicial Review?' (1987) 50 *Modern Law Review* p 432 (hereinafter Sunkin, 1987).

9   *Ibid*, pp 464–5.

10   M Sunkin, 'The Judicial Review Case-load 1987-1989' (1991) *Public Law* p 490 (hereinafter Sunkin, 1991).

Le Sueur also published an analysis of the handling of applications for leave to apply for judicial review based on two six-week sample periods in November/December 1988 and June/July 1989.[11]

In 1993 we published the preliminary findings of our study of access to and use of judicial review.[12] Publication of this research was timed to coincide with the Law Commission's further examination of judicial review and statutory appeals. Our findings were drawn on both by those who responded to the Law Commission's consultation paper[13] and by the Law Commission in its final report.

In addition to taking account of the Law Commission's proposals at various points, in this edition we present a very much revised, expanded and up-dated version of our research findings, including data published for the first time on the availability of legal aid for judicial review proceedings (Chapter 5) and new data analysis on the impact of judicial variations in leave decision on final outcomes in judicial review cases (Chapter 8).

Data sources

The research presented here is based on two separate sources of data. The first encompasses an extension of Sunkin's earlier collection and analysis of data on applications lodged with the Crown Office for judicial review. The second data source relates to applications lodged with the Legal Aid Board by those seeking financial assistance to pursue an application for judicial review. Brief details of each of these sources of data are given below, while fuller explanations of the methodologies employed in the study of Crown Office and Legal Aid Board records are set out in the Appendices.

Crown Office data

The data set employed in the present study builds on that already accumulated by Sunkin relating to all applications (both civil and criminal) for judicial review during the 1987-89 period. In particular, it involved extensive periods of data collection based in the Crown Office in London in order to complete and bring up-to-date information on applications made within this period and on their

---

11 A P Le Sueur and M Sunkin, 'Applications for Judicial Review: The Requirement of Leave' (1992) *Public Law* p 102 (hereinafter Le Sueur and Sunkin).

12 *Judicial Review in Perspective*, Public Law Project, 1993.

13 Law Commission Consultation Paper No 126, *Administrative Law: Judicial Review and Statutory Appeals*, London: HMSO, 1993.

subsequent processing and determination. In addition, a new and more comprehensive set of data was compiled on applications submitted during the first three months of 1991. A list of the information collected on each case is set out in Appendix 2.

Basic data were obtained on 1512 applications in 1987, 1224 applications in 1988, 1550 applications in 1989, and 454 applications in the first three months of 1991.[14] In addition, a short summary of the substantive issues involved in each application and any extra information on its results (eg reasons for withdrawal of application, awards of costs) were obtained in relation to the 1991 sample of cases.

Once data were collected from the Crown Office, considerable time was taken in classifying and coding this information and entering it on the computer database. This entailed not only some re-working of previous case classifications on the 1987-89 data[15] but, more important-ly, a major extension of the subject and respondent/applicant categories employed. The various categories and definitions used are described in Appendix 2. As a result of these processes, two data sets were created, one covering cases listed by number and date of inception and including a subject classification, applicant and respondent type, and the name of the applicant's legal representative (solicitors' firm but not barrister); and the second listing cases by number and showing each judicial action taken by date and judge involved. One important limitation of the database to be noted is that it divides cases into the calendar year of their inception, and it is not possible to inter-relate data across the different years covered. As a result, findings will for the most part be reported here in respect of applications filed in each of the year periods covered (1987, 1988, 1989, and the first quarter of 1991) rather than across the whole of the 4,740 judicial review cases included on the database.

It is important to emphasise at the outset that our data was compiled and analysed on a different, and in our view, more accurate and useful basis than that employed in compiling the official statistics on judicial review published each year in the *Judicial Statistics*. The official statistics provide a 'snapshot' of all decisions taken in the Crown Office list in any given calendar year, whether of not such decisions relate to applications first lodged at the Crown Office in the same year or in previous years. Thus, there is no direct relationship

---

14 This compares with 1,529 applications recorded in the official statistics in 1987, 1,229 in 1988 and 1,580 in 1989. Our data therefore provides coverage of 99% of all applications in 1987 and 1988 and 98% of those in 1989.

15 Such reclassifications partly account for the lack of direct comparability between findings reported here and Sunkin's previous analysis of the 1987–89 judicial review caseload (see Sunkin, 1991).

between the number of applications recorded in the official statistics as being received in a year and the decisions taken on leave or at substantive hearings in the same period, and it is not possible from these statistics to compute, eg accurate grant/refusal rates for applications, or to derive any information on such issues as delay in processing applications.

Our own data analysis was based instead on tracing through, as far as possible, the subsequent decisions taken on applications initiated within each of the calendar years, 1987–1989, and in the first quarter of 1991. This enabled us to compute grant/refusal rates accurately against the base figure on the number of applications made in the relevant year and also to calculate accurately the time taken to reach different decision stages. Finally, this basis of analysis provides a more useful means for examining changes in the pattern of applications and decision-making and in the extent of delay over time. As well as making direct comparisons with the official statistics difficult, it has also been necessary to allow a time gap between the most recent period covered by our research, of applications lodged in the Crown Office in the first three months of 1991, and the data collection itself, so as to ensure that sufficient information on the subsequent processing of these cases would be available. This report covers the results of cases as recorded in Crown Office records up to the end of April 1995.

Legal aid data

The second part of the study entailed the tracing, identification and gathering of data on an anonymous basis in respect of applications lodged with the Legal Aid Board's 13 Area offices relating to prospective judicial review proceedings. It had originally been hoped to collect data on applications over a full year, but for reasons described in Appendix 3 this proved impracticable, and the main data collection had to be limited to applications received in the Area office during the final three months of 1991.

A total of 905 legal aid applications relating to prospective judicial review proceedings were eventually identified as having been lodged during this three month period. The data collected on each of these cases were basically those contained in the main legal aid application form and on subsequent legal aid certificates or notices of refusal of legal aid, along with any other details of the proposed judicial reviews and substantive legal aid decisions that were available and information on the time taken to process cases through the various stages of legal aid decision-making process. Because of resource constraints, it was possible to maintain data collection only through to the end of 1992. Although the initial legal aid decision-making on the sample applications had been very largely completed by this time, in most cases information on the outcome of judicial reviews in relation to which legal aid had been granted or on the legal aid costs of such proceedings had not been reported.

In Chapter 2 we examine the changing pattern in the use of judicial review over the period covered by our research and subsequently. In Chapter 3 we analyse the use of judicial review by the type of applicant and areas of governmental activity being challenged. Here we also examine the geographical spread of applications. Chapter 4 looks at the participation of various types of legal services in judicial review cases. Chapter 5 examines the volume and distribution of legal aid judicial review applications by subject matter, geographical area and legal representative; various administrative aspects of the processing of such applications; and the nature and basis of decisions taken in relation to the grant or refusal of legal aid for judicial reviews. Chapter 6 provides a general overview of the processing of applications through the various stages of the judicial review procedure and of caseload demands at each stage. Chapter 7 analyses general policies and practices in relation to the leave stage, while Chapter 8 investigates the role of judicial discretion in leave decisions and its effects on the final outcome of applications for judicial review. Chapter 9 presents our conclusions.

Chapter 2

Changing Patterns in Use of Judicial Review

Judicial review has been increasingly celebrated, not least by the judiciary itself, as a means by which the citizen can obtain redress against oppressive government, and as a key vehicle for enabling the judiciary to prevent and check the abuse of executive power.[1] This study is concerned with exploring whether such popular images are reflected in the actual use being made of the judicial review system. In this chapter we start by considering the changing patterns in the use of judicial review. Here we examine the scale of judicial review litigation and the subject areas in which the process is used.

Nearly a decade ago Lord Justice Woolf, as he then was, commented on the growing judicial review caseload saying that:

> The statistics speak for themselves ... (they) ... show a convincing picture of an increasing need to resort to the courts for protection against alleged abuse by public bodies of their public duties.[2]

The official statistics on judicial review (see Appendix 1, Table A) appear to indicate that this observation is, if anything, even more appropriate today than it was then. They show that between 1981 and 1994 the number of applications for leave made each year increased over six-fold, from 533 to 3208, with an annual average rate of growth of 16%.[3]

Statistics relating to the number of applications for leave to apply for judicial review, however, can be somewhat misleading if read in isolation, obscuring both the way judicial review is being used and the nature of the caseload. Research in the mid-1980s, for example, showed that large numbers of applications in particular subject areas tended to

---

1   See, eg Lord Brown-Wilkinson's Foreword to M Supperstone QC & J Goudie QC *Judicial Review*, (1992) London: Butterworths. From a different perspective, see F Mount *The British Constitution Now*, (1993) London: Mandarin, p 261. For a popular example see D Rose, 'Silent Revolution', *The Observer*, 9 May 1993.

2   The Rt Hon Lord Justice Woolf, 'Public Law – Private Law: Why the Divide? A Personal View' (1986) *Public Law* 220, 222.

3   Growth was not constant throughout this period, however. In particular, in 1988 the number of applications for leave declined significantly. The most recent figures for 1994 show that the number of leave applications increased by 11% over 1993.

    The figures cited here differ in some respects from those produced in our first edition, due to the receipt of up-dated information from the Crown Office. In particular, the most recent data from the Crown Office indicate that 1,089 leave applications were received in 1986, rather than the earlier figure of 816 derived from the *Judicial Statistics* for that year.

mask the low levels of use of judicial review in many other fields.[4] Also, since such data concentrates on applications for *leave*, a procedure under which each case is subject to an initial vetting by a High Court judge to determine whether it is arguable and should be allowed to proceed to a full hearing and determination by the court[5] they do not reflect the effects of the leave stage itself in regulating the overall flow of cases through the procedure. In particular, they do not indicate what types of case are permitted to proceed past the leave stage and consequently cast little light on the nature of the issues that are actually being reviewed by the courts.

Needless to say, statistics on applications made tell us little about the scale of potential litigation. They reveal neither the volume of situations in which judicial review problems arise but are resolved without resort to the courts nor of litigants who seek but are refused legal aid and are therefore prevented from going to court. Nor do they indicate how many people have cause for challenging public bodies but whose problems are never diagnosed as raising judicial review issues.

If we turn to the official statistics with these limitations in mind, we find that although the number of applications rose over the past decade there was a steady decline in the proportion that were granted leave to proceed to a full hearing. During each of six years up to 1986 over two-thirds of applications for leave were granted. However, in 1986 the leave grant rate fell below 60% and, with the exception of 1987 and 1989, it continued to decline in each subsequent year. It fell to 37% in 1994. This decline meant that in 1994 the number of applications for leave was over six times higher than in 1981, but the number of cases granted leave was less than 3.5 times higher. This highlights the importance of the leave stage and is an issue to which we shall return in later chapters.

The official statistics (see Appendix 1, Table B) also indicate that the number of judicial reviews substantively determined each year[6] failed to keep pace with the numbers obtaining leave, at least up until 1993.

---

4   Sunkin, 1987.

5   The need to obtain leave even in order to have an initial judicial determination of a case is a particular feature of the judicial review procedure in England and Wales. The parallel procedure for judicial review in Scotland does not include a preliminary application for leave. In Northern Ireland leave is required but may in many circumstances be granted by a Master rather than a High Court judge. A requirement of leave is much more common in appellate jurisdictions. Judicial review does not involve an appeal as such, although, as its name implies, it does entail a review of decisions made by inferior courts and tribunals or other public bodies.

6   That is, those that reached a formal determination on their merits or were subject to formal consent orders, as opposed to being determined at the leave stage or being withdrawn with no determination having been made.

Diagram 2A

Numbers of Applications to Seek Leave for Judicial Review, Grants of Leave and Substantive Cases Determined, 1981-1994

1981 - 1994

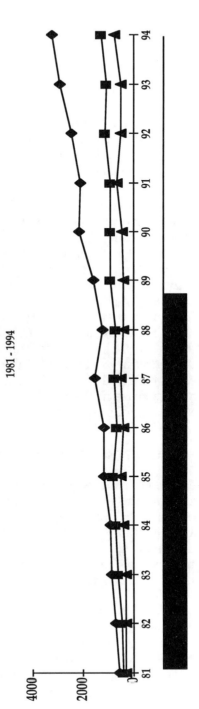

In this latter year, the number of judicial reviews substantively determined was just 1.8 times higher than in 1981. This widening gap between the number of substantive determinations made annually and the number applying for, and being granted leave (illustrated in Diagram 2A) helps to explain the lengthening delays in the judicial review procedure during the late 1980s and early 1990s. It may also be noted that the official statistics show that from 1988 onwards a significant number of applications for judicial review were withdrawn, apparently even after leave had been granted. Indeed, in 1992 such withdrawals constituted no less than 42% of the judicial review cases disposed of from the Crown Office list. By 1994 this proportion reached nearly 50%. The issue of withdrawals will be considered further in Chapter 6.

There were two years in the 1980s (1985 and 1987) when over 500 cases were substantively determined. In 1991, well over 600 cases were substantively determined, over half by way of consent orders. Many of these were probably related to the 300 applications concerning drink driving convictions lodged during the previous year. A further dramatic increase in the number of substantive determinations occurred in 1994 when 747 cases were finally resolved on their merits. This was 53% more than in 1993.[7] This increase may reflect the increase in judge time made available to judicial review cases. In 1992 there were 19 High Court judges nominated to deal with Crown Office matters. After falling to 17 in 1993 the number of nominated judges was increased to 22 in 1994 and 23 in 1995.[8] In addition there has been a substantial increase in the number of sittings and more widespread use of Deputy High Court judges.[9]

Judicial review and other forms of redress

One, albeit rather crude, way of placing judicial review in perspective is by comparing the number of applications for judicial review with the millions of decisions taken annually by government which could conceivably generate judicial review litigation. It has been said that such comparisons show that the number of judicial review cases is 'infinitesimal compared with the millions of decisions taken daily by public authorities'.[10] More revealing perhaps are comparisons between

7   20% of these were withdrawn by consent.
8   Information from the Crown Office.
9   See further Law Commission Report No 226, *op cit*, para 2.21 and Appendix C.
10   C Harlow and R Rawlings *Law and Administration* (1984) London: Weidenfeld & Nicolson, p 258.

the number of applications in particular subject areas, such as homelessness or benefits, and the numbers of potentially challengeable decisions taken by the relevant authorities. Such contrasts show, for example, that even in areas of 'mass use' the volume of judicial review litigation is tiny by contrast to the scale of administrative decision-making. In 1985 there were 66 known applications for judicial review challenging decisions of local housing authorities under the homelessness legislation.[11] During the same year 203,480 households (not individuals) applied to local housing authorities for assistance under this legislation. Less than half of these (93,980) were accepted by these authorities as entitled to assistance. This left over 100,000 whose applications were rejected and who constituted a potential pool for judicial review challenge.[12] In 1994, where there were 447 applications for leave to seek to review involving homelessness. By contrast in that year 299,053 households applied for assistance from local housing authorities and just over 127,000 were accepted as being entitled to some help.[13]

During 1993 social security tribunals received 161,208 cases, immigration adjudicators received 25,244 cases, and the Immigration Appeal Tribunal 6,559 cases.[14] When compared with the numbers of judicial reviews in each of these fields (see below) these figures also highlight the exceptional nature of recourse to judicial review.

Another contrast which may be made is that between use of judicial review and other procedures by which individuals can seek redress or complain against government, such as the Parliamentary Commissioner for Administration and the Commission for Local Administration (local government ombudsman). Diagram 2B plots applications for judicial review, complaints received by the Parliamentary Commissioner, and complaints received by the local government ombudsman in England over the period 1981-1994.[15]

The most striking feature of the diagram is the relatively rapid growth in resort to the local government ombudsman since the late 1980s. This contrasts with the much lower growth in the volume of

---

11 Now the Housing Act 1985.

12 Department of the Environment. In fact, since many litigants use judicial review to challenge the type of assistance offered, for example the quality of accommodation, the potential pool of litigants was much greater than this.

13 Data from Shelter.

14 Annual Report of the Council on Tribunals 1993–94 HC 22.

15 Another point of contrast might be with complaints handled by MPs. During the debates on the Parliamentary Commissioner Bill in 1967 it was estimated that MPs, in total, received about 300,000 complaints a year: HC Deb, 1966–67, 734, col 89. On MPs and complaints see: Richard Rawlings, 'The MP's Complaints Service' (1990) Vol 53 *Modern Law Review* 22 and 149.

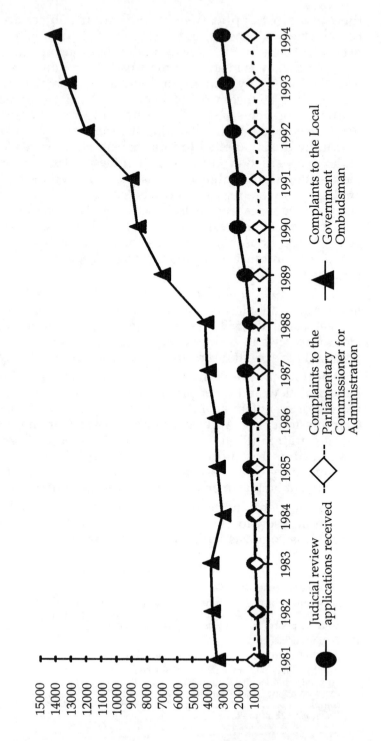

Diagram 2B

Judicial Review Receipts compared with Complaints received by the Local Government Ombudsman and the Parliamentary Commissioner for Administration, 1981-1994

matters handled by the Parliamentary Commissioner and the judicial review procedure. The growth in use of the local government ombudsman is particularly interesting in the light of our finding that much of the recent expansion in judicial review litigation has been accounted for by the increasing scale of legal challenge to decisions taken by local government rather than central government (see Chapter 3).

Subject areas of judicial review

We have seen in the introduction that the apparent rapid growth in the number of applications for judicial review has attracted a good deal of judicial comment. Such comment, however, has sometimes been unsubstantiated by empirical evidence, especially when addressed to applications in specific fields of litigation. Sunkin, in his analysis of the pre-1987 judicial review caseload, for example, was particularly critical of observations made by Lord Brightman in *Puhlhoffer v London Borough of Hillingdon*.[16] In delivering the unanimous judgment of the House, Lord Brightman said that the Housing (Homeless Persons) Act 1977 had resulted in a 'mass of litigation' and in 'the prolific use of judicial review ... [to challenge] ... the performance by local authorities of their functions under the [Act]'. He expressed hope that 'there will be a lessening in the number of challenges ... mounted against local authorities who are endeavouring in extremely difficult circumstances, to perform their duties' and called upon the High Court to grant leave in homelessness applications only if there were exceptional circumstances.[17]

Sunkin showed that despite these references to 'prolific' use of judicial review the number of homeless persons applications had up to then never exceeded 75 in any one year (1983) and that in the year prior to Puhlhoffer there had only been 66 applications. Moreover, of these applications only six had been refused leave, implying that the vast majority of these applications raised an arguable case of illegality.

The *Puhlhoffer* decision appears to have had two immediate, although temporary, effects on the caseload. First, the known number of homelessness judicial review applications fell, from 66 in 1985 to 32 in 1986. Second, there was a substantial reduction in the leave grant rate for homelessness applications, from over 90% to less than 70%, in the year following the decision.

---

16   [1986] 1 All ER 467.
17   *Ibid*, at 469, 474.

Sunkin's earlier analysis also showed that the number of judicial review cases relating to immigration had a far more significant impact on the overall caseload during the early 1980s than did homeless persons cases. Between 1981 and 1985 the immigration caseload increased more than three-fold, to a point where such cases represented nearly three-fifths of all civil judicial reviews. In fact, once immigration cases were excluded from the analysis, Sunkin's figures indicated that use of judicial review in all other civil fields actually declined by nearly a third between 1984 and 1985. This decline occurred at a time when the official statistics indicated an increase of 28% in the overall caseload. Equally, the reduction in the number of immigration judicial review applications between 1985 and 1986, from 516 to 409[18] (see Appendix 2, Table C), helped to contribute to the very limited overall growth in leave applications shown in the official statistics over those two years.

Turning to data drawn from our research, Table 2.1 shows the number of applications for leave in each subject area in which there were 10 or more applications in any one full year. As will be seen, the 23 subject areas listed in the table account for between 91% and 94% of all judicial review applications in the periods covered by our data. More significantly, applications relating to just three areas – crime, immigration and housing – dominated the use of judicial review throughout this time. These 'core areas' accounted together for between 57% and 68% of all leave applications.

General trends in immigration, housing and crime

Over the period of the research there were some significant shifts in the pattern of applications even in these major areas of use. These can best be seen in Table 2.2, which provides a simplified summary of the number of applications for leave over the study period. The number of applications for leave relating to immigration declined between 1985 and 1986 (see above), but rose sharply again in 1987, when immigration accounted for over 44% of all applications[19] and over half of those relating to civil matters. Following this peak the number of immigration applications fell sharply in 1988, after which there were smaller increases in the subsequent years covered by our research. The official statistics show that the volume of immigration cases was fairly steady during 1990-1992, at between 500 and 570 per annum. There

---

18 Or 44% of all civil cases.

19 For ease of reference, all figures in the text have been rounded up or down to a full percentage point.

Table 2.1

Applications for Leave to Seek Judicial Review by Subject Areas, 1987-1989 and 1st quarter of 1991

	1987		1988		1989		1991 (Jan-Mar)	
	No	%	No	%	No	%	No	%
Criminal:	214	14.2	164	13.4	219	14.2	71	15.6
Civil:								
Immigration	671	44.4	356	29.1	430	27.7	103	22.7
Housing	141	9.3	161	13.2	232	15.0	108	23.8
Planning	59	3.9	84	6.9	132	8.5	17	3.7
Family	42	2.8	44	3.6	26	1.7	7	1.5
Discipline	36	2.3	27	2.2	18	1.2	6	1.3
Tax	29	1.9	17	1.4	41	2.6	6	1.3
Education	27	1.8	24	2.0	46	3.0	27	5.9
Legal Process	25	1.7	43	3.5	36	2.3	20	4.4
Local Govt Affairs	25	1.7	37	3.0	38	2.5	17	3.7
Prisoners	17	1.1	25	2.0	16	1.0	5	1.1
Health	17	1.1	24	2.0	34	2.2	3	0.7
Environment	15	1.0	11	0.9	21	1.4	3	0.7
Employment	15	1.0	16	1.3	18	1.2	2	0.4
Rates	14	0.9	9	0.7	13	0.8	2	0.4
Agriculture	12	0.8	7	0.6	7	0.5	-	-
Transport	12	0.8	7	0.6	14	0.9	-	-
Legal aid	10	0.7	20	1.6	32	2.1	5	1.1
Coroners	10	0.7	9	0.7	15	1.0	3	0.7
Benefits	10	0.7	15	1.2	29	1.9	4	0.9
Trade	9	0.5	7	0.4	19	1.2	4	0.9
Compensation	6	0.4	6	0.8	11	0.9	9	2.0
Travellers	6	0.4	4	0.8	16	1.0	3	0.6
Other	90	6.0	107	8.7	123	7.9	29	6.4

was, however, further significant growth in the number of immigration applications in 1993 (668 applications) and 1994. Indeed, in 1994 the scale of immigration cases reached a new record level of 935 applications. This number represented a 40% increase over 1993 and was more than 30% higher than in 1987, the previous record year.

Table 2.2							
Applications for Leave to Seek Judicial Review by Major Subject Areas, 1987-1989 and 1st quarter of 1991							
	1987		1988		1989		1991 (Jan-Mar)	
	No	%	No	%	No	%	No	%
Criminal:	214	14.2	164	13.4	219	14.2	71	15.6
Civil: Immigration	671	44.4 (51.7)	356	29.1 (33.6)	430	27.7 (32.3)	103	22.7 (26.9)
Housing	141	9.3 (10.9)	161	13.2 (15.2)	232	15.0 (17.4)	108	23.8 (28.2)
Other	486	32.1 (37.4)	543	44.4 (51.2)	669	43.2 (50.3)	172	37.9 (44.9)

Figures in brackets show percentage of total civil applications in year represented by particular subject areas.

If we turn to the proportion that immigration cases constituted of the total judicial review caseload we find that in 1988 and 1989 immigration cases declined to below 30%, and to less than a quarter of the total caseload in the first three months of 1991. It remained at this level during the whole of 1991 and during the following two years. However, the proportion of immigration cases rose again in 1994 to just under 30% of all applications for judicial review.

The share of judicial review applications concerning housing increased throughout the period of the research, from 9% in 1987 to 24% in the first three months of 1991. It was only in the final six months of 1992 that the official statistics began to distinguish the number of one particular type of housing application, that relating to homelessness. During this half year there were 239 homelessness leave applications, representing an estimated 20% of all applications. This was a similar volume to that found by us during the first quarter of 1991. Although the actual number of homelessness leave applications in 1993 and 1994 remained constant, at 447 in each of these years, this represented a declining proportion of the overall judicial review caseload, to 15% in 1993 and 14% in 1994.

The third major area of judicial review litigation involves challenges concerning criminal matters. Our data show that criminal matters accounted for a remarkably steady percentage of all leave applications, at between 13% and 16% over our study period. The official statistics, however, indicate that in 1990, a year not covered by our data, there was a sharp rise in the number of criminal cases so that in that year these accounted for 29% of all applications. As indicated, this rise was apparently the result of a surge in challenges relating to the legality of certain drink-driving prosecutions and appears to have been an exceptional occurrence. The official statistics show that the overall proportion of leave applications relating to crime returned to between 14% and 16% during 1991-93 and declined to only 10% in 1994.

Other subject areas

Table 2.2 indicates that between 1987 and 1989 there was a 38% increase in the use of judicial review in what may be termed the 'non-core' areas, ie other than immigration, housing and crime. During this period the share of 'non-core' cases rose from 32% to 44% of the total caseload. By the first quarter of 1991, however, such applications accounted for just 38% of all cases, even though the actual number of 'non-core' applications was roughly comparable to the number in 1989.[20] In more recent years 'non-core' cases accounted for 1,229 leave applications in 1993 (45% of the total) and 1,505 in 1994 (47% of the total). These figures tend to confirm that although over half of all applications for leave to seek judicial review involved immigration, homelessness and crime, there has been a gradual expansion in the use of judicial review beyond these 'core' subjects.

Returning to the various individual subject areas listed in Table 2.1, there were only two subject areas beyond the 'core' fields of litigation that accounted for more than 5% of leave applications in any of the

20   There were 172 applications in the first quarter of 1991 representing a rate of approximately 688 per annum, compared to 669 in 1989.

periods covered by our research. These were planning (including land) and education. The former represented 7% of applications in 1988 and 9% in 1989.[21] Education accounted for 6% of applications in the first quarter of 1991. It might be speculated that the rate of applications for judicial review in planning would be sensitive to shifts in the housing and land development markets and might therefore have been influenced by the boom in property values during the late 1980s. On the other hand, the rise in judicial review applications in the field of education is likely to be explained by the 'politicisation' and 'judicialisation' of this field, particularly since the Education Reform Act 1988 which allowed schools to 'opt out' of local authority control and re-emphasised parental choice of schools. There has also been particular activity in judicial review involving challenges to local authority assessment of children with special educational needs, or their failure to carry out such assessments.[22]

Other less significant growth areas since 1987 are 'legal process',[23] local government affairs, legal aid (up to 1989), and travellers' cases (especially in 1988). Applications relating to family law matters showed an increase in 1987 and 1988 (42 and 44 applications respectively) from earlier data recorded by Sunkin,[24] but fell off in subsequent years. By contrast, prisoners' applications for judicial review, which accounted for 32, 42 and 64 cases in three six month samples in 1984, 1985 and 1986 respectively,[25] declined sharply to only 17 applications during the whole of 1987 and remained at a similar level throughout the period of the research.

Why are there so many areas where judicial review is not used?

The 23 subject areas listed in Table 2.1 (and the more than 160 included in the coding scheme covering the total sample of applications) are testimony to the potential breadth of judicial review. This presents one of the main puzzles associated with judicial review. Given the potential scope of litigation and that the procedure is perceived to be reasonably

---

21 Planning fell back to only 4% in the first quarter of 1991.

22 The incidence of judicial review applications concerning special educational needs may have been reduced since implementation of the Education Act 1993 and its introduction of new regional tribunals to deal with appeals. See further, Paul Meredith, 'Judicial Review and Education' in Brigid Hadfield (ed) *Judicial Review: A Thematic Approach* (1995) Gill and Macmillan.

23 Eg applications involving costs orders and decisions of taxing masters.

24 Sunkin, 1987, p 441.

25 *Ibid.*

accessible, and the law so dynamic, why are there so few challenges in so many key areas of governmental activity affecting vital rights and interests of individuals and groups? The decline in challenges by prisoners since the mid-1980s has already been noted, but equally significant is the fact that the whole structure of welfare benefits, encompassing millions of individual decisions about citizens' entitlements each year, produced at most 29 applications for judicial review in any of the years covered by our research. Similarly, while the 'politicisation' and 'judicialisation' of education in recent years may have led to a significant increase in judicial reviews in this area, the fields of health and environment, which have also been subject to major legislative activity and public controversy, appear to have been hardly touched by judicial review during the research period. This suggests that however accessible judicial review may seem in purely legal and procedural terms, other factors such as its geographical location (see Chapter 3), the availability of funding or of expert legal advice and assistance (see Chapters 4 and 5), or the perceived formality of the process continue to provide major barriers to its use.

It is important to stress that the data so far presented relate solely to applications for leave. As already indicated, the judicial review 'funnel' narrows sharply at the point of leave with the result that there are significant contrasts between the subject mix of the caseload before leave and after leave. This is an issue we will examine further in Chapter 6.

We now turn to look in more detail at the applications made in the two main fields of civil administrative law associated with judicial review, immigration and housing.

Judicial review and immigration

As we have seen, despite fluctuations in case numbers, immigration has remained the largest single area of use of judicial review throughout most of the past decade.

Prior to the Immigration and Asylum Act 1993, judicial review usually came into play in immigration cases in one of three ways. First, there were those situations in which individuals had rights of appeal from within the United Kingdom to an adjudicator and, with leave, to the Immigration Appeal Tribunal (IAT). These included cases in which someone was refused entry despite having obtained entry clearance and decisions affecting rights to remain in the United Kingdom after lawful entry had been obtained.[26] In this type of case judicial review

---

26   It included refusals to grant asylum to those who possessed visas.

tended to be used either to challenge the IAT's refusal to allow leave to appeal from an adjudicator or, where an appeal had been made, to challenge the ultimate decision of the IAT.

Second, there were those decisions against which there was no right of appeal from within the United Kingdom. These included most refusals of entry clearance and refusals to grant entry to those who arrived without entry clearance, as well as appeals against removal of alleged illegal entrants.[27] Unlike the first category, individuals in this group could only appeal from outside the United Kingdom, in some circumstances rendering the right of appeal 'virtually useless'.[28] Here judicial review was used either to challenge the immigration officer's decision prior to (or instead of) appealing or to challenge the IAT after an appeal from abroad had been made.

Use of judicial review prior to appealing became very common during the mid 1980s, particularly in 'genuine visitor' cases.[29] Indeed, 'genuine visitor' applications became numerically the most important single type of challenge, during 1985 accounting for approximately 20% all civil judicial reviews.[30] Mounting judicial concern that the judicial review procedure was being abused by applicants seeking to avoid the appeal procedure culminated in the Court of Appeal's decision in *ex parte Butt and Swati*.[31] In this the Court of Appeal said that however inconvenient it was to appeal, leave to seek judicial review prior to appealing would only be granted in exceptional cases. The *Swati* decision, as we shall see, had an immediate and expected impact on the use of judicial review in this area.

The third type of immigration decision, which has been unaffected by the Immigration and Asylum Act 1993, is that against which there is no right of appeal, either from within or beyond the United Kingdom. This includes refusals of entry (and entry clearance) on grounds that the Secretary of State considers the exclusion conducive to the public good, and deportations of those otherwise lawfully here on the ground that the deportation is in the interests of national security, diplomatic relations or for reasons of a political nature. Judicial review may be the only way of challenging these decisions.[32]

---

27 It also included refusals to grant asylum to those not in possession of the necessary entry documents.

28 *Per* Lord Bridge in respect of appeals under the Immigration Act 1971, s 16 (illegal entrants). *Khawaja v Secretary of State for Home Affairs* [1983] 1 All ER 765, at 786.

29 Refusal to allow entry on the grounds that the immigration officer was not satisfied that the individual was seeking entry as a genuine visitor under r 17 of the Statement of Changes in Immigration Rules (HC 169, 9 February 1983).

30 Sunkin, 1987, p 446.

31 [1986] 1 All ER 717. See further, Sunkin, 'Trends in the Use of Judicial Review Before and After Swati and Puhlhoffer' (1987) *New Law Journal* 731.

32 Or *habeas corpus*. See, eg *R v Secretary of State ex parte Cheblak* [1991] 1 WLR 890.

Unfortunately, the Crown Office records do not distinguish clearly between these three categories of decision but simply refer to immigration applications by reference to their subject matter, eg 'asylum', 'entry clearance', 'leave to remain', and it is these headings that we have adopted in Table 2.3.

Table 2.3

Immigration Applications for Leave to Seek Judicial Review by Type, 1987-1989 and 1st quarter of 1991

Subject	1987	1988	1989	1991 (Jan-Mar)
Asylum	305	85	81	34
Entry Clearance	107	94	57	19
Leave to Enter	44	29	60	19
Leave to Remain	18	24	13	5
Illegal Entry	46	42	42	6
Deportation	24	20	35	11
Removals	24	7	6	1
Others and Unclassified	103	55	136	8
Totals	*671*	*356*	*430*	*103*

It will be seen from this table that asylum decisions generated the single largest area of immigration judicial reviews in three of the four periods covered by our research, although their numbers declined sharply from a peak in 1987. The scale of judicial review applications from this group no doubt reflected delays in the processing of applications for refugee status coupled with the high rates of refusal of this status by the Home Office.[33] Up until 1985 there were approximately 20 applications for leave concerning asylum each year, but in 1987 this jumped to over 300. This increase was largely due to the number of applications brought by Tamils seeking sanctuary in the United Kingdom from the civil war in Sri Lanka.[34] The known

---

33 See further Sunkin, 1991.

34 *Ibid.* As noted in Chapter 1, the figures shown here vary slightly from those given in that paper.

numbers of Tamil asylum applications in our sample were 258 in 1987, 23 in 1988, four in 1989 and one in the first three months of 1991.

A similar, although numerically less significant, upsurge in litigation occurred in the late 1980s when large numbers of Kurdish refugees sought sanctuary in this country from repression in Iraq. The known numbers of judicial review applications from Kurds in our sample were 11 in 1987, six in 1988 and 55 in 1989.

The tremendous increase in asylum litigation echoes the growth in 'genuine visitor' cases during the mid-1980s. This is illustrated in Diagram 2C, showing trends in both asylum and entry cases during the 1980s.[35] The peaks that can be seen in these two areas highlight the degree to which judicial review is susceptible to surges in applications involving very specific issues and indicates some of the difficulties faced by judges and administrators in predicting and reacting to caseload trends. At the same time, the figures also provide a warning against either the judiciary or the Government taking precipitate action to limit access to judicial review in specific fields, since bulges in applications arising from particular issues may be relatively short-lived.

The 'leave to enter' cases concerned decisions made in the United Kingdom by immigration officers. In some of these the individual would already have obtained entry clearance and would have exercised rights to appeal within the United Kingdom prior to seeking judicial review. In other cases the individual would have arrived at a port of entry without entry clearance and then either been refused entry and left to appeal from abroad prior to seeking judicial review, or sought judicial review immediately instead of leaving the country (the *Swati* type situation). How many applications fell within these classes is difficult to determine from the records alone. If we look at the respondents we find that a relatively small (and declining) proportion of 'leave to enter' cases were known to be challenging decisions of the IAT. In 1987 there were 15 known cases of this type, but only four in 1988, five in 1989 and two in the first three months of 1991. By contrast, there were seven, none, eleven and five applications in each of these periods respectively involving challenges to refusals of 'leave to enter' where the respondent was the Home Office, that is where the challenge was directly against an immigration officer's decision without an intervening appeal. In other words, there was some evidence of a small increase in the number of *Swati* type challenges

---

34 For the purposes of the graph 'entry cases' includes both 'entry clearance' and 'leave to enter'.

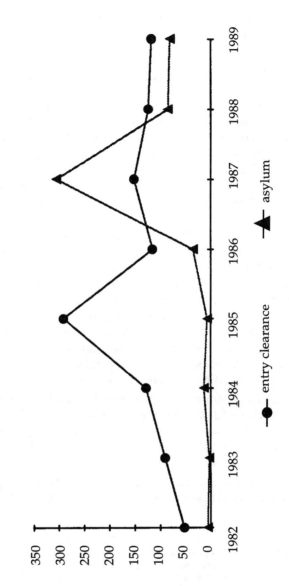

Diagram 2C

Trends in Number of Applications for Leave to Seek Judicial Review in Immigration
Entry Clearance and Asylum Cases,1982-1989

during the study period, but the numbers were clearly very much lower than they were during the mid-1980s.[36]

The Immigration and Asylum Act 1993

The Immigration and Asylum Act 1993 established, for the first time, a general line of appeal on a point of law from the IAT, with leave, to the Court of Appeal.[37] This line of appeal is also available in asylum cases. Such cases are also affected by the creation of an initial right of appeal to special adjudicators under a 'fast track' system.[38] It was anticipated that these new rights of appeal would reduce the overall number of immigration judicial reviews, and particularly the number involving asylum.[39]

However, as well as creating new opportunities for appeal, the Act also abolished rights of appeal for visitors, short-term students and those who wish to enter to study but have not accepted a place on a course.[40] The Government took this step in order to 'streamline' the system of immigration appeals and 'enable it to deal more quickly with appeals against decisions which have a fundamental impact on the lives of the persons concerned ...'.[41] In other words, the government anticipated that the changes would enable resources to be shifted from cases that were thought to be relatively unimportant to those perceived to be more important.

The decision to abolish existing rights of appeal was strongly opposed, not least by senior lawyers. Lord Ackner, for example, reflected the views of many when he told the House of Lords that it was 'wholly unjust to take away an entrenched right of appeal without compelling reasons'.[42]

Whilst it was expected that the new line of appeal from the IAT to the Court of Appeal would reduce the use of judicial review, it was

---

36 The Court of Appeal continues to impose a tight rein on the leave criteria to ensure compliance by the nominated judges with *ex parte Swati*. See, eg Lord Justice Woolf's criticism of Paul Kennedy J's approach in *R v Secretary of State for the Home Department ex parte Doorga* [1990] COD 109.

37 Section 9.

38 Section 8.

39 See Dr Christopher Vincenzi's annotations to the Act, *Current Law Statutes*, Sweet & Maxwell.

40 Section 10. Including their dependants. The Act also abolished right of appeals by those who 'are bound', under the immigration rules, to be refused entry clearance, leave to enter or a variation of leave: s 11.

41 Standing Committee A, cols 641–2, 8 December 1992.

42 *Hansard*, HL Vol 543, cols 770–1.

anticipated by many, including Ministers, that the abolition of other rights of appeal would have the reverse effect of increasing the need to resort to judicial review. It should be noted in passing, however, that access to judicial review in the type of cases affected is likely to depend to a considerable extent on the availability of legal aid and there are indications that legal aid is often refused on grounds that obtaining temporary entrance for a visitor is unlikely to provide sufficient benefit to justify the relatively high costs of judicial review proceedings (see Chapter 5).

Given these various predictions, what effect has the Act had on the use of judicial review? A definitive answer to this question will have to await a more detailed analysis of the current immigration caseload than is so far available.[43] It is, however, clear that there has been a dramatic surge in immigration leave applications since about the time the Act came into effect. This surge has been accompanied by an increase in the proportion of such applications refused leave (see further Chapter 7). What proportion of these cases involve asylum or other matters which would have benefited from the new rights of appeal or, conversely, issues which can no longer be raised on appeal is currently unknown.

Having said this, it appears that substantial numbers of these immigration cases did involve asylum. This may reflect the sheer scale of asylum requests over this period and it is possible that without the Act the number of applications might have been substantially greater, and this could well have brought the system to breaking point.[44] On the other hand, the recent surge in immigration cases may indicate that the new statutory rights of appeal have not reduced the need to seek judicial review, perhaps because the appeal procedures are perceived to be inadequate by those affected. As the Law Commission has acknowledged,[45] whether the provision of statutory appeals will in practice lessen the number of applications for judicial review very much depends on the quality of these appeal rights and of the body adjudicating them.

A third possibility is that the new rights of appeal themselves generate judicial review challenges. During the period of our research, a considerable number of immigration judicial reviews were brought

---

43   We understand that the Crown Office is monitoring the situation.

44   In 1994 there were 32,800 asylum applications received in the United Kingdom, over 10,000 more than in 1993 and more than eight times the level in 1988. The number of decisions taken on asylum cases in 1994 was, however, somewhat lower than in the previous year. There was a decrease in the numbers granted asylum or exceptional leave to remain but an increase in the number of refusals after full consideration and on safe third country grounds. Home Office Statistical Bulletin, May 1995.

45   Law Commission Report No 226, *op cit*, para 2.23.

against the Immigration Appeal Tribunal rather than the Home Office. As shown in Table 2.4 this was the case in the majority of 'entry clearance' cases. These would have involved challenges to decisions by the IAT to refuse leave to appeal as well as challenges to substantive decisions of the IAT; there may now be an increase in these types of challenge. The main point is that once new systems of appeal are established further possibilities of judicial review arise and a simple equation 'new appeal rights therefore less judicial review' cannot be assumed.

It may be that the recent surge of immigration cases includes substantial numbers of applications brought by 'visitors' and others who have lost their rights of appeal. This would be in line with

---

Table 2.4

Applications for Leave to Seek Judicial Review in Immigration 'Entry Clearance' Cases by Respondent, 1987-1989 and 1st quarter of 1991

Respondent	1987		1988		1989		1991 (Jan-Mar)	
	No	%	No	%	No	%	No	%
Home Office	46	43.0	18	19.1	14	24.6	5	50.0
Immigration Appeal Tribunal	61	57.0	75	79.8	43	75.4	5	50.0
Others	–	–	1	1.1	–	–	–	–
Total	107		94		57		10	

---

predictions and would indicate that there is likely to be a new wave of visitor cases possibly on a similar scale to the pre *ex parte Swati* 'genuine visitor' caseload. If this were to materialise it too would impose considerable new pressure on the judicial review system.

Whatever its explanation, the overall scale of immigration judicial review ought to be extremely worrying for judges and those responsible for caseload management. On the basis of our information it appears that the Immigration and Asylum Act 1993 has been a stop-gap measure that has not managed to stem the tide of dissatisfied asylum seekers using judicial review, and/or a contributing factor in generating additional applications for judicial review instituted by those who are dissatisfied with the quality of decisions taken by the appellate bodies or by those denied rights of appeal.

Judicial review and housing

The inter-relationship between appeal rights, or the lack of them, and resort to judicial review also lies at the heart of the rapid increase in applications relating to housing over recent years. Table 2.5 shows the detailed make up of judicial review housing applications over the study periods.

This table clearly shows the extent to which use of judicial review in relation to housing issues is dominated by homelessness applications; these accounted for an increasing proportion of housing judicial reviews over the study period. At least up to 1989 the growing significance of housing in the overall judicial review caseload was entirely a function of the increase in homeless persons applications.

Looking over a longer period, Diagram 2D shows the incidence of homelessness judicial review applications between 1981 and 1994. The

Table 2.5

Applications for Leave to Seek Judicial Review in Housing Cases by Type, 1987-1989 and 1st quarter of 1991

	1987		1988		1989		1991 (Jan-Mar)	
	No	%	No	%	No	%	No	%
Homeless Persons	84	59.6	105	65.2	176	75.9	77	72.6
Housing Benefits	9	6.4	11	6.8	13	5.6	15	14.2
Compulsory Purchase Order	6	4.3	5	3.1	4	1.7	2	1.9
Rates	7	5.0	5	3.1	3	1.3	2	1.9
Repairs	8	5.7	2	1.2	1	0.4	–	–
Possession	–	–	1	0.6	5	2.2	3	2.8
Grants	2	1.4	1	0.6	8	3.4	1	0.9
Transfers	1	0.7	2	1.2	4	1.7	3	2.8
Squatting	1	0.7	12	7.5	6	2.6	–	–
Other/Unclassified	23	16.3	17	10.6	12	5.2	3	2.8
Totals	141		161		232		106	

projected number of homelessness applications in 1991, based on our data for the first quarter of the year, would have been over 300, that is, some 75% higher than in 1989. Official statistics for subsequent years show a further increase in homelessness applications to well over 400 per annum. These figures clearly demonstrate that the House of Lord's decision in the *Puhlhoffer* case in 1986 (discussed above) had only a very limited and short-term impact in restricting the use of judicial review in this field.[46]

Despite these trends, the number of homelessness judicial review applications remains relatively small when placed against the background of the social crisis in this field during the late 1980s and early 1990s and the very large numbers refused access to housing by local authorities under the relevant legislation.[47] Given the lack of an independent appeal right against local authority decisions on homelessness, applicants denied accommodation have had to rely on local authorities' own internal review procedures or judicial review. While the frequent use of judicial review in homelessness cases (particularly against certain London Boroughs[48]) is perfectly understandable from the perspective of the applicants, the way in which some local authorities appear to have used the procedure as a substitute for tighter internal scrutiny of decisions received little attention from judicial and legal commentators until recently.[49]

In their 1994 report, however, the Law Commission acknowledged that 'the number of homelessness applications for judicial review and their outcome raise serious questions about the standards of decision-making in this area' and that 'steps should be taken to improve standards of decision-making and to provide for internal reviews of decisions which are challenged'.[50] The Law Commission also went on to recommend the creation of independent appeal rights in homelessness cases, on the grounds that the provision of a purely internal review could not 'be regarded as a proper substitute for a right of appeal to a court or an independent tribunal.'[51]

---

46   As will be seen subsequently, the House of Lord's decision also appears to have had little effect in influencing Crown Office list judges toward refusing leave in more homelessness cases (see Chapters 6 and 7).

47   See above p 11.

48   See discussion of geographical distribution of applicants in Chapter 3.

49   See Roy Sainsbury, 'Internal Reviews and the Weakening of Social Security Claimants' Rights of Appeal' in G Richardson and H Genn (eds) *Administrative Law & Government Action*, (1994) Oxford University Press, J Baldwin, N Wikeley and R Young *Judging Social Security*, (1992) Oxford University Press, esp Chapters 2 and 3.

50   Law Commission Report No 226, *op cit*, para 2.24.

51   *Ibid*, paras 2.25–2.26.

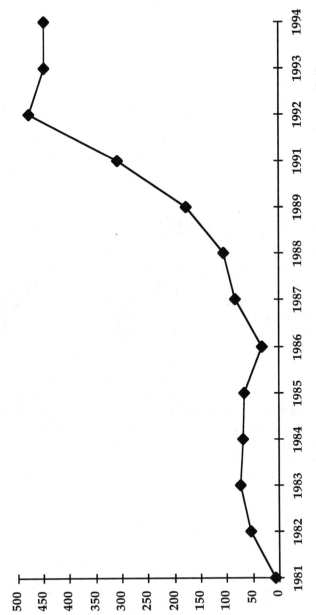

Diagram 2D

Trends in Number of Applications for Leave to Seek Judicial Review in
Homelessness, 1981-1994

Source: Sunkin, 1987 for data on 1981-1986; current research for 1987-1989 and 1991 (full year estimate based on projection from first quarter's figure); Crown Office for 1992-1994 (1992 estimate based on projection from final six months' figure); no data available for 1990.

In concentrating on homelessness we ought not to neglect the infrequent use made of judicial review to challenge decisions affecting a wide range of housing rights and benefits. Between 1987 and 1989 the number of housing judicial reviews not involving homelessness remained almost constant at 57 or 56 each year. These figures again force us to ask why judicial review is used so rarely in some areas. Earlier in the chapter we have mentioned factors such as cost. Research has also shown that a significant proportion of housing enquires handled by advice organisations such as Citizens' Advice Bureaux contain issues that are open to public law challenges, but which are not recognised.[52] A particular instance where greater use of judicial review might have been anticipated is in relation to housing benefit, which affects even more people than do decisions on homelessness. Whilst those denied housing benefit may appeal to local councillors, the independence and quality of these appeal rights have been questioned.[53]

Summary and conclusions

Much of the current drive toward the reform of judicial review appears to be based on a perceived overload of the procedure arising, it is said, from the vast increase in numbers of applications.[54] Our data call into question, not so much the fact that the machinery of judicial review is under pressure, but rather the precise causes of this pressure. The official statistics reveal a significant differential between the very rapid rate of growth over the past decade in the number of initial applications for leave to seek judicial review and the much more modest increase in the number of cases eventually being substantively determined. This highlights the importance, in particular, of the leave requirement which has become an increasingly significant barrier for applicants to surmount. We examine the working of the leave procedure in greater detail in Chapter 7. There are also important external variables impinging upon the flow of cases into and through the judicial review process. These we explore in the following three chapters.

---

52 D Forbes and S Wright, *Housing cases in Nine CABx*, (1990) unpublished.

53 See R Sainsbury and T Eardley, 'Housing Benefit Review Boards: A Case for Slum Clearance?' (1992) *Public Law* 551. Data from our separate research on legal aid applications indicates that there was a surge in the use of judicial review in relation to housing benefits late in 1991. The non-availability of funding, especially under legal aid, may have contributed to the low number of housing benefit cases. In particular, such cases may fall foul of the 'cost benefit' analysis applied under the legal aid merits test (see Chapter 5).

54 This was highlighted in the recent Law Commission Report No 226, *op cit*, which contains an 11-page appendix dealing with issues of 'case-load management'. See Appendix C, pp 163–73.

Use of judicial review, at least in terms of numbers of applications for leave, is dominated in non-criminal cases by immigration and housing. Together these two fields account for around half of all applications. The immigration caseload has been subject to wide fluctuations and to surges in litigation focusing on particular issues, such as 'entry clearance' or, more recently, asylum seeking. These surges in litigation in specific fields are difficult to predict, and for this reason they do not constitute a sensible basis on which to plan reform of the overall procedure.

Nor have past efforts by the judiciary to stem the flow of litigation in specific areas proved to have lasting effect. Despite the judicial sentiment expressed in *Puhlhoffer* in 1986, urging stricter control over the use of judicial review in relation to homelessness, this has in fact been the most significant growth area for judicial review over recent years. In this respect, judicial review provides a 'safety net' for asserting basic rights to fair treatment within the system of administrative decision-making where no other appeal mechanism is available. At the same time, the continued frequent use of judicial review to challenge decisions of the immigration adjudicators and Immigration Appeal Tribunal may serve as a reminder that it is as much the perceived inadequacy of alternative appeal rights as their non-availability that produces a demand for judicial review.

Despite its growing importance in the overall judicial review caseload, the rate of homelessness applications remains low when compared with the much wider potential to challenge decisions in this and related housing fields. This is even more true of the other subject areas covered by judicial review which, while they theoretically span the whole scope of governmental and other public decision-making, tend to produce relatively few applications. Possible explanations for this under-use of the system will be considered in the following chapters where we examine in more detail precisely who uses judicial review and against which public bodies and how patterns of use may be affected by the availability of different forms of legal assistance including, in particular, legal aid.

Chapter 3

The Parties in Judicial Review Proceedings

The popular image of judicial review stresses its role as a mechanism for imposing the rule of law on executive power. Within this image the typical challenge is brought by citizens, or increasingly in recent years, interest groups against the executive. But, as we asked in the previous chapter, does this image reflect reality? Who is it that seeks judicial review and which agencies are being challenged?

Judicial review is widely perceived as being used by a broadening spectrum of litigants. In particular, it is commonly associated with 'test cases' brought by citizens' groups to exert pressure on government decision-making.[1] Commercial concerns are also thought to be resorting to judicial review more often to challenge government regulation. Are these perceptions accurate? Although government bodies are the target for judicial review, how often do they also act as applicants, instigating challenges to other public bodies?

Turning to those against whom the process is used, central government is an obvious target for judicial review, but does judicial review directly touch the whole of Whitehall or does it leave some departments unaffected?[2] Local government has also been another obvious target of judicial review, but again, how often and in what areas?

Increasingly, government powers are being allocated to non-departmental agencies and even to private bodies.[3] This raises important issues of control and accountability.[4] One of these is the degree to which the courts will supervise the actions of such bodies. During the 1980s the courts accepted that non-statutory bodies performing public functions may be amenable to judicial review, but recent decisions have shown them reluctant to extend the scope of

---

1   See generally, C Harlow and R Rawlings *Pressure Through Law* (1992) London: Routledge.

2   *Cf* the question of impact, on which see, eg, M Sunkin & AP Le Sueur, 'Can Government Control Judicial Review?' (1991) 44 *Current Legal Problems* 161; R Cranston, 'Reviewing Judicial Review' in G Richardson and H Genn, *op cit*.

3   See, for eg, G Drewry, 'Revolution in Whitehall' in J Jowell & D Oliver (eds) *The Changing Constitution*, (1994) Oxford University Press.

4   For a discussion of the implications of self-regulation on issues of accountability, see C Graham, 'Self-Regulation' in G Richardson and H Genn, *op cit*.

their supervisory powers.[5] We were therefore concerned to explore the extent to which non-governmental organisations become involved in judicial review, either as respondents or applicants.

In this chapter we look at the applicants and respondents to judicial review during the period covered by the research. We have divided applicants into six main types: individuals; companies; non-governmental bodies, such as voluntary organisations or pressure groups; local authorities; central government; and other non-departmental public bodies. Respondents have been grouped into five major categories: central government; local government; courts and tribunals; other non-departmental public bodies; and non-governmental organisations. The definitions and the criteria used to allocate applicants and respondents into these groupings are explained in Appendix 2.

Applicants for judicial review

As might be expected, the vast majority of applications for judicial review are brought in the name of individuals. Indeed, during the periods covered by our research between 84% and 88% of all applications were made in the name of individuals. These figures, however, reveal little about the true nature of the applications made or the capacity in which the individuals were seeking judicial review. They do not show, for example, whether applications made in the name of individual were in fact made on behalf of a wider group or organisation. Bearing in mind that legal aid is only available to individuals,[6] and since few non-commercial organisations have sufficient resources to support lengthy litigation or risk substantial orders for costs if a case is unsuccessful, many 'test cases', although supported by pressure groups, are likely to be made in the name of individual applicants. Using individuals as named applicants also helps avoid questions of standing (that is, whether the applicant has a sufficient interest in the subject matter of the application to be allowed

---

5   See in particular, *R v Panel on Take-overs and Mergers, ex parte Datafin plc* [1987] QB 815, *cf R v Panel on Take-overs and Mergers ex parte Guinness plc* [1990] 1 QB 146; *R v Chief Rabbi ex parte Wachmann* [1992] 1 WLR 106; *R v Code of Practice Committee of the British Pharmaceutical Industry, ex parte Professional Counselling Aids Ltd* [1991] COD 42; *R v Disciplinary Committee of the Jockey Club ex parte Aga Khan* [1993] WLR 909; *R v Insurance Ombudsman Bureau and the Insurance Ombudsman, ex parte Aegon Life Assurance Ltd* (1994) *The Times* 7 January. But, *cf R v The Governors of Haberdasher's Aske's Hatcham College Trust ex parte Tyrell*, 10 October 1994 (unreported) where it was held that a City Technology College would be subject to judicial review.

6   See Chapter 5.

to proceed) that might otherwise be raised if a case were taken in the name of an organisation or a group.[7]

With this in mind, we concentrate our analysis in this chapter on applications brought expressly in the name of non-individual litigants. Table 3.1 sets out details on non-individual applicants for judicial review during the study period.

Companies and other non-governmental organisations

The figures in Table 3.1 testify to the growing significance of commercial involvement in judicial review (at least until the end of 1989) especially when compared to figures derived from earlier studies. Sunkin found that in three six-monthly periods in 1983, 1984 and 1985 there were respectively 35, 26 and 33 applications for judicial review taken in the name of companies.[8] This compares with 98, 111 and 141 company applicants respectively in 1987, 1988 and 1989. In these three years, companies constituted by far the largest category of non-individual applicants, accounting for between 50% and 60% of this group. Indeed, in 1988 and 1989, one-in-eleven of all applications for judicial review were initiated by companies.

As might be expected, the main areas in which companies pursued judicial reviews were town and country planning, tax and licensing. Taking the caseload across the three-and-a-quarter year study period as a whole, 21% of applications by companies were in the field of town and country planning, 16% related to tax, 12% to various forms of licensing, and 7% to criminal matters. No other subject area accounted for more than 5% of applications by companies, and the remaining 44% of such cases were widely spread across a number of fields.

Other non-governmental organisations constitute a relatively small group among total applicants for judicial review, accounting for between 1% and 2% of all cases during the study period. Of the 84

---

7   The courts have recently taken a very liberal approach to standing. See, *R v Secretary of State for Foreign Affairs ex parte Rees-Mogg* [1994] 1 All ER 457; *R v Inspectorate of Pollution ex parte Greenpeace (No 2)* [1994] 4 All ER 29; *R v Secretary of State for the Home Department ex parte Fire Brigades Union* [1995] 2 All ER 244; *R v Secretary of State for Foreign Affairs ex parte World Development Movement Ltd* [1995] 1 All ER 611. For recent discussions of standing see in particular: Sir Konrad Schiemann, 'Locus Standi' (1990) *Public Law* 42; David Feldman, 'Public Interests Litigation and Constitutional Theory in Comparative Perspective' (1992) 55 *MLR* 44; Peter Cane, 'Standing, Representation and the Environment' in Ian Loveland (ed) (1995) *Lessons From America: Studies in Public Law*, Oxford University Press, forthcoming; Peter Cane, 'Standing Up for the Public' (1995) *Public Law*, 276. Also, Robinson and Dunkley (eds) *Public Interest Perspectives in Environmental Law*, (1995) Chichester: Wiley Chancery, esp Chapters 10 and 11.

8   Sunkin, 1987 p 47.

applications made by such organisations across the whole three-and-a-quarter years, 20 (24%) were initiated by pressure groups. This included one 'block booking' of nine applications by Friends of the Earth in 1989. These data suggest that judicial review was not widely used by pressure groups to undertake 'test cases' in their own names, either on their own behalf or as representatives of others. This is a tendency which may change if the courts continue to adopt a liberal approach to standing.

Government bodies as applicants

Central government as applicant

In all the rhetoric about judicial review as a protection for the individual against government illegality, it can be forgotten that judicial review may also be an important weapon for government, both central and local, and an instrument for mediating and regulating inter-governmental relations. Recent years have seen an increasing centralisation of political power, supported by a far more legalistic political culture. This has been particularly evident in the context of the relationship between central and local government.[9] One manifestation of this has been the number of high profile and well publicised cases of judicial review which have arisen when one public authority (often a Labour controlled local authority) has sought to challenge the actions of another (often Conservative central government).[10]

Given that central government has a variety of legal, administrative and political tools at its disposal for ensuring that others comply with its policy, including its ability to initiate legislation providing it with new powers, it is not surprising that central government tends to apply for judicial review very infrequently. During our research no more than about 1% of all applications in any of the years, and around 6% of non-individual applications in two of the years (1988 and 1989), were instituted by central government.

---

9   This has been well documented in the literature, see for example: M Loughlin *Local Government in the Modern State,* (1986) London: Sweet & Maxwell; S Leach and J Stoker, 'The transformation of central–local relations' in C Graham and T Prosser (eds) *Waiving the Rules: The Constitution Under Thatcherism* (1988) Milton Keynes: Open University Press; L Bridges *et al Legality and Local Politics* (1987) Avebury.

10 Eg *Nottinghamshire CC v Secretary of State for the Environment* [1986] 1 AC 240; *R v Secretary of State for the Environment ex parte Brent LBC* [1982] QB 59; *R v Secretary of State for the Environment ex parte Hammersmith & Fulham LBC* [1991] 1 AC 521; *R v Secretary of State for the Environment ex parte Hillingdon LBC* (1991) 90 LGR 425; *R v Secretary of State for the Environment ex parte Tower Hamlets* [1993] QB 632.

Table 3.1

Non-individual Applicants for Judicial Review, 1987-1989 and 1st quarter of 1991

	Companies	Non-governmental organisations	Central government	Local authorities	Non-departmental public bodies
1987:					
No of applications	98	28	3	46	23
% of all applications	6.5	1.9	0.1	3.0	1.5
% of non-individual applications	49.5	14.1	1.5	23.2	11.6
1988:					
No of applications	111	20	11	26	13
% of all applications	9.1	1.6	0.9	2.1	1.1
% of non-individual applications	61.3	11.0	6.1	14.4	7.2
1989:					
No of applications	141	32	17	55	17
% of all applications	9.1	2.1	1.1	3.5	1.1
% of non-individual applications	53.8	12.2	6.5	21.0	6.5
1991 (Jan-Mar):					
No of applications	23	4	1	19	7
% of all applications	5.1	0.9	0.2	4.2	1.5
% of non-individual applications	42.6	7.4	1.9	35.2	13.0

Taking the three-and-a-quarter year study period as a whole, a total of nine central government departments applied for judicial review, but only six of these did so more than once. These were: the Home Office (nine times); Customs and Excise and the Department of the Environment (three times each); the Ministry of Defence and the Department of Social Security (twice each); and the Attorney General, who instituted seven applications all in 1989 against the Licensing Authority for the Eastern Traffic Area. The other central government applications were made by the Ministry of Agriculture, the Department of Employment, and the Department of Health.

Local government as applicant

By contrast, local government was a relatively frequent initiator of judicial review litigation throughout the 1980s. During three six monthly periods in 1983, 1984, 1985 local authorities commenced a total of five, eight and 27 judicial review applications respectively.[11] Although the number of local authority applications declined in 1988, the figures for 1987 and 1989 were generally in line with the earlier data. During the first quarter of 1991 there was a marked increase in local authority applications to an annual rate of approximately 76.

Of the total local authority applications over the three-and-a-quarter year study period: 36% were against the Department of the Environment, primarily in relation to town and country planning issues; 18% were against other local authorities relating to town and country planning, housing, rates, and (since 1989) education; and 15% were against magistrates' courts in respect of such matters as crime, family law matters, housing and licensing. The sharp rise in local government-initiated education cases (there were only three in 1987 but 13 in 1989) is further evidence of the effect of the Education Reform Act 1988 in 'politicising' and 'judicialising' this field of governmental activity.

Non-departmental public bodies

The main non-departmental public bodies involved in judicial review proceedings as applicants were the Director of Public Prosecutions and the Crown Prosecution Service. These together accounted for 38 of the 60 applications by such bodies (63%) in the three-and-a-quarter years. Most of these applications related to criminal court matters. There were also eleven applications in 1987 instituted by the Welsh Water Authority against the Department of the Environment.

Geographic distribution of applicants

The machinery of judicial review is highly centralised, with all applications having to be lodged and heard in London. As the Law Commission recognised, this concentration of judicial review raises 'access to justice issues'[12] for those who are not in London or the South East and who may as a result of their geographical location be

---

11 Sunkin, 1987 p 47.

12 Law Commission Report No 226, *op cit*, para 2.28.

disadvantaged in using the process or discouraged from attempting to do so.

It has not always been possible to determine, from our data, the location of the applicant. This is because, for reasons of confidentiality, no personal details of individual applicants were collected as part of the research and because addresses of applicants are not normally recorded on Crown Office records. Moreover, where the respondent is a national body, such as a central department or a tribunal, the geographical source of the application may not be clear from the application itself. The most complete information available to us on geographical distribution of cases is that on applications begun in the first quarter of 1991, on which extended data were collected. We sought to determine the geographical source of applications first by reference to the identity of the applicant or respondent and, where this was insufficient, by the address of the applicant's legal representative.

Table 3.2 shows the overall geographical distribution of judicial review applications during the first quarter of 1991. Of those cases where the geographical source of the application could be determined, 55% originated within London. This figure, however, needs to be treated with some caution for it may exaggerate concentrations in

Table 3.2

Applications for Leave to Seek Judicial Review by Geographical Origin, 1st quarter of 1991

	No	%
London	241	55.4
Out-of-London:		
South East	42	9.7
East Anglia	13	3.0
South West	29	6.7
West Midlands	26	6.0
East Midlands	14	3.2
Yorkshire and Humberside	7	1.6
North West	45	10.3
North East	6	1.4
Wales	12	2.0

*   Excludes 19 cases where geographical origin not ascertained or applicable. % based on total of all applications where origin known.

London. There may, for example, be a tendency for non-London applicants to instruct London solicitors on the grounds that they will have better access to the Crown Office or have become specialist in particular fields of judicial review litigation. As will be seen in the next chapter, specialisation is particularly notable in immigration cases and since many immigration applications involve challenges to decisions taken by the Home Office or the Immigration Appeal Tribunal (neither of which are geographically specific) we had to rely on the solicitors' address in order to classify the geographical source of these applications. On this basis, no fewer than 85% of immigration applicants were identified as originating in London. By contrast only 5% of immigration applicants appeared to come from the West Midlands and the North West.

Homeless persons cases were also heavily concentrated, with 73% of all applications in the first three months of 1991 originating from within London. In fact, just one authority, the London Borough of Southwark, was the respondent in no less than one-in-six of all homeless person cases during this period. The remaining 44 homeless persons applications originating in London came from across 19 local authorities. There were 19 non-London homeless persons cases (27%) which came from regions across the country; although it is notable that in this three month period there were no judicial review applications in this field against any local authority in the North East or in Yorkshire and Humberside.

Once immigration and homeless persons cases are disregarded, the use of judicial review in other fields was more widely distributed across the country as a whole. Of individual applicants in fields other than immigration and homelessness, 63% were from beyond London. Similarly, about a two-thirds of applications taken in the name of private organisations or public bodies originated outside London. The South West accounted for 15% of non-immigration and non-homelessness individual applicants in the first quarter of 1991; the South East (other than London) for 14%; and, the West Midlands for 10% of these cases. Around 18% of applications from organisations also originated both in the South East (other than London) and in the West Midlands.

Respondents to judicial review

We now turn to consider which public bodies were the main targets for judicial review challenges. Table 3.3 shows the distribution of applications across the main categories of respondent. The data are arranged so that they identify the effect of the three major subject areas of judicial review on the distribution of applications between the different respondent categories: immigration cases are found under central government (the Home Office) and courts and tribunals (the Immigration Appeal Tribunal); crime constitutes a large category of applications against courts and tribunals; and, homeless persons cases are included under challenges to local government.

Table 3.3

Applications for Leave to Seek Judicial Review by Type of Respondent, 1987-1989 and 1st quarter of 1991

	1987		1988		1989		1991 (Jan-Mar)	
	No	%	No	%	No	%	No	%
Central Government:	686	45.4	355	29.1	517	33.4	121	26.7
Immigration	539	35.6	226	18.5	328	21.2	85	18.8
Other	147	9.7	129	10.6	189	12.2	36	7.9
Local Government:	295	19.5	345	28.3	479	31.0	159	35.1
Homeless Person	84	5.5	105	8.6	176	11.4	77	17.0
Other	211	14.0	240	19.7	303	19.6	82	18.1
Courts & Tribunals:	451	29.8	434	35.6	439	28.4	146	32.2
Crime	185	12.2	153	12.6	201	13.0	69	15.2
Immigration	131	8.7	129	10.6	101	6.5	18	4.0
Other	135	8.9	152	12.5	137	8.9	59	13.0
Non-departmental Public Bodies*	44	2.9	45	3.7	66	4.3	10	2.2
Non-governmental Organisations	36	2.4	40	3.3	45	2.9	17	3.8

*   Because of a change during the research period in the classification of certain bodies, such as the transfer of legal aid from the Law Society (a non-governmental organisation) to the Legal Aid Board (a non-departmental public body), cases in some subject areas may have been switched between different respondent categories.

Central government

Central government departments constituted the largest category of respondents during the period 1987 to 1989. Their predominance, however, was primarily due to the high number of immigration cases. Challenges to central government in other fields accounted for around 10% to 12% of all judicial review applications during this period and for less than 8% in the first quarter of 1991. In fact, in this latter period the annual rate of non-immigration applications against central government departments was almost 25% lower than in 1989, and even with immigration cases taken into account central government was no longer the most frequent target for challenge, having been overtaken in this respect by local government.

Table 3.4 shows a detailed breakdown of the main central government departments challenged during the study periods. The Home Office alone accounted for 74% of all challenges to central government across the whole three-and-a-quarter years. The next most frequently challenged department was the Department of the Environment which attracted 7% of all challenges to central government over the study period. The number of applications against this department increased substantially in each of the years covered by our data. The Inland Revenue accounted for 4% of challenges to central government, but unlike the Department of the Environment, the number of applications against it varied sharply from year to year.

Only three other central government departments were the subject of 10 or more judicial review challenges during any one year covered by the research: the Department of Social Security (in each of the three years 1987–1989); the Department of Transport (1988 only); and the Welsh Office (1987 only). The remaining eight departments listed in Table 3.3 were challenged no more than between three and eight times, even in their 'busiest' years. For most central government departments, therefore, judicial review challenges were a very infrequent occurrence, happening at most only once or twice a year.

Before leaving challenges to central government departments, it is interesting to note that it is the Department of Social Security and the Inland Revenue which are the main targets for complaints to the Parliamentary Commissioner for Administration. These are followed by the Department of the Environment and the Home Office.[13]

---

13 They were the subject of 9%, 10%, 5% and 4% of the complaints during 1994: Annual Report of the PCA for 1994 HC 07, p 45.

Table 3.4

Number of Applications for Leave to Seek Judicial Review Against
Selected* Central Government Departments,
1987-1989 and 1st quarter of 1991

	1987	1988	1989	1991 (Jan-Mar)	Totals
Home Office	563	254	335	89	1241
Environment	21	32	55	13	121
Inland Revenue	22	6	39	3	70
Social Security	11	10	11	-	32
Transport	4	14	5	3	26
Agriculture	5	7	5	-	17
Education	4	6	6	1	17
Health	8	-	6	-	14
Customs and Excise	6	3	5	-	14
Welsh Office	11	2	-	1	13
Foreign Office	-	2	6	2	10
Trade and Industry	4	-	4	-	8
Defence	5	2	-	-	7
Employment	-	3	-	1	4

* Table includes all departments that were respondents in 0.5% or more of applications against central government in any one of the years 1987–1989. In 1987 there were a further 19 applications against a total of 12 departments; in 1988 a further 10 applications each against a separate department; and in 1989 an additional 19 applications against 16 departments. In the first quarter of 1991, there were a further eight applications against five departments.

Local government

Once the very high numbers of immigration cases have been disregarded local government emerges from our data as a more frequent respondent to judicial review than central government. Local government was the target for large numbers of applications relating to homelessness, which was the most rapidly growing area of judicial review over the study period. But even if homeless persons cases are discounted, the number of applications against local government increased significantly over the period of the study. The estimated annual rate of non-homelessness applications against local authorities, based on the first quarter figures for 1991, was 55% higher than the number of such applications in 1987.

The comparison between central and local government as targets for judicial review can best be illustrated by examining the ratio between the number of non-homelessness applications against local government to the number of non-immigration challenges to central government (see Diagram 3A). In 1987 there were 1.4 non-homelessness applications against local government for every one non-immigration application against central government. In 1988 the ratio was 1.9 to one, in 1989 1.6 to one, and in the first quarter of 1991 2.3 to one.

The main fields in which local government was challenged are summarised in Table 3.5. The single most significant area was homeless persons, accounting for 35% of applications against local authorities in the whole three-and-a-quarter years covered by our data. Other housing matters accounted for 11%, town and country planning for 10%, education for 7%, licensing for 6%, and family matters for 4% of applications against local government. As noted previously, other than in homelessness, the most dramatic growth in challenges to local government over the research periods was in education. The annual rate of applications against local government in this area in the first quarter of 1991 was four times higher than in 1987 and 2.5 times higher than in 1989.

Table 3.5

Subject Areas of Applications for Leave to Seek Judicial Review Against Local Authorities, 1987-1989 and 1st quarter of 1991

	1987	1988	1989	1991 (Jan-Mar)
Homeless Person	84	105	175	77
Other Housing	33	41	46	21
Town & Country Planning	45	46	18	13
Licensing	24	23	24	4
Education	17	16	35	22
Family	14	19	14	6
Other	78	95	166	16

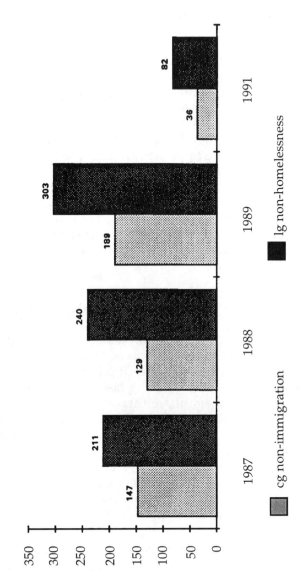

Diagram 3A

Judicial Review Applications
Non-Immigration/Non-Homelessness against Central/Local Government,
1987-1989 and 1st Quarter 1991

lg non-homelessness

cg non-immigration

Courts and tribunals

Traditionally, one of the primary functions of judicial review has been to enable the High Court to exercise supervision over the conduct of inferior courts and tribunals. This remains one of the most important tasks of judicial review. Taken as a group, courts and tribunals were respondents in between 28% and 36% of all applications across the study periods, with criminal courts accounting for between 12% and 15% of all applications. Immigration applications against the Immigration Appeal Tribunal also accounted for a significant proportion of the applications against courts and tribunals. Challenges to decisions of courts and tribunals outside the fields of crime and immigration accounted for between 9% and 13% of all judicial review cases in the study periods; these included 41 housing cases and 55 applications concerning various forms of licensing (both figures are out of 1,460 challenges to courts and tribunals in the whole three-and-a-quarter years).

Other public bodies and non-governmental organisations

Despite the fragmentation of public service provision, in particular the separation of the 'purchaser' and 'provider' functions of government and the effects of privatisation, up to the first quarter of 1991 there was little evidence of there having been a significant growth in the use of judicial review against either non-departmental public bodies or private organisations. Over the study periods, challenges to public bodies other than central government departments, local authorities, or courts and tribunals constituted only between 2% and just over 4% of all applications. Of course, many of the new agencies created over recent years, especially those established to take over departmental functions, do not have separate legal identity so that the respondent in judicial review proceedings would continue to be the department or its Minister.

The most frequent field of challenge to non-departmental public bodies was health, with Area Health Authorities and Family Practitioner Committees being challenged in 28% of the applications against this category of respondent. The Director of Public Prosecutions was the respondent in 11% of the applications against non-departmental public bodies.

Non-governmental organisations

Private bodies may be subject to judicial review where they are performing statutory functions or other public purposes.[14] A good example is the Law Society, a private professional body, which until 1989 was responsible under statute for administering the legal aid scheme and which was therefore amenable to judicial review in respect of its decisions concerning the grant or refusal of legal aid, or the payment of costs under the scheme. Once responsibility for legal aid was transferred to the Legal Aid Board in 1989, such challenges would have been classified in our research as being against a non-departmental public body: there were 40 applications against the Law Society/Legal Aid Board in the study periods; five in 1987, 12 in 1988, 18 in 1989, and five in the first quarter of 1991.

Legal aid challenges, however, were not the most frequent type of application against non-governmental bodies. Those arising from professional and other disciplinary proceedings accounted for nearly 30% of the applications where a non-governmental body was the respondent over the whole three-and-a-quarter years.

Summary and conclusions

Applications for judicial review are very largely taken in the name of individuals. In many instances, especially in the field of immigration and homelessness, this reflects precisely the individualistic nature of the interest involved. But applications taken in the name of individuals may well raise wider public interest issues; they may also be brought on behalf of a wider group or as a surrogate for an organisation. The bias towards applications being made in the name of individuals is reinforced both by the current rules on legal aid which emphasise its availability primarily for asserting individual private interests and by rules of standing which have traditionally emphasised the need for applicants to show they are directly adversely affected by the decision being challenged (see Chapter 5). As a result, the visible incidence of judicial review applications taken in the name of pressure groups has been very low. The recent liberalisation of standing, particularly if accompanied by reforms recommended by the Law Commission aimed at better equipping judicial review to handle public interest

---

14   See note 5 above.

litigation, may result in more explicit use of the procedure by groups.[15] Whilst groups may not have been making much explicit use of the process, private companies were resorting to judicial review more often, although primarily in the traditional commercial fields of town and country planning, tax and licensing.

There is no evidence that central government frequently resorts to judicial review. This probably reflects the availability to central government of other legislative, administrative and financial resources. Local government on the other hand is an increasingly frequent applicant; well over half of its cases being against central government, or other local authorities.

Judicial review is highly centralised in London. The vast majority of immigration applications and nearly three-quarters of homelessness cases appear to have had their origin in London. Although applications not involving immigration or homelessness were more widely distributed, about a third of these also originated from within London. Overall, 55% of all applications for judicial review came from within London. As respondents to the Law Commission's consultation paper and the Law Commission itself have recognised, these findings highlight problems of access to judicial review for those outside London and South East.[16] In the specific context of homelessness these may be alleviated if a system of local appeals is introduced. There is, however, a more general need to make judicial review more accessible, perhaps by enabling High Court judges to consider oral applications for leave whilst on circuit.[17]

Whilst judicial review has undoubtedly shown itself to be a potentially potent weapon for those seeking to challenge areas of decision-making in Whitehall, in fact the growth of judicial review litigation over the study period tended to be at the expense of local government rather than central government. Challenges to central government are dominated numerically by immigration cases and, as we saw in Chapter 2, homelessness applications against decisions by local authorities have been the most significant growth area in recent years. Beyond these two fields of mass use of judicial review, local government appears likely to be challenged over twice as often as

---

15 In this context note the Law Commission's criticism of *R v Darlington BC ex parte Association of Darlington Taxi Owners*, (1994) *The Times*, 21 January in which it was held that unincorporated associations have no capacity to apply for judicial review. See Law Commission Report No 226, *op cit*, paras 5.8–5.41.

16 Law Commission Report No 226, *op cit*, paras 2.19–2.20, 2.28.

17 Since early 1995, judges have been able to consider written applications for leave whilst on circuit.

central government; and only a handful of central government departments face more than 10 applications against them in any one year.

These data highlight that it is misleading to view judicial review as being primarily a tool for challenging and constraining central government. Rather, it appears more accurate to view it as an additional constraint on local government.[18] If this is correct it probably reflects both that local government has carried much of the administrative burden of recent pressures on the social welfare system, particularly in the field of housing, and also that local government has been a target of some of the most controversial areas of governmental reform carried out over recent years, including those in the fields of public finance and education. Both of these are areas in which judicial review has played a significant role.

18 Note also the contrast between the caseload of the Parliamentary Commissioner for Administration and that of the Local Government Ombudsman, Chapter 2, Diagram 2B.

Chapter 4

Judicial Review and Legal Representation

The extent to which use is made of judicial review by the general populace is heavily dependent on the answers to two questions. First, how much access do ordinary citizens have to lawyers and advisers who can recognise the public law implications of decisions and who are aware of the opportunities offered by judicial review proceedings? Second, how are the costs of such proceedings to be met?

In the past judicial review had a reputation for being an esoteric process of little relevance to most legal practitioners. Indeed, very few of them would have claimed to possess any more than a rudimentary knowledge of administrative law principles, and up to the mid-1980s very few firms of solicitors were involved in judicial review litigation with any regularity. On the other hand, a few specialist firms processed large numbers of applications, particularly involving immigration and housing.

The link between the litigation strategy of small numbers of lawyers and the make-up of the judicial review caseload had a number of important implications. First, the work of little more than a handful of lawyers was very influential in determining the nature and scale of public law litigation. There is also the possibility that judicial review was being under-used in other areas because potential applicants did not have access to the appropriate advice.[1]

More recently, judicial review has gained a higher profile and the public and the legal profession appear to be far more aware of its implications than they were a few years ago. To what extent was this reflected in higher levels of professional participation in the process over the period covered by our Crown Office data? Was judicial review litigation being handled by a wider range of lawyers or was it still the case that a substantial proportion of cases was being processed by a few lawyers? And what roles did private solicitors and law centres respectively play in relation to judicial review litigation?[2]

In this chapter we seek to answer these questions by looking first at the patterns of legal representation of individuals who lodged applications for judicial review in our study period. Of course, not all individuals who seek judicial review will be legally represented, and

---

1   Sunkin, 1987 p 462.
2   It should be noted that we have not examined the role and influence of barristers.

litigants in person appear to have grown in numbers over the years. Also, as shown in Chapter 3, many judicial review applications are taken in the name of governmental bodies and other institutional applicants, who are often represented by their own 'in-house' legal staff.[3] This is less true of company or commercial applicants for judicial review, who often make use of private solicitors' firms to prepare their cases for court. The patterns of legal representation of company applicants, and of use of the judicial review procedure by litigants in person, will also be examined in this chapter.

As well as requiring expert advice in order to embark on judicial review proceedings, the costs involved in such cases are likely to be well beyond the means of most individuals. This is especially so since, once leave has been obtained from the court for an application for judicial review to proceed, the same costs rules apply as in most other forms of civil litigation. This means that the losing side will normally be required to pay their opponent's legal costs. As noted in Chapter 3, even where interest groups support applications for judicial review, they will often regard it as essential that the proceedings are taken in the name of individuals who are themselves eligible to receive legal aid.[4] Legal aid not only provides financial assistance in meeting the applicant's own legal expense, but it usually provides a form of protection against the applicant being required to pay the respondent's costs in the event of the application being unsuccessful.

For the ordinary person, therefore, access to judicial review may very much depend on his or her eligibility for legal aid to take such proceedings. This raises the question of how far the separate rules governing eligibility for legal aid act to facilitate or hinder individuals' access to the procedure. And how do these rules and the machinery for their administration inter-relate with the judicial review procedure itself? In the next chapter we examine these questions by considering our separate data relating to applications made to the Legal Aid Board for potential judicial review cases during the final three months of 1991.

---

3   Such staff will perform the functions ordinarily carried out by solicitors for other applicants. Governmental bodies and other institutional applicants will still be required to retain the services of a private barrister (or now a private solicitor) to present their application for judicial review in court, as employed lawyers do not have rights of audience in the High Court.

4   Organisations are ineligible to receive legal aid by virtue of the Legal Aid Act 1988, s 2(10).

Distribution of judicial review work: private practice and law centres

Legal representation for individuals can be provided either by solicitors in private practice or law centres with salaried legal staff. One interesting question is the extent to which law centres (which have in Britain traditionally concentrated their efforts in areas of 'social welfare law', including immigration and housing) can be said to have performed a leading or at least a distinctive role in judicial review litigation. Table 4.1 shows the number of private practice solicitors and law centres handling judicial review applications on behalf of individual applicants during periods covered by our research.

For the purposes of analysis we classified the firms and law centres into five groups according to the number of applications they handled in any one year: those who made 'very low' use of the procedure (only one application per year); those who made 'low' use of the procedure (between two and four applications per year); those who made 'medium' use of the procedure (between five and nine applications per year); those who made 'high' use of the procedure (between 10 and 19 applications per year); and those who made 'very high' use of the procedure (20 or more applications per year).

Our data shows that no fewer than 56 separate law centres, divided equally between those in London and the rest of the country, undertook at least one judicial review application over the whole of the three-and-a-quarter years covered by the research. This included 30 law centres making applications in 1987, 26 in 1988, 30 in 1989, and 17 during the first quarter of 1991. These figures indicate that over half of the law centres in the country were involved in at least one judicial review application in any one year.

This compares with 526 private practice solicitors in 1987, 503 in 1988, 629 in 1989; and 226 in the first quarter of 1991 who represented an individual applicant for judicial review. Although far greater than the number of law centres involved in the process, these figures show that a much smaller proportion of private practice solicitors undertake judicial review cases. Compared, for example, with the 11,000 solicitors' offices that were receiving legal aid payments per annum during these periods, it would appear that less than 6% of private practitioners were involved in judicial review litigation in any one year.

Moreover, for most private practitioners who did undertake judicial review work, involvement in the field was clearly a fairly uncommon occurrence. Over three-quarters of the private practitioners who represented individual applicants in each of the three years 1987 to

Table 4.1

Solicitors in Private Practice and Law Centres Providing Representation for Individual Applicants for Judicial Review, 1987-1989 and 1st quarter of 1991

	Very low (1 only pa)	Low (2-4 pa)	Medium (5-9 pa)	High (10-19 pa)	Very High (20+ pa)	Totals
1987						
Private Solicitors	415	83	18	6	4	**526**
Law Centres	16	11	2	1	-	**30**
All Representatives	431	94	20	7	4	**556**
% Representatives	*77.5*	*16.9*	*3.6*	*1.3*	*0.7*	
No of Cases	431	238	129	99	290	**1187**
% Cases	*36.3*	*20.1*	*10.9*	*8.3*	*24.4*	
1988						
Private Solicitors	397	84	14	7	1	**503**
Law Centres	9	15	1	1	-	**26**
All Representatives	406	99	15	8	1	**529**
% Representatives	*76.7*	*18.7*	*2.8*	*1.5*	*0.2*	
No of Cases	406	245	95	110	52	**908**
% Cases	*44.7*	*27.0*	*10.5*	*12.1*	*5.7*	
1989						
Private solicitors	491	108	21	7	2	**629**
Law Centres	13	13	4	-	-	**30**
All Representatives	504	121	25	7	2	**659**
% Representatives	*76.5*	*18.4*	*3.8*	*1.1*	*0.3*	
No of Cases	504	308	161	91	83	**1147**
% Cases	*43.9*	*26.9*	*14.0*	*7.9*	*7.2*	
1991 (Jan-March)						
Private Solicitors	*185*	34	4	3	-	**226**
Law Centres	11	6	-	-	-	**17**
All Representatives	196	40	4	3	-	**243**

1989 undertook only one case in the year, while that was true of less than half of the law centres involved in judicial reviews in each of these three years. Overall, 95% of private practice solicitors doing judicial review in each year were 'low' or 'very low' users. On the other hand, there were a number of more frequent users of judicial review among private practitioners. In 1987, there were 10 private practice firms (but only one law centre) that undertook 10 or more judicial review applications for individuals. In 1988 there were eight 'high' or 'very high' private practice users (but, again only one law centre), and in 1989 there were nine private practice firms in this category (but no law centres). In the first quarter of 1991, there were seven private practitioners (but no law centres) that had undertaken five or more individual applications for judicial review in this three month period alone.

Specialisation and private practice

Levels of specialisation are particularly evident in several subject areas, especially immigration (see Table 4.2). In 1987, there were 153 private practice firms that undertook at least one immigration judicial review application, of which 102 did only one case in the year. But, taken together, these 102 firms accounted for only 18% of the private practice immigration judicial review applications. At the other end of the spectrum, there were nine private practice firms that did 10 or more immigration judicial reviews in 1987, and these firms together accounted for no less than 58% of the private practice immigration judicial review applications. This included four firms which were 'very high' users in the immigration field, alone handling respectively 26, 63, 81, and 118 applications in each of the years. Such concentrations of cases were clearly associated with the upsurge in asylum cases during 1987.

Even in immigration, however, where the levels of specialisation among private practice solicitors have perhaps been greatest, there was a gradual dispersal of the judicial review caseload among private practitioners over the period of our research. In 1989, when the overall number of private practice immigration judicial reviews was some 38% lower than in 1987, the number of private practice firms undertaking judicial reviews in this field was slightly higher than two years earlier. By then, the 105 firms doing only one immigration case in the year accounted for 27% of the private practice immigration judicial review applications, while the four firms doing more than 10 cases handled 28% (half the proportion dealt with by such firms in 1987). In 1989 the two 'very high' private practice users in the field of immigration handled 26 and 55 such applications respectively.

Table 4.2

Solicitors in Private Practice and Law Centres Providing Representation to Individual Applicants for Judicial Review in Immigration Cases, 1987-1989 and 1st quarter of 1991

	Very low (1 only pa)	Low (2–4 pa)	Medium (5–9 pa)	High (10–19 pa)	Very High (20+ pa)	Totals
1987						
Private Solicitors	102	30	12	5	4	**153**
Law Centres	17	7	1	-	-	**25**
All Representatives	119	37	13	5	4	**178**
% Representatives	*66.9*	*20.8*	*7.3*	*2.8*	*2.2*	
No of Cases	119	100	84	70	288	**661**
% Cases	*18.0*	*15.1*	*12.7*	*10.6*	*43.6*	
1988						
Private Solicitors	97	35	6	4	1	**143**
Law Centres	4	9	-	-	-	**13**
All Representatives	101	44	6	4	1	**156**
% Representatives	*64.7*	*28.2*	*3.8*	*2.6*	*0.6*	
No of Cases	101	105	38	57	52	**353**
% Cases	*28.6*	*29.7*	*10.8*	*16.1*	*14.7*	
1989						
Private Solicitors	105	39	10	2	2	**158**
Law Centres	13	3	2	-	-	**18**
All Representatives	118	42	12	2	2	**176**
% Representatives	*67.0*	*23.9*	*6.8*	*1.1*	*1.1*	
No of Cases	118	111	79	27	81	**416**
% Cases	*28.4*	*26.7*	*19.0*	*6.5*	*19.5*	
1991 (Jan–Mar)						
Private Solicitors	49	7	4	1	-	**61**
Law Centres	3	1	-	-	-	**4**
All Representatives	52	8	4	1	-	**65**

As noted, homelessness is an area where there was a growing number of judicial reviews over the period of our research, and this increased volume was accompanied by a growth in the number of private practitioners becoming involved in such cases (see Table 4.3). The overall number of firms, however, still remained relatively small. Although there was some concentration of homelessness cases among individual firms, this was certainly on a much smaller scale than in the immigration field.

In 1987, there were 46 private practice solicitors who represented applicants for judicial review in homelessness cases, and 40 of these undertook only one case. Together, these 40 firms accounted for two-thirds of the private practice homelessness cases. The most homelessness cases undertaken by any one representative was eight, and this was a law centre; the largest private practice user handled seven cases in the year. By 1989, the number of homeless person judicial reviews undertaken by private practitioners had increased by 160% and the number of private practice firms undertaking such cases had increased by 120%, to just over 100. However, 82 of these firms had handled only one homeless persons case in the year, accounting for 54% of the private practice homelessness caseload. By this stage, there were two private practice firms that each represented 11 homeless person applicants, and the largest caseload undertaken by a law centre in this field in 1989 was just five cases.

Further evidence of limited concentrations of homelessness cases building up among particular private practitioners is to be found in the data for the first quarter of 1991. During this period, one firm undertook nine such applications in the three months. However, especially when compared to immigration, homelessness judicial reviews were fairly widely dispersed among firms that undertook such cases, although by no means across the private profession as a whole.

When we turn to consider non-homelessness and non-immigration cases (see Table 4.4), the extent of dispersal of judicial review cases among private practice firms was even more marked. In 1987, there were no less than 291 private solicitors who undertook only one judicial review outside the fields of immigration and homelessness on behalf of individual applicants, and those firms accounted for two-thirds of all such cases involving private practitioner representation. There were only four firms that handled more than five cases in this category, and they accounted for only 7% of the private practice non-immigration and non-homelessness cases, on behalf of individuals.

Table 4.3

Solicitors in Private Practice and Law Centres Providing Representation to Individual Judicial Review Homelessness Applicants, 1987-1989 and 1st quarter of 1991

	Very low (1 only pa)	Low (2-4 pa)	Medium (5-9 pa)	High (10-19 pa)	Very High (20+ pa)	Totals
1987						
Private Solicitors	40	5	1	-	-	**46**
Law Centres	5	3	1	-	-	**9**
All Representatives	45	8	2	-	-	**55**
% Representatives	*81.8*	*14.5*	*3.6*	-	-	
No of Cases	45	21	15	-	-	**81**
% Cases	*55.6*	*25.9*	*18.5*	-	-	
1988						
Private Solicitors	46	8	1	1	-	**56**
Law Centres	7	4	1	-	-	**12**
All Representatives	53	12	2	1	-	**68**
% Representatives	*77.9*	*17.6*	*2.9*	*1.5*	-	
No of Cases	53	29	11	10	-	**103**
% Cases	*51.4*	*28.2*	*10.7*	*9.7*	-	
1989						
Private Solicitors	82	14	3	2	-	**101**
Law Centres	9	3	1	-	-	**13**
All Representatives	91	17	4	2	-	**114**
% Representatives	*79.8*	*14.9*	*3.5*	*1.8*	-	
No of Cases	91	41	20	22	-	**174**
% Cases	*52.3*	*23.6*	*11.5*	*12.6*	-	
1991 (Jan-Mar)						
Private Solicitors	39	3	1	-	-	**43**
Law Centres	8	2	-	-	-	**10**
All Representatives	47	5	1	-	-	**53**

Table 4.4

Solicitors in Private Practice and Law Centres Providing Representation to Individual Applicants for Judicial Review in Non-Immigration and Non-Homelessness Cases, 1987-1989 and 1st quarter of 1991

	Very low (1 only pa)	Low (2–4 pa)	Medium (5–9 pa)	High (10—19 pa)	Very High (20+ pa)	Totals
1987						
Private Solicitors	291	53	5	-	-	349
Law Centres	5	1	-	-	-	6
All Representatives	296	54	5	-	-	355
% Representatives	*83.4*	*15.2*	*1.4*	-	-	
No of Cases	296	120	34	-	-	450
% Cases	*65.8*	*26.7*	*7.6*	-	-	
1988						
Private Solicitors	279	45	4	2	-	330
Law Centres	7	5	1	-	-	13
All Representatives	286	50	5	2	-	343
% Representatives	*83.4*	*14.6*	*1.5*	*0.6*	-	
No of Cases	286	111	25	26	-	448
% Cases	*63.8*	*24.8*	*5.6*	*5.8*	-	
1989						
Private Solicitors	345	47	7	2	-	401
Law Centres	2	6	1	-	-	9
All Representatives	347	53	8	2	-	410
% Representatives	*84.6*	*12.9*	*2.0*	*0.5*	-	
No of Cases	347	128	49	24	-	548
% Cases	*63.3*	*23.4*	*8.9*	*4.4*	-	
1991 (Jan-Mar)						
Private Solicitors	113	11	1	1	-	126
Law Centres	7	-	-	-	-	7
All Representatives	120	11	1	1	-	133

By 1989, the extent of dispersion of non-immigration and non-homelessness cases had hardly changed, despite an increase of 17% in the number of such cases undertaken by private practitioners. The 345 firms handling only one non-immigration or non-homelessness judicial review for individual applicants in the year still accounted for 64% of all such private practice cases, and there were still only eight firms doing more than five cases of this type in the year. In the first quarter of 1991, however, one private practice firm undertook 12 non-immigration/non-homelessness cases. These all involved judicial reviews in the field of education.

Perhaps all of this adds up to a comforting message for the barristers practising administrative law. Despite the overall growth in public law litigation, there was evidence of only very limited specialisation among private solicitors in judicial review litigation during the period covered by our research. Over nine out of 10 private solicitors firms appeared to handle no judicial review cases, and the vast majority of those who did, handled only the odd case and were no doubt very much dependent on the skills and expertise of the Bar in doing so.

Role of law centres

This leaves the question of the role of law centres in judicial review litigation. As noted, over half of all law centres handled at least one judicial review in each of the years studied, and overall law centres handled between 6% and 8% of all applications brought by represented individuals in the years covered by our data.

Between 1987 and 1989 law centre involvement in immigration judicial reviews was about the same level, between 6% and 8%, although in the first quarter of 1991 they handled only 4% of such applications. Of course, by 1987 immigration was already very well established as a major field of judicial review with a number of specialist private practice providers. It may, however, be that law centres had a more significant role in developing judicial review as a remedy in immigration at an earlier stage.

The role of law centres in homelessness judicial review has been more notable, certainly given their numbers in comparison to private practice. In 1987, law centres accounted for a quarter of such cases, and for a fifth in 1988. However, by 1989 the proportion of homelessness judicial reviews handled by law centres had dropped to just below 10% and, in fact, in that year they handled fewer homelessness cases than in 1987. In other words, as the volume of homelessness judicial reviews increased, the role of private practice solicitors in providing representation in this field expanded. It is open to question whether, given the constraints of their small numbers and resources, law centres could have coped with much of the increasing volume in homelessness cases.

What was the role of law centres in other subject areas? Is there, for example, evidence of their being particularly active in opening up new fields of challenge? In this respect, the evidence from our research is at best patchy. In 1987 only seven out of 77 law centre judicial reviews (9%) were concerned with non-immigration or non-housing matters, although by 1988 this had increased to 23 out of 97 cases (24%), falling back to 21 out of 96 (22%) in 1989, and seven out of 30 (23%) in the first quarter of 1991. Taking the three-and-a-quarter years covered by the research as a whole, law centres were responsible for 17 judicial reviews relating to welfare benefits out of a total of 58 such cases in the period, 10 education judicial reviews out of a total of 124 such cases, and seven judicial reviews in relation to utilities. In no other field did law centres, taken as a group, represent applicants in more than five judicial reviews in the whole three-and-a-quarter years.

Litigants in person

As can be seen from Table 4.5, litigants in person constituted a significant and apparently growing minority of applicants for judicial review. In 1987 they accounted for 9% of applications made in the name of individuals, 13% in 1988, 12% in 1989, and 15% in the first quarter of 1991.

Table 4.5

Litigants in Person as Applicants for Judicial Review, 1987-1989 and 1st quarter of 1991

	1987	1988	1989	1991 (Jan-Mar)
No of Applications by Litigants in Person	120	139	159	62
% of Individual Applications	9.2%	13.3%	12.2%	15.1%
% of All Applications	7.9%	11.4%	10.3%	13.7%

The fact that nearly one-in-six individual applications for judicial review, and over one-in-eight of all applications, in this latter period were instituted by persons without legal representation is perhaps surprising, given that this is considered to be a fairly complex field of law and procedure and one which is confined to the High Court in London. It may be that the increasing proportion of judicial review applications from unrepresented individuals is a reflection of the growing publicity and public awareness of the procedure, although it may also reflect financial and other restrictions on the availability of legal aid.

Certainly, in terms of the types of decision which were being challenged by litigants in person, very few cases were in the field of immigration and homelessness where, because of the subject matter and the low incomes of many of those likely to be affected, one would expect legal aid to be more widely available for judicial review proceedings (see Chapter 5). Between a fifth and a third of all applications by litigants in person during the periods covered by our research were in relation to criminal matters.

Representation of commercial applicants

Legal representation of company applicants for judicial review appeared to be as widespread as that for individual applicants. In 1987 the 98 applications by companies were spread across no less than 75 different solicitors' firms, with two-thirds of these applications being handled by firms representing only one company applicant in the year. Only two firms dealt with more than five company applications in 1987. The 114 company applications in 1988 were represented by 91 different firms, and 77 of these firms dealt with only one company applicant in the year, and these again accounted for two-thirds of such applications. No firm in 1988 handled five or more company applications. Slightly more concentration of company representation was found in 1989, when there were still 77 firms each dealing with a single company applicant in the year, but these accounted for only 55% of such cases. In this year there were three firms representing five or more company applicants for judicial review.

Summary and conclusions

The overall impression gained from our research is that only very limited degrees of specialisation in judicial review have been developed by solicitors in private practice, whether representing individuals or companies, or indeed by law centres. The main fields in which particular firms handled large numbers of judicial review applications on behalf of individuals were in immigration and, to a lesser degree, homelessness and education (in particular educational special needs cases).[5] Law centres played a significant role in relation to homelessness cases during the earlier years covered by our research, but their share of such cases declined as increasing numbers of private practitioners became involved.

Of course, our data relate only to the role of private solicitors and of law centres in representing those who did apply for judicial review, and it is not possible from this to say how many more might have been seeking to break into judicial review but were denied the opportunity to do so by a lack of available finance for their clients, particularly under legal aid. We examine how far the processes for obtaining legal aid were masking a hidden demand for judicial review, both among individuals and their legal representatives, in the next chapter.

Nor can we say how often legal representatives (perhaps particularly those in law centres) were advising their clients not to apply for judicial review but to employ other means of resolving their disputes with public authorities, or were themselves dealing with public law matters at other levels (eg providing advice or representation at tribunals). Nevertheless, the general impression from our research is that relatively few private solicitors were extensively involved in judicial review or had any particular expertise in use of the procedure. Contrary to the view that law centres played a leading role in relation to the development of new fields of judicial review, our evidence suggests that, like private practice solicitors, much of their caseload was confined to the fields of immigration and housing. In fact, the small number of law centres and their limited resources seem likely to have constrained their role in judicial review litigation as such, although they may well have been a significant source of referrals of potential judicial review applicants to private practitioners.

There is also very little evidence of concentration of representation of company applicants for judicial review. Very few private practitioners provided representation to more than one or two such applicants in any one year. Finally, litigants in person constituted a significant and apparently growing minority of judicial review applicants, especially among those involved in criminal cases, over the period covered by our research.

---

5   The issue of concentration of judicial review work among particular firms of solicitors will be discussed further in the next chapter in relation to legal aid, where it will be seen that during one three-month period a firm in Liverpool processed no less than 106 applications relating to potential judicial reviews on the non-determination of housing benefit.

Chapter 5

Legal Aid and Judicial Review

The lodging of an application for judicial review is the culmination of a preliminary process through which an individual first seeks help in relation to his or her problem with a public body, is advised that there may be a potential remedy in judicial review, and in most instances then successfully makes an application for legal aid in order to initiate legal proceedings. For the potential applicant for judicial review, legal aid can provide both the means of meeting the legal costs of such a case and a form of protection against having to pay the other side's costs in the event of the judicial review being unsuccessful. This is not the only significance of legal aid, however. The legal aid decision-making process, in which the applicant's potential case for judicial review will undergo a preliminary vetting as to its merits, can serve as an early filter of unmeritorious cases, even before the courts consider this issue at the leave stage.

Because legal aid acts as a pre-litigation filter of potential challenges, research in this area allows us to take one step back from the court process and from the demand for judicial review that surfaces there. In other words, it brings us closer to the hidden demand that may exist in the community for challenging the decisions of, and seeking redress against, public authorities. In particular, it enables us to address the following questions: how does the demand for legal aid for judicial review compare with the numbers of applications to seek leave lodged with the Crown Office? Is the composition of the body of legal aid applications significantly different from the make up of judicial review cases, in terms of factors such as their subject matter or the types of public authorities being challenged? If so, how are such differences to be explained? Does legal aid filter out more of some type of case than others, perhaps because of the nature of the criteria that are employed by the legal aid authorities to test the merits of cases? Are there other intervening variables that prevent cases where legal aid has been granted from being transformed into applications to the court for judicial review?

There are also a number of issues concerning the administration of legal aid in relation to judicial review. As we shall see, in contrast with judicial review itself, legal aid administration is decentralised across the country and depends to some extent on the availability of expertise among local legal practitioners in deciding in which cases to grant or refuse legal aid. Not only does this raise the possibility of inconsistency in decision-making on legal aid applications, but in light of the evidence presented in the previous chapter on the limited extent of specialisation in judicial review among solicitors (and the probable concentration of specialist barristers in London), there may be questions as to the availability of relevant expertise in some parts of the country.

Legal aid criteria and administration

The availability of legal aid is governed by criteria laid down in the Legal Aid Act 1988 and in regulations made under that Act, as administered by the Legal Aid Board. The criteria for granting or refusing legal aid have remained little changed ever since the modern legal aid scheme was established in this country in 1950. The criteria applicable to judicial review cases are the same as those that apply to other forms of civil legal proceedings. Applications for civil legal aid must be made through a solicitor to one of the 13 Area offices maintained by the Legal Aid Board.[1] Once an application has been submitted, it is subject to two different tests of eligibility. One of these relates to the *financial means* of the applicant and is effectively administered on behalf of the Legal Aid Board by a special unit of the Department of Social Security located in Preston. The second test of eligibility concerns the merits of the case to which the application relates, and decisions on this are made by each Area office. The grant or refusal of legal aid is governed directly by the relevant Act and regulations,[2] under which decisions are delegated to Area Directors and their staff and, on appeal, to Area Committees. Although the national Legal Aid Board can itself issue guidance to its Area offices on the standards to be applied in determining applications, and indeed does so each year in the form of Notes for Guidance published in the *Legal Aid Handbook*,[3] such guidance is purely advisory in character[4] There is no machinery under which decisions relating to particular legal aid applications can be appealed, or referred, to a national level for review.

---

1   The offices are in London, Brighton (South Eastern), Reading (Southern), Bristol (South Western), Cardiff (South Wales), Birmingham (West Midlands), Manchester (North Western), Newcastle (Northern), Leeds (North Eastern), Nottingham (East Midlands), Cambridge (Eastern), Chester (Chester and North Wales), and Liverpool (Merseyside).

2   In particular, the Legal Aid Act 1988, s 15(2), (3) and the Civil Legal Aid (General) Regulations 1989.

3   For the most recent version of these Notes for Guidance, see *Legal Aid Handbook* 1994, London: Sweet & Maxwell, pp 3–167.

4   For a discussion of this issue, see The Public Law Project, *The Applicant's Guide to Judicial Review*, (1995) London, Sweet & Maxwell, Chapter 7 and O Hansen 'Disappearing Merits Test Guidance', (1993) *Legal Action*, August p 13.

The decision whether or not to grant legal aid on the merits of the case to which the application relates is taken in the first instance by an employed officer of the Legal Aid Board acting in the name of each Area Director. This decision entails a two-limbed test. Under the first limb, the applicant is required to show that he or she has 'reasonable grounds for taking, defending of being a party to the proceedings'[5] in question. The second limb requires the officer to consider whether 'in the particular circumstances of the case' it is 'unreasonable that [the applicant] should be granted representation'.[6] The first of these requirements is usually referred to as the *legal merits test* and the second as the *general reasonableness test*. The officer of the Legal Aid Board also has a discretion to grant legal aid on an emergency basis, and this can be done at very short notice either over the telephone to the solicitor, or in response to a postal application. A grant of legal aid may be subject to specified limitations, relating either to the particular procedural steps that may be taken in the proceedings or to the costs that can be incurred, although it will be open to the solicitor to apply subsequently to have these restrictions removed.

Where an application for legal aid is refused on its merits, either under the legal merits or the general reasonableness test, the applicant has a right of appeal to an Area Committee consisting of solicitors and barristers drawn from ordinary practice within the relevant locality. No right of appeal exists against a refusal of legal aid on the grounds of the applicant's financial ineligibility. As noted, there is no further appeal from an Area Committee decision to refuse legal aid, although the regulations do permit new applications to be made in respect of the same proceedings, especially where there has been a change in circumstances or new information can be provided. Like any other body exercising statutory responsibilities, the Legal Aid Board is potentially open to judicial review. Indeed, as we shall see, legal aid may be available to fund applications for judicial review of decisions taken in the name of the Legal Aid Board.

Volume and distribution of legal aid applications

There were 905 applications[7] relating to judicial review known to be received by the Legal Aid Board's Area offices between October and

---

5   Legal Aid Act 1988, s 15(2).

6   *Ibid*, s 15(3).

7   All further reference in this chapter to 'legal aid applications' or 'legal aid grants' will refer to those relating specifically to judicial review unless otherwise specified.

December 1991. This figure can be compared with the total of 454 applications for leave to seek judicial review lodged in the Crown Office during a similar three month period at the beginning of 1991. As we have seen, 54 of these were taken in the name of organisations which would not have been eligible to receive legal aid and a further 58 were made by individuals who were not legally represented. Of course, some of this latter group may have sought legal aid before making their application for judicial review but been refused. Nevertheless, these comparative figures show that in these similar periods there were well over twice as many applications to fund judicial review cases as there were actual applications to seek judicial review. This is significant because it indicates that a large number of potential judicial reviews were not being brought to court.

Table 5.1 shows the distribution of applications across the 13 Legal Aid Area offices in the final quarter of 1991. It also breaks them down by the subjects in which there were more than five such applications. Crown Office data has shown that use of the judicial review procedure itself has tended to be dominated by challenges in just three subject areas: immigration, homelessness and criminal court proceedings, and as shown in Chapter 2, these three fields accounted for 23%, 24% and 16% respectively of all applications to seek leave for judicial review during the first three months of 1991. At the same time, the judicial review procedure is administratively centralised on the High Court in London, and some 55% of applications during the first quarter of 1991 originated in London (see Chapter 3).

Applications for legal aid for judicial review show similar concentrations by area and subject matter. The London Area office accounted for 47% of cases (423) during the final quarter of 1991. This indicates that the concentration of judicial review cases in London is substantially greater than for other areas of civil litigation. It compares, for example, with only 16% of general civil non-matrimonial legal aid applications that were processed through the London Area office during 1991-92.[8] The second largest concentration of judicial review legal aid applications was found in the Merseyside Area office in Liverpool, which handled 152 cases or 17% of the national total, although in this instance the figures were greatly affected by one mass group of applications relating to the non-payment of housing benefit. Indeed, 'other housing' cases (eg those not relating to homelessness) constituted three-quarters of all applications made to the Liverpool office in this period. Other Area offices which handled sizeable

---

8   Estimate derived from *Legal Aid Board Annual Report* 1991-92, London: HMSO, Table General 1, p 84.

Table 5.1

Applications for Legal Aid for Judicial Review Proceedings, October – December 1991 by Legal Aid Area and Subject Matter of Application

Subject	London		South East (Brighton)		Southern (Reading)		South West (Bristol)		S Wales (Cardiff)		W Midlands (Birmingham)		North West (Mancheser)		Northern (Newcastle)		North East (Leeds)		E Midlands (Nottingham)		Eastern (Cambridge)		N Wales (Chester)		Merseyside (Liverpool)		Totals	
	No	%	No	%	No	%	No	%	No	%	No	%	No	%	No	%	No	%	No	%	No	%	No	%	No	%	No	%
Homeless	198	46.8	11	33.3	11	33.3	8	28.6	3	27.3	10	17.5	9	15.0	4	25.0	8	44.4	23	53.5	1	6.3	6	40.0	8	5.3	300	33.1
Other Housing	24	5.7	2	6.1			1	3.6	1	9.1	5	8.8	3	5.0					3	7.0	2	12.5			114	75.0	155	17.1
Immigration	106	25.4			1	3.0			2	18.2	8	14.3	3	5.0	4	25.0	2	11.1	3	7.0	1	6.3			2	1.3	130	14.4
Criminal Courts	19	4.5	5	15.2	2	6.1	3	10.7			5	8.8	18	30.0	2	12.5			4	9.3	5	31.3			5	3.3	70	7.7
Education	27	6.4	1	3.0	9	27.3	4	14.3	1	9.1	1	1.8	6	10.0			1	5.6	1	2.3			3	20.0	4	2.6	58	6.4
Prisons	10	2.4					1	3.6			9	15.9	2	3.3	2	12.5	2	11.1							1	0.7	27	3.0
Benefits	4	0.9	2	6.1	2	6.1	1	3.6	1	9.1			3	5.0			1	5.6	2	4.7					6	3.9	20	2.2
Legal Aid	10	2.4	2	6.1	1	3.0			1	9.1	2	3.5	1	1.7			1	5.6	1	2.3					1	0.7	20	2.2
Children in Care	5	1.2	3	9.1					2	18.2	1	1.8	2	3.3	1	6.3	2	11.1			1	6.3	1	6.7			18	2.0
Mental Hlth	2	0.5	6	18.2							3	5.3	1	1.7							1	6.3			1	0.7	14	1.5
Planning	3	0.7			2	6.1	2	7.1													5	31.3			1	0.7	13	1.4
Poll Tax	1	0.2					1	3.6			3	5.3	2	3.3											5	3.3	12	1.3
Crim Injury	2	0.5			2	6.1	1	3.6					3	5.0													8	0.9
Travellers							2	7.1			3	5.3							2	4.7							7	0.8
Other	9	2.1	3	9.1	3	9.1	3	10.7			6	10.5	6	10.0	2	12.5	1	5.6	3	7.0			4	26.7	2	1.3	42	4.6
Not Ascertained	3	0.7					1	3.6			1	1.8	1	1.7	1	6.3			1	2.3			1	4.7	2	1.3	11	1.2
Totals No	423		33		33		28		11		57		60		16		18		43		16		15		152		905	
%	46.7		3.6		3.6		3.1		1.2		6.3		6.6		1.8		2.0		4.8		1.8		1.7		16.8			

numbers of applications during the final quarter of 1991 were the North Western Area in Manchester (60 cases or 7% of the national total); the West Midlands Area in Birmingham (57 cases or 6%); the East Midlands Area in Nottingham (43 cases or 5%); the South Eastern Area in Brighton and the Southern Area in Reading (33 cases or 4% each), and the South Western Area in Bristol (28 cases or 3%).

At the same time, the legal aid data confirm the relatively low rate of demand for judicial review in other parts of the country, some of which contain very large centres of population. The Northern Area office in Newcastle and the North Eastern Area office in Leeds, for example, dealt with only 16 and 18 applications respectively (each 2% of the national total) in the three month period. Interestingly, data on the number of applications for leave to seek judicial review, discussed in Chapter 3, also point to these two areas as having a low demand for judicial review at the relevant time. The remaining three Legal Aid Areas with low rates of applications were the Eastern Area in Cambridge (16 applications or 2%), the Chester and North Wales Area in Chester (15 applications or 2%), and the South Wales Area in Cardiff (11 applications or 1%).

Turning to the subject matter of legal aid applications, the largest group related to homelessness, which constituted a third of all applications. There was a particular concentration of homelessness cases in the London Area office, which dealt with two-thirds of such applications nationally. As a result, nearly half of the London Area office's judicial review caseload was made up of applications relating to homelessness. Although all Area offices received at least one legal aid application relating to homelessness, the numbers in some areas were still very small. The second largest subject group related to other housing matters, although here the effect of a large group of applications concerning non-payment of housing benefit in Liverpool must again be noted. As a result, the Merseyside Area office accounted for nearly three out of four of all applications nationally in this subject area. There was, however, a fairly wide distribution of such applications across the other areas of the country, with all but four of the 13 Legal Aid Area offices handling at least one in the sample period.

By contrast, legal aid applications relating to potential judicial reviews of immigration decisions, which accounted for 14% of cases, were very much concentrated in London. Over 80% of the legal aid applications in this field were processed through the London Area office, and such cases constituted a quarter of this Area's overall judicial review caseload. Applications relating to potential judicial reviews of criminal legal proceedings accounted for 8% of cases, with particular concentrations of such cases in the London and Manchester

Area offices (each dealing with around a quarter of such cases nationally).

The fifth largest group of applications was related to education, which constituted 6% of the sample. The London Area office dealt with almost half of all such applications nationally, while the Southern Area office in Reading handled approximately one-in-six. In this instance, the concentration of legal aid applications in particular Area offices may well be related to the location of the small number of solicitors in the country known to specialise in education judicial reviews. At the time, there was one solicitor in London and another in Stroud in Gloucestershire who were regarded as specialists in challenging decisions on assessment of educational special needs through judicial review, while another solicitor located in Oxford was a national expert in education law in general. A similar explanation may lie behind the relative concentration of legal aid applications for judicial reviews relating to mental health in the South Eastern Area office in Brighton, which dealt with six out of the 14 such cases in the sample. The London Area office and the West Midlands Area office in Birmingham also each handled a third of the applications relating to potential judicial reviews on prison issues.

Because of special arrangements regarding challenges to decisions of legal aid authorities, the distribution of applications relating to legal aid issues must be treated with some caution. Where an application involves a case in which the Legal Aid Board would be the respondent, it is considered by an Area office other than the one involved in the original decision being questioned. There were 13 such cases in the sample, and one other case where the respondent would have been the Department of Social Security's special legal aid unit in Preston. The remaining six applications in this category involved challenges relating to criminal legal aid where the respondents would have been magistrates' courts. The Legal Aid Areas whose initial decisions were potentially being challenged in these cases were the South Eastern Area (five cases), the Southern Area (two cases), with one case each in the West Midlands, North Western, South Western, North Eastern, Chester and North Wales, and Eastern Areas.

There were as many applications relating to potential judicial reviews of legal aid decisions as for all other types of social welfare benefits; this again highlights the paucity of litigation in the latter field and one of the main puzzles associated with judicial review, namely why are there so few challenges in many key areas of governmental activity affecting vital rights and interests of individuals and groups. In this respect, it may be noted that the 20 judicial review legal aid applications in the final quarter of 1991 involving welfare benefits

Table 5.2
Legal Aid Applications for Judicial Review, October-December 1991
by Prospective Respondents

Prospective Respondent	Number of Applications	(% of Applications)
Central Government Departments:		
Home Office		
Immigration	*112*	
Prisons	*21*	
Other	*5*	
Total	138	
Department of Social Security	18	
Department of Education and Science	5	
Department of the Environment	3	
Department of Transport	2	
Department of Health	2	
Inland Revenue	1	
Total	168	(19.0)
Local Authorities:		
Homelessness	*300*	
Other Housing	*155*	
Education	*48*	
Other	*50*	
Total	553	(62.5)
Courts and Tribunals:		
Magistrates' Courts	81	
Immigration Appeals Tribunal	17	
Mental Health Review Tribunals	7	
Social Security Commissioners	5	
Coroners' Courts	2	
Special Commissioners for Tax	1	
County Court	2	
Crown Court	1	
Total	116	(13.1)
Other Bodies:		
Legal Aid Board	13	
Crown Prosecution Service	11	
Criminal Injuries Compensation Board	7	
Prison Governors/Boards of Visitors/Doctors	4	
Council for Legal Education	2	
Police Complaints Authority	1	
Education and Library Board	1	
Polytechnic	1	
Special Hospital Authority	1	
Gaming Board of Great Britain	1	
Health Authority	1	
Sickness Benefit Society	1	
Working Men's Club	1	
British Athletics Association	1	
British Show Pony Society	1	
Labour Party	1	
Total	48	(5.4)

compares with only five applications for leave lodged in the Crown Office in this field during the first quarter of the same year. On the other hand, the sample did contain 12 cases relating to potential judicial reviews on poll tax, and this was perhaps an indication that this highly controversial subject was beginning to emerge as a growth area for judicial review.

As shown in Chapter 3, it is local government rather than central government, that has tended to be the main target of judicial reviews over recent years. This is confirmed by the data on legal aid applications (see Table 5.2). Local authorities were the intended respondents in 62% of the legal aid applications where the respondent could be identified, with over 80% of the prospective actions against them relating to homelessness or other housing issues. On the other hand, less than 20% of the applications involved prospective actions against central government departments, with 80% of these being against the Home Office, primarily in relation to immigration. Courts and tribunals were identified as the respondents in 13% of applications and various non-departmental public bodies in 5%. Among individual local authorities, there were nine London boroughs (Southwark, Camden, Tower Hamlets, Newham, Hackney, Westminster, Lambeth, Ealing and Haringey) and three non-London authorities (Liverpool, Birmingham and Dyfed County Council) who were named as the prospective respondents in 10 or more judicial review legal aid applications in the three month period.

Distribution by legal representatives

Table 5.3 shows the distribution of legal aid judicial review applications across firms of solicitors in private practice and among solicitors employed within law centres, advice agencies and national interest groups. A total of 377 private firms of solicitors and 27 law centres, advice agencies and interest groups were involved in representing the 905 applicants for legal aid, an average of just over two applications for each firm or agency. In fact, two-thirds of the private firms and half of the law centres, advice agencies and interest groups handled only one legal aid judicial review application in the sample period, and a further quarter of the private firms and all but one of the law centres, advice agencies and interest groups dealt with between two and five such applications. There was one firm of solicitors in Liverpool that submitted a total of 106 legal aid judicial review applications in relation to the non-payment of housing benefit within the city. Otherwise, all the private firms and the one law centre that handled more than 10 applications in the sample were in London.

Table 5.3

Distribution of Legal Aid Applications for Judicial Review, October–December 1991 by Legal Representatives

No of Applications	1	2	3	4	5	6	7	8	9	10	12	17	19	106	Totals
Solicitors in Private Practice:															
No of Firms	254	56	24	7	10	8	3	3	4	3	1	2	1	1	377
% of Firms	67.4	14.9	6.4	1.9	2.7	2.1	0.8	0.8	1.1	0.8	0.3	0.5	0.3	0.3	
(% of Applications)															(93.5)
Law Centres, Advice Agencies and Interest Groups:															
No. of Outlets	14	7	1	4							1				27
% of Outlets	51.9	25.9	3.7	14.8							3.7				
(% of Applications)															(6.5)
% of Total Applications	29.6	13.9	8.3	4.9	5.5	5.3	2.3	2.7	4.0	3.3	2.7	3.8	2.1	11.7	100.0

On the other hand, the 19 firms dealing with between six and 10 applications were evenly distributed between London and other parts of the country. It may be noted that not all the firms within this group were located in major centres of population. They included firms based in Hereford, Evesham in Worcestershire and Mansfield in Nottinghamshire, and this may be indicative either of particular pockets of public law expertise or the incidence of local issues throwing up a demand for judicial review.

It is interesting to compare the distribution amongst solicitors of legal aid applications with that of actual judicial review cases. As noted, the number of legal aid applications in the sample was over twice the number of applications made by individuals for leave to seek judicial review at the Crown Office over a similar period in 1991. Of the 400 individual applicants for leave in the first quarter of 1991 58 were litigants in person, with the remaining 342 being represented by a total of 226 private firms of solicitors and 17 law centres. The vast majority of such offices handled only one judicial review case in the relevant period. In view of the concentrations of cases in particular subject areas shown in Chapter 4, we were interested in the question whether the much greater volume of legal aid applications for judicial review found in the final quarter of 1991 was the product of the same number of firms handling larger numbers of cases at this preliminary stage or a larger number of firms attempting to make use of the procedure. The evidence would appear to suggest that both factors were at work. As shown in Table 5.4, the average number of leave applications per representative in the first quarter of 1991 was 1.4, and this compares with an average of 2.2 legal aid applications per representative in final quarter of the same year. Of course, the latter figure was greatly influenced by the one Liverpool firm that dealt with 106 applications, but even when this firm is eliminated from the calculations the average number of applications per representative was still 2.0. Put another way, a 165% difference in the number of cases between the two samples was associated with only a 66% variation in the number of representatives. It would therefore appear that although there was some evidence of greater concentration of legal aid applications in particular solicitors' firms than found in our sample of judicial review applications, the greater volume of legal aid applications was also the result of many more firms, often doing only one or two cases, being involved at this stage.

It is also notable that the proportion of legal aid judicial review applications submitted by solicitors in law centres, advice agencies and interest groups, at 7% of the total, was the same as the proportion of judicial review applications they appear to have handled. There were only six applications in the sample (less than 1%) made in the name of

Table 5.4

Comparison of Distribution of Judicial Review Leave and Legal Aid Applications by Legal Representatives

	Judicial Review Leave Applications by Represented Individuals January-March 1991	Legal Aid Judicial Review Applications October-December 1991*	
No of Applications	342	905	(799)
No of Representatives	243	404	(403)
Average No of Applications per Representative	1.4	2.2	(2.0)

*Figures in brackets exclude one representative that submitted 106 (11.7%) of all applications.

a solicitor directly employed by a national interest group. On the other hand, there were a total of 64 cases (7%) where there was an indication on the application form that a national or local interest group had some involvement, for example having advised the applicant earlier or referred the matter on to a solicitor.

Overall these findings confirm the impression that only very limited degrees of specialism in judicial review had developed among either private solicitors or law centres, advice centres and interest groups. Moreover, the majority of legal aid applications were submitted in fields where the use of judicial review had become routine, such as immigration and housing, and most of the solicitors dealing with such applications appeared to do so only relatively infrequently, at least in comparison with other areas of legally-aided litigation. Thus, 30% of judicial review legal aid applications were submitted by solicitors dealing with only one such case in the three month sample period, and a further 33% by solicitors handling between two and five such applications. On the other hand, other than the one firm that handled 106 separate applications (12% of the total), the further 25 solicitors who submitted more than five judicial review legal aid applications over the three month period accounted for about a quarter of all such cases nationally. As we shall see, these findings on the routine nature of most legal aid judicial review applications and on the relative lack of specialism in judicial review may have significant implications for the legal aid decision-making process itself.

Information on the identity of the barrister involved in the case was often not available. There were only 207 cases where the barrister could be identified, and these involved a total of 127 separate barristers. There was one barrister who handled 11 cases; one, nine cases; one, eight cases; one, six cases; three, five cases; five, four cases; two, three cases; and 19 two cases. The remaining 94 barristers identified each handled only a single case in the three month period.

The processing of applications

Applications for judicial review are subject to tight time limits (see Chapter 6), and this places a premium on the efficiency of both solicitors in completing and submitting legal aid applications, where this is required, and on the legal aid authorities processing and deciding on the application. This is especially the case where there has been any substantial delay between the decision giving rise to the potential judicial review and the date when the person affected contacts a solicitor and submits a legal aid application. The length of time between the date of the decision being challenged and the receipt of the legal aid application in the Area office could be determined in only just over half of the cases in the sample. And in 22% of these it amounted to a week or less, in 25% to between two and three weeks, in 15% to between four and six weeks, and in 26% to between seven and 13 weeks. There were 14% of the applications in which the delay from the date of the decision could be determined (7% of all sample cases) where more than three months elapsed before the legal aid application was submitted.

Although the courts have recognised delay in obtaining legal aid as grounds for allowing an application for judicial review to proceed out-of-time, this is a matter of discretion for the court considering the case and therefore cannot be relied upon by applicants or their legal representatives.[9] Also, in some types of case, such as those involving imminent deportations of applicants from the country or their eviction from temporary accommodation, there may be more pressing reasons for obtaining legal aid for judicial review urgently and getting the

---

9   *R v Stratford on Avon DC, ex parte Jackson* [1985] 1 WLR 1319.

matter before the court. The Home Office, for example, will often only agree to stay a deportation for a matter of days subject to an application for leave being lodged with the court in this time. In these circumstances, it is hardly surprising that most judicial review legal aid cases involve an application for emergency legal aid. This was the case in 82% of the applications, with a fifth of such emergency applications being made over the telephone. In addition, in two-thirds of cases the solicitor also made use of the Green Form Legal Advice and Assistance scheme in order to provide preliminary help to the applicant. There were also 63 cases (7%) where the applicant had previously received legal aid in connection with the same matter, no doubt frequently to cover proceedings from which the grounds for the potential judicial review had arisen.

Of course, it is open to a solicitor to start judicial review proceedings prior to lodging an application for legal aid, and this in fact happened in 66 cases (7%) in the sample. Almost two out of every five such cases involved challenges arising out of criminal court decisions, 18% were in immigration cases, and 15% involved homelessness cases. There are, however, fairly compelling reasons why solicitors would be reluctant to initiate judicial review proceedings, even to the extent of applying for leave, without legal aid. Not only would there be a danger of any work done going unremunerated, but there is some risk of the applicant having to pay the other side's costs if the application for judicial review is unsuccessful.[10]

As noted, solicitors are themselves part of the machinery through which legal aid is administered, and the legal aid authorities are dependent on them to provide adequate information from which to determine the potential merits of any application for judicial review as part of their decision as to the grant or refusal of legal aid. The most important part of the application in this respect is that requiring a 'statement of case'. The practices of solicitors in completing this section of the application appear to vary a good deal. Some will simply include a statement of the facts as presented by the applicant, while others might accompany this by appending copies of various documents (eg a formal decision letter) or possibly correspondence with the prospective respondent. Another approach would be for the solicitor to complete, either on the application form or in an

---

10 For a further discussion of the issue of costs, see Chapters 6 and 7 and The Public Law Project, *The Applicant's Guide to Judicial Review, op cit*, Chapter 6. Cost implications can arise even on leave applications; see Tim Kerr, 'Questions of practice and costs' (1993) *Solicitors' Journal* 2 April. The risk of applicants having to pay respondents' costs may increase if the Law Commission's proposals for such costs to be ordered more frequently on unsuccessful renewed applications for leave are implemented. These proposals are discussed in greater detail in Chapter 7.

accompanying letter, a resumé of the facts and of the legal grounds on which it was considered that the matter might be open to judicial review.

In some cases the application might be further accompanied by counsel's opinion. Indeed, at one stage the legal aid authorities appear to have encouraged the obtaining of counsel's opinion prior to an application for full legal aid and would grant an extension under the Green Form scheme for this purpose. The practice in recent years has been to discourage the use of the Green Form for undertaking formal pre-litigation steps such as obtaining counsel's opinion, in preference to obtaining a civil legal aid certificate,[11] which may itself be limited only to undertaking certain steps leading to formal proceedings. In the sample, there were only 72 cases (8%) where counsel's opinion had been obtained prior to the legal aid judicial review application being submitted, with 38% of such cases involving potential challenges to criminal court decisions, 21% challenges under homelessness legislation, 14% immigration challenges, and 8% each potential judicial reviews in the fields of education and 'other housing' matters.

Given the variations with which solicitors approached the task of completing the 'statement of case' on the application form, we decided to include in our data collection questionnaire an item asking whether the legal aid application or any accompanying letter or documents contained a statement of the legal grounds for seeking judicial review. In fact, such a statement appeared in only just over half (55%) of all applications, and in as many as 29% there was no apparent attempt by the applicant's solicitor to state the legal basis on which judicial review might be sought. In the remaining 16% of cases it was unclear whether such a statement had been made, for example, because documents that had originally accompanied the application were no longer available for inspection.

Two factors may go some way to explain the relatively frequent failure of solicitors to include on the legal aid application what may seem to the most basic statement of the legal grounds for a potential judicial review. First, as indicated, in most cases there was an application for emergency legal aid, an indication that solicitors themselves are often under considerable pressure of time when completing applications. Indeed, when an application for emergency legal aid is made by telephone, the solicitor may be required to give a verbal statement of the grounds for seeking judicial review, and these may then be reproduced only in summary form, or not at all, on the

---

11   See *Legal Aid Handbook, op cit*, Notes for Guidance, para 2.21(f) and (g).

written application. A second factor may be the relative infrequency with which most solicitors undertake judicial review cases, even in the fields where such litigation is itself fairly routine, combined with solicitor's dependence on counsel to identify and draft grounds for judicial review. An interesting question to be examined further below is how far the absence of a clear statement of the legal grounds for judicial review actually prejudices the chances of the case being granted legal aid.

The very high proportion of legal aid judicial review cases that entailed an emergency application was reflected in figures for the time taken by Legal Aid Area offices to process them through to the initial decision on whether to grant or refuse legal aid. In about a third of cases this decision was made on the same day or the day following the receipt of the application, and in a further two-fifths of cases it was taken within two weeks. Less than 5% of applications had not been initially determined within 10 weeks.

More serious problems with delays in the administration of legal aid can arise where an application is initially refused other than on grounds of the applicant's financial ineligibility and it is necessary to lodge an appeal. Appeals are heard before committees consisting of solicitors and barristers drawn from ordinary practice, and for this reason it can be difficult to arrange hearings at short notice. Moreover, an appeal is likely to require additional preparation by the applicant's solicitor in order to provide further justification or supporting evidence as to why there are reasonable grounds for taking judicial review proceedings. Thus, although approximately half of the appeals against refusals of legal aid were lodged by solicitors within a week of the notification of the initial decision on the application, there were a further 40% where the appeal was only lodged within two or three weeks and 10% where it took longer than three weeks. The hearing itself was held within four weeks of receipt of the notice of appeal in just 17% of the cases where information was available on this point. A further 35% of appeals were heard within five to eight weeks, 28% within nine to thirteen weeks, and 20% took over three months to be heard. When combined with the time that may already have elapsed prior to the initial legal aid decision on the application, these figures tend to confirm that where an appeal against a refusal of legal aid is required, there are likely to be very substantial difficulties in the applicant meeting the time limit of three months from the date of the decision being challenged for filing the application for leave.

Applicants have a right to attend and/or to be represented at appeal hearings, although their legal representatives will not be remunerated under legal aid for this. Information on attendances at hearings was available in only just over half of the cases involving an appeal, and neither the applicant nor any other representative appeared in 41% of the appeals in these cases. The applicant appeared on his or her own in a further 20%, and in the remaining 39% of appeals where information could be obtained on this point the applicant was represented by someone else. In three-quarters of the cases where a separate representative attended it was a solicitor and in the remaining cases it was a non-legally qualified person. There were no cases in the sample where the applicant was represented by a barrister on an appeal against a refusal of legal aid.

The granting of legal aid

As has already been shown, the demand for legal aid for judicial review, as measured by the volume of applications, is considerably greater than the number of leave applications made to the court. This raises the question of how the supply of legal aid, in terms of actual grants, relates to the demand both in general and in particular fields of potential judicial review. Is the legal aid decision-making process cutting out significant numbers of potential judicial reviews and therefore suppressing the demands made on the courts? Given the current decentralised basis of legal aid decision-making, there is also the possibility that rates of granting legal aid for judicial review may vary from one area of the country to another, thereby adding to the inconsistency known to affect other parts of the judicial review process (see Chapter 8).

Table 5.5 shows the results of applications in the sample for each of the thirteen Area offices. Just over two-thirds of judicial review legal aid applications were granted on the legal aid officer's initial decision, although in the majority of such cases legal aid was only granted on a limited basis. A further 6% of applications were granted on appeal. The overall grant rate of nearly 75% in judicial review applications compares with a national average of 67% for all non-matrimonial civil legal aid applications in 1991-92.[12] The main difference, however, was that whereas over 5% of general non-matrimonial civil legal aid applications were refused on grounds of the applicants' financial ineligibility, this was the case in only three of the judicial review legal aid applications in the sample (0.3%). Also, a further 5% of general non-matrimonial civil legal aid applications were abandoned or

---

12 *Legal Aid Board Annual Report*, 1991-92, Table Civil 3, p 49.

Table 5.5

Legal Aid Applications for Judicial Review Proceedings, October-December 1991 by Legal Aid Area and Result of Application

Result of Application	London		South East (Brighton)		Southern (Reading)		South West (Bristol)		S Wales (Cardiff)		W Midlands (Birmingham)		North West (Mancheser)		Northern (Newcastle)		North East (Leeds)		E Midlands (Nottingham)		Eastern (Cambridge)		N Wales (Chester)		Merseyside (Liverpool)		Totals	
	No	%	No	%	No	%	No	%	No	%	No	%	No	%	No	%	No	%	No	%	No	%	No	%	No	%	No	%
Granted on Initial Application																												
Unlimited	51	12.1	1	3.0			9	32.1	1	9.1	18	31.6	6	10.0			8	44.4	5	11.6	2	12.5	1	6.6	2	1.3	104	11.5
Limited	276	65.2	8	24.2	13	39.4	11	39.3	2	18.2	23	40.4	16	26.7	6	37.5	3	16.7	31	72.1	7	43.8	12	80.0	101	66.4	509	56.2
Granted on Appeal																												
Unlimited	2	0.5	4	12.1	1	3.0							2	3.3											7	4.6	16	1.8
Limited	14	3.3			7	21.2	2	7.1	2	18.2	1	1.8	2	3.3	1	6.3	1	5.6							14	9.2	44	4.9
Refused and Not Appealed																												
Financial	2	0.5																	1	2.3							3	3.3
Legal	57	13.5	8	24.2	6	18.2	3	10.7	1	9.1	9	15.8	19	31.7	9	56.3	4	22.2	3	7.0	6	37.5	2	13.3	27	17.8	154	17.0
Refused on Appeal	14	3.3	5	15.1	6	18.2	3	10.7	4	36.4	6	10.5	12	20.0			2	11.1	1	2.3	1	6.3			1	0.7	55	6.1
Refused and Appeal Result Not Ascertained	6	1.4	1	3.0					1	9.1			3	5.0					1	2.3							12	1.3
Not Ascertained	1	0.2	6	18.2															1	2.3							8	0.9
Totals	423		33		33		28		11		57		60		16		18		43		16		15		152		905	

withdrawn before a decision. There were no cases so categorised in our sample of judicial review legal aid applications,[13] although there were 31 cases (3%) where legal aid was formally refused following a reported settlement of the dispute giving rise to the potential judicial review. Thus, the 23% of judicial review legal aid applications that were eventually refused on legal grounds (that is, even after appeals) is very similar to the proportion of all non-matrimonial civil legal aid applications so refused nationally in 1991-92.

Over 90% of the legal aid judicial review applications that are successful are granted on the basis of the officer's initial decision, without the necessity of an appeal. The proportion of judicial review legal aid applications initially refused on the merits that were taken to appeal, at 43%, was higher than the national average for all non-matrimonial civil legal aid application in 1991-92 at 33%. There was also a higher rate of success in appeals against refusals of legal aid in judicial review cases (52%) than in general non-matrimonial cases (40%).[14] Put another way, 22% of all legal aid judicial review applications that were refused initially on the merits were eventually granted legal aid as the result of an appeal, as compared with only 13% of initial legal refusals relating to general non-matrimonial civil legal aid applications. These figures appear to show that, while there is little overall difference in rates at which judicial review and general non-matrimonial civil legal aid applications were eventually refused on legal grounds, applicants in judicial review cases were somewhat more dependent on the appeal process to achieve this result.

As in the judicial review data, the national statistics on legal aid mask very significant variations in the grant rates for legal aid judicial review applications between the different subject matter of cases (see Table 5.6) and, even more markedly, across the 13 Area offices (see Table 5.7). Applications for legal aid in connection with homelessness judicial reviews, which constituted the largest subject category of cases, had one of the highest grant rates overall, with six out of seven such cases receiving legal aid. Other subject areas with similarly high grant rates were mental health and travellers cases. One common feature of the subject areas associated with high grant rates is that the judicial reviews are likely to relate to obviously vital interests of the applicants, such as their accommodation (homelessness and travellers) or liberty (mental health). Similar considerations would also apply in relation to immigration judicial reviews, legal aid applications for

---

13 There were, however, 2% of applications in the sample where the final result of the application could not be ascertained.

14 The figures relating to appeals in non-matrimonial civil legal aid cases are calculated from *Legal Aid Board Annual Report*, 1991-92, Table Civil 4, p 50.

Table 5.6

Legal Aid Applications for Judicial Review Proceedings, October-December 1991 by Subject Matter of Application and Grant and Refusal Rates

Subject (No of Applications)	% Granted on Initial Application	% Granted on Appeal	Total % Granted	% Refused	% Not Ascertained
Homelessness (300)	79.3	5.3	84.7	12.3	3.0
Other Housing (155)	67.1	10.3	77.4	21.9	0.7
Immigration (130)	74.6	0.8	75.4	23.1	1.5
Criminal Courts (70)	62.9	5.7	68.6	27.1	4.3
Education (58)	55.2	22.4	77.6	20.7	1.7
Prisoners (27)	51.8	11.1	63.0	33.3	3.7
Benefits (20)	40.0	25.0	65.0	35.0	-
Legal Aid (20)	40.0	-	40.0	60.0	-
Child Care (18)	44.4	5.5	50.0	44.4	5.5
Mental Health (14)	85.7	-	85.7	14.3	-
Planning (13)	23.0	7.7	30.8	69.2	-
Poll Tax (12)	44.4	8.3	50.0	50.0	-
Criminal Injuries (8)	37.5	-	37.5	62.5	-
Travellers (7)	85.7	-	85.7	14.3	-
Other (42)	64.3	2.4	66.7	31.0	2.4
All Subjects (905)	67.7	6.6	74.4	23.4	2.2

Table 5.7

Legal Aid Applications for Judicial Review Proceedings, October-December 1991 by Legal Aid Area and Percentage of Applications Granted on Initial Application and Appeal

	Granted on Initial Application	Granted on Appeal	Total Grant Rate
London -			
Immigration (106)	*78.3*	-	*78.3*
Homeless (198)	*84.3*	*4.5*	*88.9*
Other (119)	*64.7*	*5.9*	*70.6*
Total (423)	77.3	3.8	81.1
South East (Brighton) (33)	27.3	12.1	39.4
Southern (Reading) (33)	39.4	24.2	63.6
South West (Bristol) (28)	71.4	7.1	78.6
South Wales (Cardiff) (11)	27.2	18.2	45.5
West Midlands (Birmingham) (57)	71.9	1.8	73.7
North West (Manchester) (60)	36.7	6.7	43.3
Northern (Newcastle) (16)	37.5	6.3	43.8
North East (Leeds) (18)	61.1	5.6	66.7
East Midlands (Nottingham) (43)	83.7	-	83.7
Eastern (Cambridge) (16)	56.3	-	56.3
North Wales (Chester) (15)	86.7	-	86.7
Merseyside (Liverpool)			
Other Housing (114)	*71.0*	*12.3*	*83.3*
Other(38)	*57.9*	*18.4*	*76.3*
Total (152)	67.8	13.8	81.6
All Areas (905)	67.7	6.6	74.4

which were granted at a near average grant rate of 75%. As will be discussed in the next chapter, this can be contrasted with the relatively low rate at which applications for leave to seek judicial review in immigration matters are granted leave by the courts.

The judicial review subject areas with relatively low legal aid grant rates were child care (50%), poll tax (50%), legal aid (40%), criminal injuries compensation (38%), and planning (31%). The reasons for refusals of legal aid are examined in detail below. As noted, in order to prevent legal aid Area offices having to decide applications for legal aid to challenge their own decisions, such cases are transferred to another legal aid Area for decision, but they still had one of the lowest grant rates of any subject area. Half of the initial refusals of legal aid in this category were appealed, but none successfully.

Although most of the remaining subject areas of potential judicial reviews had overall legal aid grant rates near to the national average, some of these were only achieved through the use of the appeals process. For example, applications for legal aid for judicial reviews in the fields of education, prisons and welfare benefits all had initial grant rates well below the national average. However, around a quarter of all applications in respect of education and prison judicial reviews, and about a third of those that were eventually granted, received legal aid only as a result of an appeal against an initial refusal.

Regional variations

The London Area, which accounted for nearly half of all judicial review legal aid applications nationally, had a grant rate of 81%, somewhat higher than the national average. This was partly due to the very high grant rate for homelessness judicial review cases in this area (89% as compared to a national average of 85%) and the fact that such applications constituted 47% of the judicial review caseload of the London office. Immigration applications in London were also granted at a slightly higher rate (78%) than on average in the country as a whole (75%), but this was also the true of judicial review applications in all other subject areas (other than homelessness and immigration) where the London grant rate was 71% compared to the national average of 68%.

Other legal aid Areas with high grant rates in respect of judicial review cases were the East Midlands, Chester and North Wales, and Merseyside, although the rate in the latter was boosted by the fact that the 83% of the very large group of 'other housing' applications were granted compared to a national average of 77% in this subject category. By contrast, offices with low grant rates for judicial review legal aid applications were the Eastern Area (56%), the South Wales Area (46%), the Northern Area (44%), the North Western Area (43%) and the South Eastern Area (39%). Indeed, in the South Eastern and South Wales Areas fewer than one-in-three legal aid judicial review applications were granted on the officer's initial decision. There was also a low initial grant rate in the Southern Area, although here a high rate of applications granted on appeal, especially in the field of education, brought the overall grant rate to 64%.

There is no clear explanation why there should have been such wide variations between Area offices in their rates of granting legal aid for judicial review. There were no particular regional concentrations of applications in subject areas which themselves had high or low grant rates. One factor which might have been thought to be important is the relative familiarity of Area offices and committees in dealing with applications relating to prospective judicial reviews. The relatively high grant rate in London has already been noted. Here there is a large concentration of legal aid judicial review applications and decision-making on them may have become somewhat routine. Outside London, however, there were three Areas that dealt with more than 50 legal aid judicial review applications in the sample period, and of these two had average or higher grant rates (West Midlands at 74% and Merseyside at 82%) and one a very much below average rate (the North Western Area at 43%). On the other hand, there were five Areas that dealt with less than 20 legal aid judicial review applications in the period, and of these only one had an above average grant rate (Chester and North Wales at 87%), compared with three with grant rates considerably lower than the national average (Eastern at 56%, South Wales at 46% and Northern at 43%).

These data provide *prima facie* evidence that legal aid area offices and committees operated, at least implicitly, different policies or standards in deciding whether to grant legal aid for judicial reviews. The overall chance of an applicant obtaining legal aid for judicial review in some of the lowest grant rate Areas was about half of that for applicants in the high grant rate Areas. When combined with variations that exist at other stages of the judicial review process, in particular between judges in granting leave for a case to proceed (see Chapter 8),[15] the impression that access to judicial review is something of a lottery for the individual applicant becomes even stronger.

The higher rate of appeals against initial refusals of legal aid in judicial review cases, when compared to general non-matrimonial cases, and their higher rate of success on appeal, has been noted. The

---

15   See also Law Commission Report No 226, *op cit*, Appendix C, para 8.4 and Annex 1.

appeals process, which is itself confined within the Area office where the original decision on the application has been taken, does not appear sufficient to counter-balance the sharp variations between Areas in their initial grant rates. In fact, there was only one Area where legal aid applicants in judicial review cases had a significantly higher success rate than the national average for such cases, and this was in Merseyside where 21 out of 22 appeals were successful. The effect here was to bring an initial grant rate slightly below the national average for legal aid judicial review applications up to a point above it. On the other hand, there were two Areas where legal aid applicants in judicial review cases had notably low rates of success on appeal. These were the West Midlands, an area with an above average initial grant rate, where only one out of seven appeals was successful, and the North Western Area, with a very much below average initial grant rate, where only four out of 16 appeals were successful.

Success at appeals was influenced by the attendance or representation of the applicant. Of those appeal cases in the sample where information could be obtained on this point, 62% of appeals attended by a solicitor or some other representative (with or without the applicant) were successful, compared with 42% of those appeals where the applicant attended but was not represented, and only 23% where no one attended the appeal hearing.

Limitations on legal aid

The fact that legal aid has been granted does not necessarily mean that the individual can immediately apply for judicial review. Most grants of legal aid in judicial review cases are subject to a limitation on the formal steps that can be taken in the proceedings. Nearly a third of grants of legal aid for judicial reviews were initially limited so as to prevent an application for leave being lodged prior to the matter being referred back to the legal aid authorities for further consideration, usually after having obtained counsel's opinion on the merits of the case and sometimes also settling with counsel the basis of the prospective proceedings. A further 30% of legal aid grants had initial limitations restricting the proceedings to an application for leave and, if successful, the service of the papers in the case on the prospective respondent, and in a further 20% the initial limitation extended to the receipt of the respondent's evidence and obtaining counsel's opinion on the merits of allowing the case to proceed to a full substantive hearing. Finally, there were only 18% of grants of legal aid for judicial review made on an unlimited basis, so as to enable the matter to proceed to a full hearing without further reference back to the legal aid authorities.

Refusals of legal aid

As discussed above, although the overall refusal rate for legal aid judicial review applications was about the same as for general non-matrimonial civil legal aid applications, there were substantial variations in rates of refusal of legal aid for judicial review both between subject areas and in different parts of the country. There are various reasons why legal aid might be refused, the most important relating to the two-limbed test that is applied to the merits of the prospective legal action involved in the application: the *legal merits test* and the *general reasonableness test*. As we shall see, the criteria to be applied under each of these tests are by no means unproblematic, especially in legal aid applications for judicial review.

Table 5.8 shows the reasons given for refusals of legal aid for judicial review, both at the stage of the officer's initial decision and by committees on appeal. The first thing to be noted is that no fewer than 23% of initial refusals are based on an insufficiency of information provided with the application. This finding can be related back to the earlier observation that 29% of legal aid judicial review applications were put forward without a clear statement of the legal grounds on which judicial review might be sought. In fact, applications lacking a clear statement of grounds for judicial review were more likely to be refused on the initial officer's decision (44%) than those containing such statements (25%), and they also accounted for 33 of the 64 or 52% of the applications initially refused on grounds of an insufficiency of information.

Nevertheless, it is significant that a majority of applications which appeared to lack a statement of grounds for judicial review were still granted legal aid on the initial officer's decision. The relatively high rate of initial grants of legal aid, even in applications lacking a clear statement of the grounds for judicial review, may be testimony to legal aid officers' ability to discern the potential for this type of legal action on the basis of limited information (eg on the facts of cases as presented in applicants' statements), especially in those subject areas where there are considerable numbers of applications. A less generous interpretation is that decisions on insufficient evidence were based on impression rather than on an informed view of the legal merits of the case. Of course, the fact that a grant of legal aid can be limited as to the steps to be taken leading up to or in formal proceedings may itself contribute to the apparent liberality of legal aid officer's decisions and willingness to overlook inadequacies in the presentation of applications. Of the 64 legal aid judicial review applications initially refused for an insufficiency of information, 23 (36%) were taken to appeal, 13 successfully. Put another way, nearly 80% of such refusals

Table 5.8

Legal Aid Applications for Judicial Review, October-December 1991 by Reasons for Refusal of Legal Aid

Reason for Refusal	Initial Application		Appeal Decision	
	No	%	No	%
Insufficient information with application	64	22.9	3	5.9
No reasonable grounds shown for judicial review	75	26.9	12	23.5
Decision challenged not *Wednesbury* unreasonable	25	9.0	7	13.7
Insufficient prospect for success	30	10.8	10	19.6
Judicial review would be premature	8	2.9	3	5.9
Judicial review application would be out-of-time	8	2.9	3	5.9
Other remedies not exhausted	7	2.5	1	2.0
Other legal reasons	4	1.4	1	2.0
Insufficient benefit to applicant	17	6.1	8	15.7
Persons other than applicant would benefit	3	1.1	1	2.0
Applicant's behaviour raises questions of standing	1	0.4	-	
Judicial review not appropriate	1	0.4	2	3.9
Case would result in same outcome for applicant	1	0.4	-	
Costs not considered justified	1	0.4	-	
No emergency in case	1	0.4	-	
Separate legal aid application required	1	0.4	-	
Legal aid application premature - should use Green Form for counsel's opinion	1	0.4	-	
Dispute resolved by settlement	31	11.1	-	
Totals	279		51	

were either not taken to appeal or upheld on appeal. This may suggest that the insufficiency of information on the application forms masked more substantive weaknesses in the prospective judicial reviews to which many of these applications related.

Refusals on legal merits

The traditional view of the criteria to be applied to legal aid applications under the legal merits test has been that the applicants are required to show more than that they have *prima facie* or arguable case and to demonstrate that there are reasonable prospects that their case will be ultimately successful.[16] The Legal Aid Notes for Guidance state that:

> The area office must be satisfied that, on the facts put forward and the law which relates to them, there is a case ... which should be put before a court for a decision. The availability and strength of evidence to support the facts alleged will be taken into account.

> However, the area office sees only one side of the case and it is for the court to adjudicate on the issues. If the ultimate prospects for success are unclear, a limited grant may be appropriate, although the area office must, in every case, be satisfied that the applicant has reasonable grounds for taking ... the proceedings. The likelihood of success is a factor which the area office must bear in mind but it is of the essence of litigation that there are two opposing points of view on which the court is required to adjudicate. Litigation is also notoriously uncertain so that any attempt to restrict legal aid to certainties or near certainties would not only be doomed to failure (if the aim was 100% success) but would also be a denial to many applicants of an opportunity to obtain justice.

> The aim therefore must be not to be over-cautious but not to grant legal aid for cases where there is little or no hope of success. If legal aid is granted in hopeless cases it raises the expectation of assisted persons too high, forces opponents to defend their rights and wastes public money ...[17]

A total of 56% of initial refusals of legal aid for judicial review were made under the legal merits test. These included a number of standard situations in which it would be expected that legal aid would be refused on this basis: where, on the facts as presented, there is no decision open to challenge by way of judicial review or the application for judicial review would be premature; where alternative remedies have not been exhausted; or where the application for judicial review would be out-of-time. As is shown in Table 5.8, however, these specific reasons for refusing legal aid for judicial review occurred relatively

---

16 EJT Matthews and ADM Oulton *Legal Aid and Advice* (1971) London: Butterworths, pp 122–3.

17 Legal Aid Notes for Guidance, *op cit*, para 6-06.

infrequently and accounted for only 8% of all initial refusals and 15% of those made on grounds of legal merits. Of the 23 initial refusals on these specific legal grounds, only six were appealed, four of them successfully.

Far more commonplace were legal refusals based on more general reasons that no reasonable grounds had been demonstrated for taking judicial review proceedings or that the decision prospectively being challenged by way of judicial review had not been shown to be *Wednesbury* unreasonable.[18] These grounds accounted for 36% of all initial refusals of legal aid for judicial review and 64% of those made under the legal merits test. Appeals against the initial refusal of legal aid were lodged in 45 out of the 100 cases falling into these categories, 26 of which were successful. Thus, in nearly three out of four applications where legal aid was refused for reasons of a general lack of legal merit in the prospective judicial review, the decision was either not appealed or upheld on appeal.

There were an additional 30 applications, constituting 11% of all initial refusals and 19% of those made under the legal merits test, where the reason cited was that the proposed judicial review had little prospect of success. Only 12 of these refusals of legal aid were taken to appeal, with just two being successful. This relative lack of success at appeal is perhaps surprising, given the problematic nature of this particular ground for refusing legal aid in judicial review cases. In the case of *R v Legal Aid Board, ex parte Hughes*,[19] which was decided after the completion of our research fieldwork, the relationship between the legal merits test for determining applications for legal aid and the criteria for the High Court granting leave to seek judicial review was considered. Here an application was lodged though Oldham Law Centre for legal aid to challenge a local authority's decision to withdraw an offer of accommodation from a homeless person and their refusal to make an alternative offer. Legal aid was refused on an initial officer's decision and this refusal was taken to appeal. Before the legal aid appeal could be heard, however, an application for leave to seek judicial review was lodged with the High Court, and leave was granted on the papers. Despite this, the Area Committee upheld the refusal of legal aid, on the basis of the legal merits test, and the applicant then applied for judicial review of this decision.

At first instance Kennedy J dismissed the application for judicial review against the Legal Aid Board, endorsing the view that the legal

---

18   In one instance this was transcribed onto the notice of refusal as 'not unreasonable on Wednesday'.

19   (1992) 142 *New Law Journal* 1304.

aid authorities had to apply a different test from that used by the courts in deciding whether or not to grant leave to seek judicial review, in that the legal aid test required the applicant to show not just an arguable case but one that had a reasonable prospect of success. This decision was overturned by the Court of Appeal where, in a judgment by Lord Donaldson MR, it was held that the legal merits test for legal aid and that applied by the High Court in determining applications for leave to seek judicial review were essentially the same. As was stated in the Court of Appeal judgment:

> Lord Diplock may well have been right in 1981 to have said in *IRC v National Federation of Self-Employed and Small Businesses Ltd* that:
>
> > If, on a quick perusal of the material then available, the court thinks that it discloses what might on further consideration turn out to be an arguable case in favour of granting the applicant the relief claimed, it ought, in the exercise of judicial discretion, to grant him leave to apply for that relief.
>
> However, things have moved on since then. This was an *ex parte* application. In such a case leave is or should now only be granted if *prima facie* there is already an arguable case for granting the relief claimed. This is not necessarily to be determined on 'a quick perusal of the material', although clearly any in-depth examination is inappropriate. Furthermore, a *'prima facie* arguable' case is not established by disclosure of 'what *might on further consideration* turn out to be an arguable case'. It is only when there is a clearly arguable case that leave should be granted *ex parte*.[20]

In other words, Lord Donaldson was distinguishing between potential and actual arguability, with the test both for granting leave and for obtaining legal aid under the legal merits test being equated with actual arguability; a levelling up rather than a levelling down of the burden facing applicants.

Lord Donaldson also drew a parallel between the option open to High Court judges, when there is doubt as to whether an application for leave to seek judicial review should be either granted or refused, to adjourn the matter to an *inter partes* hearing in order to obtain more information, and that available to the legal aid authorities to grant legal aid for the limited purposes of obtaining counsel's opinion on the merits of the prospective judicial review. As has been shown, about a third of legal aid grants for judicial review were made subject to just such a limitation, with a further 30% allowing the case to proceed only to the extent of receiving a judicial decision on arguability under the

---

20 *Ibid* p 1305.

leave procedure. The judgment in *ex parte Hughes* should also be considered in light of the fact that there is a degree of uncertainty as to how High Court judges interpret the leave criteria in judicial review, with a great deal of variation between individual judges (see Chapters 7 and 8).

Refusals under the general reasonableness test

Whatever the implications of the decision in *ex parte Hughes* for future decision-making on legal aid judicial review applications under the legal merits test, it is important to bear in mind that legal aid may also be refused on the grounds that it is unreasonable to grant it in the particular circumstances of the case.[21] This second limb of the legal aid merits test confers a wide discretion on officers and committees to consider the general context of a prospective legal action. As we shall see, however, the general reasonableness test tends to be applied on a relatively narrow, individualised basis, even in judicial review cases which may raise issues of wider public interest. Despite this, the incidence of refusals of legal aid for judicial review under the general reasonableness test is much smaller than under the legal merits test. Other than cases recorded as refusals where there had in fact been a settlement prior to the legal aid application being determined, there were only 27 initial refusals of legal aid for judicial review under the general reasonableness test, accounting for just 10% of all refusals. Appeals against the initial refusal of legal aid were lodged in 10 of these cases, only two of which were successful.

By far the most common ground for refusing legal aid for judicial review under the general reasonableness test was that there would be insufficient benefit to the applicant. This was given as the reason for initially refusing legal aid in 17 cases, and there was one other case where it was considered that the costs of the proceedings would not be justified. In fact, as the Legal Aid Notes for Guidance make clear, the general reasonableness test often involves the application of a 'cost-benefit' analysis to prospective legal proceedings:

Legal aid is likely to be refused as unreasonable if:

...

(b) the proceedings are not likely to be cost effective, ie the benefit to be achieved does not justify the costs ...

---

21 In the recent case of R *v Legal Aid Board ex parte Belcher*, 15 July 1994 (unreported) it was confirmed that *ex parte Hughes* was not applicable to the general unreasonableness test under the Legal Aid Act 1988, s 15(3).

The cost effectiveness factor may be outweighed by other matters—the importance of the case to the applicant ...

Examples of cases which are not likely to be cost effective are:

(i)   the amount of the claim is small ...

(ii)   the estimated costs of the proceedings are likely to exceed the benefit to the client ...

(iii)   the only matter at stake is loss of stature, dignity or reputation.[22]

Recently, the Legal Aid Board has attempted to introduce greater consistency in the application of this 'cost-benefit' test by issuing, as part of the Notes for Guidance, 'performance standards' to legal aid officers and committees and also altering the emphasis as to how far factors other than direct material gains should be weighed in the balance in deciding on the cost effectiveness of cases. Under the 'performance standards' it is now stated that legal aid should be refused in *all* cases where the monetary benefit to the applicant would be less than £1,000 and in other cases where the monetary benefit would not exceed the likely costs by more than £1,000 unless the prospects of success are high and the opponent is likely to indemnify the applicant for legal costs or there is a benefit which, although not quantifiable in monetary terms, is of such importance to the applicant that it would justify the costs of the proceedings.[23]

The Notes for Guidance also state that legal aid is likely to be refused where 'the applicant would get no personal benefit out of the proceedings'[24], and this relates to the provision under the Civil Legal Aid (General) Regulations 1989 that 'an application *may* be refused where it appears ... that (a) only a trivial advantage would be gained by the applicant from the proceedings in question'[25] (emphasis added). The legal aid authorities have traditionally taken the view that the scheme is not intended to enable cases to be pursued for the purposes of clarifying the law or to advance some general public interest not related to the benefit for the individual applicant. In fact, the authority

---

22 Legal Aid Notes for Guidance, *op cit*, para 6-08(b).

23 *Ibid*, pp 69–70. It is questionable whether the specific sums set out under these 'performance standards' and the mandatory language in which they are cast are appropriate to what legally should be no more than advice and guidance to officers and committees on how to exercise their discretion under delegated powers of decision-making. The comments of Woolf J in *R v Social Security Fund Inspector, ex parte Sherwin, Stitt and Roberts*, 20 February 1990, unreported, at p 32 of the transcript may be relevant to this issue: 'If the Secretary of State is seeking to give guidance, then he must use the language of guidance and not the language of direction.'

24 Legal Aid Notes for Guidance 1994, *op cit* para 6-08(I).

25 Regulation 29.

cited for this rule provides very obscure and at best only indirect support for it.[26] Nor should acceptance of the proposition that legal aid should not be given *solely* or *primarily* for the purposes of pursuing a general public interest necessarily prohibit officers and committees from having regard to any wider benefit that may be achieved in a case, *in addition* to that likely to be gained by the individual applicant, in assessing whether legal aid should be granted under the 'cost-benefit' or general reasonableness test.

The application of the 'cost-benefit' test to prospective judicial review cases may be regarded as particularly problematic precisely because such litigation is not directly related to the substantive merits of decisions being challenged or to their effects on individual rights. Nevertheless, there are many cases where there is a fairly clear link between the issues involved in a judicial review and the material interests of applicants, such as their right in immigration cases to enter or remain in the country or in homelessness cases to obtain accommodation for their families. As has been shown, the vast majority of legal aid judicial review applications relate precisely to these types of case, so that questions of the sufficiency of the benefit the applicant may gain from the prospective proceedings do not arise. On the other hand, there are a number of situations in which, although they may not occur in great numbers, the decision to grant or refuse legal aid does typically involve considerations of the benefit to be gained in relation to the likely costs of a judicial review.

For example, four of the 18 applications in our sample that were initially refused legal aid because of a lack of 'cost-benefit' related to challenges to the denial of various forms of social welfare benefits. These included refusals of housing benefit, of prescription benefit, and of a late application under the Social Fund. In these instances it was the relatively small sum involved for the individual applicants that was cited as the basis for the refusal of legal aid, typically on the grounds that:

---

26 *United Dominion Trust Ltd v Bycroft* [1954] 3 All ER 355. In this case the plaintiffs, a finance company, were appealing against the lower court ruling in favour of a legally-aided defendant, that a promissory note was not separately enforceable from the hire purchase agreement to which it originally related. At the appeal, the plaintiffs sought to introduce new grounds not raised in the County Court and advanced the argument that, as the point was one of general interest and the defendant was legally-aided, the Court of Appeal should not apply its normal rule against raising a new point of law on appeal. The Court of Appeal rejected the appeal because it raised a new point of law not argued in the court below and stated that the fact that the defendant was legally aided was 'an entirely irrelevant consideration.' Evershed MR went on to say: 'Nor does it [the defendant's legal aid] affect the case, as I think, that the issue now raised is one of importance to the *plaintiffs*. The Legal Aid Act was designed to assist those whom it finances in the course of litigation and not indirectly to assist other parties or even the general public in determining points of interest.' (emphasis added) at 459–60.

A relatively small sum is involved and a fee paying client would not be advised to issue judicial review proceedings.

The analogy that is drawn here with the advice that would be offered to a private, fee-paying client is one that has traditionally been relied on by legal aid officers and committees in deciding whether a grant of legal aid would be reasonable, although in fact it has no basis in the Act or regulations.[27] Interestingly, earlier versions of the Legal Aid Notes for Guidance published up to 1989 cautioned against a rigid application of the private client analogy, since even a small amount of financial gain, say in weekly welfare benefits, could be of considerable importance to someone of very limited means. In fact, the example of challenges to welfare benefits decisions was specifically cited as a situation where use of the private client analogy 'would not comply with the statutory criteria' for granting or refusing legal aid because 'it would be unrealistic to consider what decision a properly advised client of adequate means would make, and attention has to be directed to the benefit for [the] particular applicant, bearing in mind the chances of success and costs of achieving it'.[28] It is also notable that two of the four potential judicial reviews relating to welfare benefits in which legal aid was initially refused on grounds of insufficient benefit to the applicant were put forward as 'test cases' which could potentially have a wider impact.

Legal aid might also be refused where the non-financial benefit is considered too insignificant to justify the costs of the proceedings. One example of this in our sample was a case involving a potential judicial review of a refusal of a visitor's visa to a New Zealand citizen to re-enter the United Kingdom following a holiday abroad. This case is of particular interest since, as discussed in Chapter 2, the Immigration and Asylum Act 1993 subsequently removed the right of appeal to Immigration Adjudicators in visitor cases, a step that was thought at

---

27 It has, however, been endorsed by the courts in numerous cases. See, eg *R v Legal Aid Area No 8 (Northern) Appeal Committee, ex parte Angell* [1990] *Medical LR* 394. It has also been suggested that the Legal Aid Act 1988, s 1, which defines its purpose as establishing 'a framework for the provision ... of advice, assistance and representation which is publicly funded with a view of helping *persons* who might otherwise be unable to obtain advice, assistance and representation on account of their means' (emphasis added) restricts legal aid from being granted to fund cases generally perceived to be in the public interest. Against this, it may be noted that while the Act clearly does restrict legal aid to be granted to 'persons' it does not specify the nature of the purposes for which such grants can be made or rule out considerations of general public, as well as personal, interests.

28 See, eg Legal Aid Notes for Guidance 1989 as published in *Legal Aid Handbook 1989, op cit,* para 9(c) p 25. Such changes to the Notes of Guidance have been made even though the statutory criteria for granting or refusing legal aid have remained virtually the same ever since the inception of the Legal Aid Scheme in 1950. For a discussion of this point and other recent changes made to the Notes for Guidance, see O Hansen, 'Disappearing merits test guidance' (1993) *Legal Action,* August p 13.

the time as likely to produce a spate of applications for judicial review as the only remaining means of challenging such decisions. Anecdotal evidence from solicitors indicates, however, that legal aid is being regularly refused for judicial reviews in visitor cases on grounds that entry to the country for relatively short periods would be 'insufficient benefit' to justify the costs of the proceedings.

Another situation in which the 'cost-benefit' test would typically be applied in order to refuse legal aid for a judicial review is where the prospective challenge relates to a procedural impropriety, such as the denial of a fair hearing or the failure to carry out proper consultations, but where there is only a limited financial or other material benefit involved for the particular applicant. For example, there were six cases in our sample where legal aid was refused on these grounds for potential judicial reviews of magistrates' decisions on such matters as bail conditions, procedures in relation to the trial of Road Traffic Act offences, refusal to transfer legal aid, the effective denial of jury trial, and a suspended committal to prison for community charge arrears. In one of these cases the applicant had initially been represented at court by a duty solicitor, in whose name a subsequent legal aid order had been granted. When the applicant later requested that legal aid be transferred to another solicitor of his choice (having not previously been aware of the option of not using the duty solicitor), the court refused to do so and revoked the legal aid order. Legal aid to judicial review this decision was refused on the grounds that a 'private-paying client would not be advised to embark on expensive High Court proceedings' when the alternative of re-applying to the court for legal aid in the name of the new solicitor and, if necessary, appealing any refusal to the Legal Aid Area Committee was available. Another case involved a potential judicial review of magistrates' refusal to consider as an abuse of process the Crown Prosecution Service's decision to reduce charges on an 'either way' offence to summary only, following the defendant's election for jury trial. Legal aid was again refused on the grounds that a 'fee-paying client would not take judicial review proceedings in these circumstances bearing in mind the potential costs and benefit'.

There were three cases in our sample where legal aid was refused on grounds of insufficient benefit for potential judicial reviews of prison discipline proceedings or policy. In one of the prison discipline cases, in which gross procedural impropriety was alleged against a deputy governor, the legal officer commented on the file that, as the life prisoner concerned had been 'sentenced' to only three days confinement in his cell, 'no paying client would go to court for that however insulted he felt.' Similar grounds were also cited for the refusal of legal aid in the second prison discipline case, again relating to a life prisoner, and on appeal the solicitor argued that it would be 'highly unlikely to find anyone in prison facing a Board of Visitors with the means to pursue' such a case and that the 'significance of Boards of Visitors for inmates should not be under-estimated.'

A final circumstance in which legal aid for judicial review might be refused on grounds of insufficient benefit is where the case is intended to clarify or test the law but the individual applicant would gain only limited advantage from the case. One case from our sample illustrates this situation very well. The applicant sought legal aid to judicially review the terms of a statement of special educational need that the pupil should have ancillary support 'for up to five hours per week' on the grounds that this was too vague to comply with the requirements of the Education Act 1981 and could enable the local education authority to 'whittle away' the extra help to be provided. Legal aid was initially refused on grounds of legal merit, and on appeal the solicitor submitted that both the school and the Department of Education and Science acknowledged the significance of the legal point raised and wished the case to proceed. Despite this, legal aid was again refused, this time on the basis that 'insufficient benefit would be derived to justify the costs'. It does appear, however, that following national press publicity about this case, the Legal Aid Board reconsidered the matter and subsequently decided to grant legal aid.

Another ground for refusing legal aid on the basis of general unreasonableness relates to the provisions of Civil Legal Aid (General) Regulation 32 that where there are persons other than the applicant who are 'concerned jointly with' or have 'the same interest as the applicant' in the proceedings, the legal aid authorities must determine whether it would be reasonable for these other persons to defray 'so much of the costs as would payable from the [legal aid] fund in respect of the proceedings' and, furthermore, whether to refuse legal aid if 'the rights of the applicant' would not be 'substantially prejudiced' by doing so. As the Notes for Guidance make clear, this provision is intended to relate to cases where a number of persons have the same and not just a similar interest in the case, ie where 'each person (including the applicant) is seeking an identical outcome to the proceedings, eg an order, injunction or declaration which would benefit all equally without the need for them to issue separate proceedings'.[29] Given the fact that judicial reviews can often involve challenges to general policies of public authorities or decisions which have a wider impact than on a particular individual, it is perhaps

---

29 Legal Aid Notes for Guidance 1994, *op cit*, para 6–10.

surprising that there were only three cases in our sample (1% of initial refusals) where Regulation 32 was invoked as a basis for refusing legal aid.

The effect of this rule on potential judicial reviews is well illustrated by one of these cases involving an application by a local councillor seeking to challenge the validity of a meeting where the Community Charge was set for the year and the council's failure to comply with provisions on public access to information. Legal aid was refused because this was considered to be 'a matter in which all the poll tax payers in [the large urban authority] had a similar interest.' Despite the misuse of the word 'similar' on the notice of refusal, it is clear that this was a situation in which all the persons concerned would have in fact had the same interest in the proceedings, in that an order to quash the decision to set the Community Charge granted to any one of them would have equally benefited the others. Other situations in which Regulation 32 might be applied would be in relation to potential judicial reviews of a lack of proper consultation on decisions affecting large groups of persons, such as school or hospital closures. Indeed, a dilemma inherent in the application of this rule is that the more general the potential impact of a judicial review and the larger the number of possible beneficiaries, the less likely it may be that legal aid will be granted to any individual to pursue the case.[30]

A related rule under which legal aid may be refused on grounds of general unreasonableness concerns applicants who have other rights or facilities available in order to fund the case, or a reasonable expectation of receiving financial or other help from some other body.[31] This can arise where an applicant is the member of a trade union or other organisation which gives entitlement to legal assistance or there are other bodies, including statutory ones such as the Commission for Racial Equality or the Equal Opportunities Commission,[32] which might be expected to provide legal or financial help with a case falling in their area of competence. In fact, there were no cases in our sample where this ground was invoked as the basis for refusing legal aid for a judicial review.

The final point to be noted in relation to the general reasonableness test is that the issue of the eventual prospects of success in the case can again be raised as a factor to be taken into account in assessing the overall cost-benefit. This may happen where the grounds for challenging a particular decision by way of judicial review are not in

---

30 Similar issues arise in respect of questions of standing in judicial review. On this see the numerous cases cited in Chapter 3, n 7.

31 Civil Legal Aid (General) Regulations 1989, reg 29.

32 *R v Secretary for Employment ex parte Equal Opportunities Commission* [1994] 2 WLR 409.

question under the legal merits test, but there are doubts as to whether, even if the original decision was quashed, the applicant would eventually succeed in, or gain any benefit from, the re-consideration of the merits of his or her substantive claim. Thus, in one case legal aid was sought to judicially review a decision by the Immigration Appeal Tribunal to uphold the refusal of an entry certificate for a father in a 'primary purpose' case. The grounds on which it was intended to seek judicial review were that, due to an administrative error by the IAT, a request for an adjournment in the case had not been registered and the hearing had gone ahead without the appellant being properly notified or represented. The IAT admitted to the administrative error in handling the appeal but for technical reasons required that an order be obtained by way of judicial review to quash the original decision before it could re-hear the case. In this instance, legal aid was initially refused not on the basis that the prospective judicial review would be unsuccessful (in fact, it was likely to be uncontested) but because the applicant's ultimate chances of succeeding in the re-hearing of the immigration appeal were considered to be poor.

In fact, it appears that this case was one that gave rise to a subsequent application to seek judicial review of the Legal Aid Board, with the solicitor concerned lodging an application for leave without seeking legal aid for this purpose. Leave was granted, and following this the legal aid authorities invited the solicitor to re-apply in relation to the proposed judicial review of the IAT. Legal aid was granted and an order to quash the IAT's original decision was obtained, and the Home Office subsequently agreed to allow the applicant an entry certificate.

The outcome of legally-aided cases

Because our fieldwork was completed in 1992, before many of the cases in which legal aid was granted for judicial review had been completed or the results reported to the Legal Aid Board, the outcome of 70% of the relevant cases remained unknown. There were, however, 50 cases (7% of legal aid grants) where the applicant was subsequently advised by counsel that there were no grounds for judicial review, and a further 33 cases (5%) where for various reasons it appears that the grant of legal aid did not result in a formal application for leave being made to the court. There were just six cases where legal aid was granted and a refusal of leave or of the substantive judicial review application had been reported to the Legal Aid Board by the time our fieldwork had been completed. Taking all of these categories together, the grant of legal aid can be said not to have resulted in 'success' for the applicant in 12% of cases or 41% of those where the outcome was ascertained. There were a further 39 cases (5% of all grants and 18% where the outcome was known) in which the applicant withdrew, or the certificate was discharged, in circumstances in which it was unclear what substantive outcome had been achieved.

On the other hand, there were 88 cases where legal aid for judicial review was granted and the case appeared to have been settled at least partly in favour of the applicant. Such cases accounted for 12% of all grants and 41% of those in which the outcome was known at the time of the completion of our fieldwork. As we shall see in the next chapter, a substantial proportion of applications to the court for judicial review result in withdrawals or settlements either prior to the leave application being determined or following a grant of leave by the court. Unfortunately, it was not possible to determine in many of the cases in our legal aid sample whether the favourable settlement had been achieved prior to an application for leave being lodged with or determined by the court, or subsequent to a grant of leave.

Table 5.9 shows the distribution of these various known outcomes across grants of legal aid for judicial review in various subject areas during the final quarter of 1991, and also compares these with the volume of formal leave applications lodged with the Crown Office by legally represented individuals during the first quarter of the same year. Of the grants of legal aid for immigration judicial reviews, 13% were known to have resulted in negative advice on the merits of the case, compared with only 9% of the grants of legal aid for homelessness judicial reviews and 5% of those in other areas. In addition, 10% of legal aid grants for immigration judicial reviews were known to have resulted in legal aid being revoked or discharged or the applicant withdrawing in circumstances where no effective action appears to have been taken in pursuing the case, as compared with only 4% of grants of legal aid for homelessness judicial reviews and those in other subject areas. The pattern of known settlements in favour of applicants shows that these most often occurred in relation to grants of legal aid for welfare benefit judicial reviews (23%), followed by those relating to homelessness (20%), education (17%) and then immigration (10%).

Although the two periods covered are different, the comparison between the volume of grants of legal aid for judicial review in the final quarter of 1991 and the number of leave applications lodged in the first quarter of the same year is useful in considering the role of legal aid decision-making in determining, and possibly controlling, access by individuals to judicial review. As will be seen, the overall number of grants of legal aid for immigration judicial reviews in the final quarter of 1991, at 98, was very similar to the number of leave

Table 5.9

Legal Aid Grants for Judicial Review, October–December 1991 and Applications for Leave, January–March 1991 by Subject Matter

	Legal Aid for Judicial Review, October–December 1991				Leave Applications Lodged with Crown Office, January–March 1991
	Total Number of Grants	Advised No Case	Legal Aid Discharged/Revoked/Withdrawn with No Effective Result	Known Settlement in favour of Applicant	
Immigration	98	13	10	10	103
Homelessness	254	22	9	50	76
Other Housing	120	–	4	6	18
Criminal Courts	48	2	4	3	50
Education	45	5	1	8	23
Prisons	17	3	–	2	5
Benefits	13	2	–	3	4
Mental Health	12	–	–	1	2
Legal Aid	8	1	1	1	–
Other	58	2	4	4	61

applications lodged with the Crown Office in a comparable period earlier in the same year (103). If those grants which proved to be ineffective, either because negative advice was received on the merits or legal aid was subsequently revoked/discharged, or the applicant withdrew in circumstances unlikely to have resulted in a leave application, are discounted, the number of effective grants of legal aid for immigration judicial reviews (75) was somewhat less than the volume of actual leave applications in the earlier period. The only other main subject area where there was a relatively close equivalence between the volume of grants of legal aid for judicial review and the number of leave applications lodged by represented individuals was in cases relating to criminal court proceedings. In all the other main subject areas the volume of grants of legal aid for judicial review, even when those unlikely to have resulted in proceedings are discounted, far outnumbered the volume of leave applications actually lodged with the Crown Office by legally represented individuals during a comparable period of time. For example, the 254 legal aid grants for homelessness judicial reviews in the final quarter of 1991, and the 223 of these likely to have been effective, compares with only 76 formal leave applications lodged in this subject area during the first quarter of the same year.

There are at least two possible explanations for this apparent gap between the number of leave applications lodged with the Crown Office and the much larger number of grants of legal aid for judicial review in most subject areas. One would be that a far higher proportion of legal aid grants for judicial review prove to be ineffective, either because no substantive grounds for judicial review are found or for other reasons that our limited data on outcomes do not reveal. If this is the case, it would suggest that legal aid decision-making, at least at the initial stage, does not operate *in general* as a major barrier to access to judicial review or as an effective means of filtering out unmeritorious applications; although as we have seen, in particular circumstances the legal aid criteria, and especially the general unreasonableness test, can prevent individual applicants from obtaining legal aid for cases that may otherwise be meritorious on legal grounds.

On the other hand, the above data may be indicative of a significant volume of 'hidden' settlements of potential judicial reviews. As indicated, data derived from Crown Office records have shown a high rate of withdrawal/settlement in judicial review applications, and it would not be unreasonable, therefore, to speculate that there is also a significant number of cases where settlements are achieved following a (possibly limited) grant of legal aid, even without the necessity of an application being lodged with the court. If this is the case legal aid, rather than being ineffective as a preliminary filter of potential judicial reviews, may be functioning to facilitate settlements and therefore saving the court from dealing with an even greater volume of formal applications for leave.

Summary and conclusions

Our study of legal aid judicial review applications has provided confirmation of a number of findings arising from our earlier analysis of applications for judicial review lodged with the Crown Office. It has shown that the 'demand' for judicial review among legal aid applicants also fell predominantly within a limited range of subject matters, including immigration, homelessness and 'other housing' issues and, to a lesser extent, crime and education. The findings similarly demonstrate that the heavy geographical concentration of judicial review applicants in London and the very low level of use of the procedure originating from some other heavily-populated areas of the country were replicated among legal aid judicial review applicants. The legal aid data also tend to confirm that only limited degrees of specialisation in judicial review had developed among private solicitors and law centres, with the majority of legal aid applications in this field being processed through solicitors apparently dealing with such matters only on an occasional basis.

Obtaining legal aid to pursue a judicial review case did not appear to be any more difficult than for other types of non-matrimonial civil litigation, although there is evidence to indicate that legal aid judicial review applicants were required to rely on appeals against initial refusals of legal aid more often than those in other fields. The most common reason why legal aid for judicial refuse was likely to be refused was a lack of general legal merits in the case put forward on behalf of the applicant, this was followed closely by an insufficiency in the information contained in the legal aid application itself. In fact, a surprisingly high proportion of legal aid applications in this field failed to present any clear legal grounds for taking judicial review proceedings. Despite this, the vast majority of legal aid grants for judicial review were made, usually following an emergency application, as the result of a legal aid officer's initial determination without the necessity of an appeal; and this was even true in a majority of the applications which appeared to have provided no legal justification for the prospective judicial review.

A combination of factors may help to explain the relative success of applicants in obtaining legal aid for judicial reviews. As noted, most judicial review applications were made on an emergency basis, with the result that the initial decisions whether to grant or refuse legal aid were made relatively quickly and on the basis of limited information. Second, the fact that there was such a predominance of applications in a few subject areas, such as immigration and homelessness, meant not only that legal aid officers were able to build up a certain expertise in these fields but also that there were usually very clear and vital interests involved for the individual applicant and his or her family. This would imply that, once the legal merits for taking judicial review proceedings had been established, no question would arise in the great majority of applications as to the general reasonableness of granting legal aid at least to pursue the case through its initial stages. In these circumstances, it was perhaps to be expected that legal aid officers would take the option open to them of granting legal aid initially subject to limitations on the steps to be taken leading up to or in pursuing formal proceedings, rather than refusing the applications outright. As we have seen, no less than a third of grants of legal aid for judicial review were limited initially to pre-litigation steps short of formally lodging an application for leave, and most of the remainder were restricted to the leave stage or other steps short of a full substantive hearing of the case. Of course, a proportion of such legal aid grants would have resulted in the applicants subsequently receiving advice that they had no grounds for seeking judicial review or otherwise dropping the case without making a formal application to the court for leave.

Nevertheless, a comparison between our two sets of data indicates that, in most subject areas other than immigration and crime, there were far more legal aid grants for judicial review than actual applications for leave lodged with the Crown Office. This suggests that the initial legal aid decision-making process was not as effective as it might have been in sifting out unmeritorious cases at this early stage and/or that the rate of settlement of potential judicial reviews, once legal aid had been granted but before an application for leave was made to the court, was higher than our limited data on outcomes would indicate. In either case, the data confirm that there is a far greater level of initial demand (albeit much of it in the familiar subject areas) for judicial review than would be suggested by Crown Office data alone.

Although the availability of legal aid to pursue judicial reviews did not appear to be problematic for the generality of applicants, our data point to at least two worrying aspects of the legal aid decision-making process. First, there were very wide variations between the 13 Legal Aid Area offices in their grant/refusal rates for such applications. These variations cannot be explained by differentials between the Areas in the subject matters of the legal aid judicial review applications that they handled. Rather, it would appear that in practice the criteria for granting and refusing legal aid were being interpreted differently between Area officials and committees. It is not clear what additional steps might be taken to reduce these regional variations in decision-making. Certainly, some would argue that the Legal Aid Board's recent efforts in altering the emphasis of its Notes for Guidance and introducing tighter 'performance standards' for such decisions have only resulted in making it more difficult for applicants in certain types of judicial reviews to obtain legal aid (see below). The Legal Aid Scrutiny which reported in 1986 proposed that legal aid administration in 'public interest' cases, including judicial review, might be centralised in a single national office, so as to enable greater consistency in decision-making.[33] A further advantage that might come from such an arrangement would be that members of legal aid appeal committees could more easily be drawn from solicitors and barristers with particular public law expertise. On the other hand, there could be disadvantages in such a centralised system. Without provision to assist applicants and their legal representatives in attending appeal hearings, it could serve to disadvantage precisely those applicants involved in the most problematic and possibly distinctive cases where legal aid officials and committees are currently less familiar with the subject matter or legal basis of the potential judicial review.

The second issue arising from our research concerns the way in which the criteria under the general reasonableness test for deciding legal aid applications fail to relate to the purposes of judicial review in an important, yet numerically small, group of cases. These are cases where, although there may be clear legal grounds for seeking judicial review, it is adjudged that the potential benefit for the individual applicant would not be sufficient to justify the costs of the proceedings. As we have seen, the way in which this 'cost-benefit' criterion is applied tends to overlook issues of small but often very vital significance for individual applicants, such as in the payment of welfare benefits or the assertion of procedural rights, and it appears to take no account whatsoever of the wider public interest that may be involved in a judicial review.

This highlights what may be regarded as at least a lack of correspondence, if not a major contradiction, between the way in which the general reasonableness test for granting legal aid is currently interpreted, on the one hand, and what may be regarded as the fundamental purpose of judicial review proceedings, on the other. Judicial review owes its origins to the supervisory role of the High

---

33   Lord Chancellor's Department, *Legal Aid Scrutiny*, June 1986.

Court to ensure that subordinate courts and tribunals and other bodies exercising administrative decision-making functions perform their functions within the rule of law. Conceptualised in this way, there is an inherent public purpose in judicial review proceedings which can be said to transcend the individual applicants' interests in particular cases or the direct benefit they may gain from them. As the Law Commission has noted in discussing the question of liability for costs in judicial reviews:

> The applicant, by initiating the issue of Crown side proceedings is enabling the court to exercise its supervisory jurisdiction at the behest of the Crown. It is the Crown that has a major interest in the courts exercising proper supervisory control of decision-making bodies ...[34]

Indeed, many of the distinctive legal features of the judicial review procedure, including the requirement that applicants obtain leave to proceed with their cases and the wide discretion of the court to deny relief on grounds of the interests of good public administration, stem from its unique function in upholding the public interest in proper standards of public decision-making rather than providing a mechanism for the enforcement of individual legal rights.

The Law Commission has now recommended that the unique purpose of judicial review should be acknowledged in the criteria for granting or refusing legal aid for such proceedings by amending the Civil Legal Aid (General) Regulations 1989 to enable consideration to be given to the wider public interest in having a judicial review case heard.[35] In fact, it would appear that the statutory criteria for granting legal aid, as laid down in the Legal Aid Act 1988 and the relevant regulations, are already sufficiently flexible to accommodate such a change in interpretation at the discretion of legal aid officers and committees (in much the same way as these criteria have been reinterpreted and tightened up by the Legal Aid Board in their re-writing of the Notes for Guidance over recent years). It would arguably also fit in with the Government's recently stated objective that the legal aid scheme should 'provide the most effective and economical solutions to problems in the interests of the client *and the tax payer*' (emphasis added),[36] since this appears in itself to introduce a concept of the 'public interest' into considerations of when legal aid should be made available for particular cases. Indeed, the Green Paper on legal aid also proposes that the criteria for granting legal aid might

---

34 Law Commission Consultation Paper No 126, *op cit*, p 69.
35 Law Commission Report No 226, *op cit*, para 10.9.
36 Lord Chancellor's Department, *Legal Aid – Targeting Need*, London, 1995, para 4.2.

differ from one type of case to another and that the 'cost-benefit' test should be reformulated so that it would be assessed 'both individually and in relation to other cases'.[37] This suggests that it would be possible to develop a 'public interest' test to be applied specifically to legal aid judicial review applications, as the Law Commission has proposed, and that this should enable applicants to argue, where their judicial reviews can legitimately be claimed to involve benefits for a wider group or for the general public interest and that it would be appropriate and, indeed, economical to grant legal aid to the one individual to pursue the matter rather than having numerous potential applications placed before the courts for decision.

37 *Ibid*, para 7.9.

Learning Resources
Centre

Chapter 6

The Progress and Outcome of Applications for Judicial Review

In the previous chapters we have examined the types of governmental decisions and bodies being challenged, the types of applicants undertaking these challenges, the nature of their legal representation, and the availability of legal aid for judicial review. We now move from an examination of the various inputs into judicial review to consider and analyse the outcomes of the judicial review procedure itself. We begin, in this chapter, by providing a broad statistical overview of the process, tracking cases through the various stages of judicial review. We also consider here the issue of delay and the time taken to dispose of cases at each stage. As will be seen, our statistical analysis identifies the leave stage and the withdrawal of applications before and after leave as being of far greater importance to the judicial review litigation process than might previously have been assumed. We therefore go on in the following chapters to look in more detail at the operation of the leave stage and the role of judges in this process.

An overview of the judicial review process

The judicial review procedure contains a number of features which are particularly pertinent to this study. In particular, potential litigants face a short time limit within which they must initiate legal action. They must also obtain the leave (permission) of the court in order to proceed.

An application for judicial review must be made promptly and in any event within three months of the date of the decision being challenged.[1] Judges have a discretion to refuse leave (or subsequently deny relief) to applicants considered not to have made their challenge promptly. The obligation to act promptly means that even applications filed within the three month period may be turned away.[2] The courts, however, can allow applications to proceed beyond this time limit if the applicant can show good reason for the delay.[3]

---

1   Supreme Court Act 1981, s 31(6) and RSC Order 53, r 4(1). See further, Alistair Lindsay, 'Delay in Judicial Review Cases: a Conundrum Solved?' (1995) *Public Law*, 417.

2   Eg *R v The Independent Television Commission ex parte TVNI Ltd* (1991) *The Times* 30 December.

3   It might also be necessary for the applicant to show that the application would not substantially cause hardship or prejudice rights or good administration. Such issues would normally be dealt with at the substantive hearing: *R v Dairy Produce Quota Tribunal ex parte Caswell* [1990] 2 AC 738; *R v Secretary of State for Health ex parte Furneaux* [1994] 2 All ER 652.

The purpose of this time limit (which compares with the six years allowed for starting most ordinary civil legal actions) is to protect government from being left vulnerable to challenge for long periods, thereby creating uncertainty in public administration and potential delay in the implementation of government policies. The Law Commission considered recommending an extension to the time limits, but concluded that the 'the principle of certainty' justified not doing so.[4]

Short time limits might further certainty, but they can also affect the scale and quality of judicial review litigation in ways which are not necessarily immediately obvious. For example, the effect of reducing the numbers of challenges that might otherwise have been made could be to lead to some forms of government illegality going unchallenged, possibly to the detriment of the quality of public administration. On the other hand, short time limits might also stimulate premature or weak applications for leave, thereby increasing the burden on the court system.

The second key feature of judicial review in England and Wales is that all applications must pass through an initial vetting stage by a High Court judge to determine whether they should be given leave (or permission) to proceed to a full, substantive hearing.[5] In Scotland there is no leave requirement built into the judicial review procedure, while in Northern Ireland the leave requirement operates differently.[6] Of course, both these jurisdictions have much smaller numbers of applications to deal with, although as a proportion of the population the volume of cases dealt with is similar to that in England and Wales.[7]

Currently applicants for leave have a choice whether to ask for their applications to be considered at an oral hearing, normally before a single judge, or to have it initially decided only on written submissions (a paper or table application).[8] The advantage of making a table application is that it is cheaper and possibly quicker for the applicant. When considering a table application a judge will, on a quick perusal of the papers submitted by the applicant, decide whether to grant or refuse leave immediately, or to submit the case to a full oral hearing on

---

4   Law Commission Report No 226, *op cit*, paras 5.23-5.30.

5   The Law Commission have recommended changing the name of the leave requirement to the 'preliminary consideration' stage. *Ibid*, para 5.11.

6   See Chapter 2, n 5.

7   B Hadfield and E Weaver, 'Trends in Judicial Review in Northern Ireland' (1994) *Public Law* 12; B Hadfield and E Weaver, 'Judicial Review in Perspective' (NI) (1995) *Northern Ireland Law Quarterly* (forthcoming); T Mullen, K Pick and T Prosser, 'Trends in Judicial Review in Scotland' (1995), *Public Law* 52.

8   The Law Commission has recommended that applicants should no longer have a choice of procedure for seeking leave, and that most applications should be initially considered only on the papers: Law Commission Report No 226, *op cit*, paras 5.23-5.30.

leave. If a table application for leave is refused, the applicant has an automatic right to renew the application to an oral hearing. If renewed the application is considered afresh as if the application were being made for the first time; this is why this procedure is described as a renewal rather than an appeal.

There are circumstances where the applicant is required to proceed immediately by way of an oral application for leave without the opportunity of first making a table application. This is normally required where the applicant is seeking some form of interim relief along with the decision on leave.[9] An example of such interim relief would be an injunction preventing the applicant in a homelessness case from being evicted from temporary accommodation provided by a local authority pending their initial decision whether to re-house the applicant on a permanent basis. Another would be an immigration case where the applicant is held in custody pending deportation and seeks bail along with leave to apply for judicial review. Also, if it is intended to ask the court to expedite the full hearing of the substantive case, the applicant may choose to do so immediately at an oral leave hearing rather than applying separately for expedition subsequent to the grant of leave.

It may be noted in passing that in Northern Ireland initial applications for leave are considered (unless the application relates to the liberty of the subject) by a Master, who may grant leave or refer the application to a judge. If minded to refuse leave the judge will invite the applicant to be heard. The advantage of this procedure is that it ensures applicants an oral hearing before they are denied access.

Where leave is refused in a civil application following an oral hearing (whether or not there was a previous table application), the applicant may again renew the application for leave to the Court of Appeal. This right to renew to the Court of Appeal does not apply, however, in criminal judicial review applications; although in such cases the applicant has the right to ask that the leave application be considered again by a two-judge Divisional Court.

Applications for leave are normally considered on an *ex parte* basis. This means that they are considered on the basis of the applicant's submissions only, without the respondent being present to argue against the grant of leave. In submitting the initial application, the applicant must file a standard form (Form 86A) setting out the nature of the decision being challenged and the grounds for that challenge and the relief (including interim relief) being sought. This form will be

9   Such applications will still be considered orally if the Law Commission's recommendations are implemented.

accompanied by 'affidavits in support', including a sworn statement from the applicant setting out the facts behind the application. It is on the basis of these documents that the application for leave will normally be considered. The court, however, has a discretion to request the respondent to be present at the leave stage in order to assist in the presentation of factual information, and in certain circumstances the court may allow *inter partes* argument on preliminary points at the leave hearing. It is also open to the respondent, once leave has been granted, to apply to have it set aside or the case struck out.[10]

As can be seen from the above description, whilst intended to speed up the disposal of applications and protect the process and public bodies from unmeritorious cases, the leave requirement has itself introduced considerable procedural complexities at the preliminary stage. In this respect, a key question is whether the requirement of leave actually saves court time by filtering out weak applications at an early stage, or generates extra, and perhaps unnecessary, work for the court. This might be the case, eg if there was evidence that public bodies are using leave as a shield protecting them, until leave has been granted, from the need to undertake a substantive internal review of cases or from engaging in proper negotiations toward settlement with applicants and their legal representatives. The possibility that this may be occurring points to a need to examine the inter-relationship between leave decisions and withdrawals of applications. There is, of course, also the question whether in the interest of protecting public administration meritorious applications for judicial review are being rejected prematurely.

By contrast to the procedural complexities of the preliminary leave stage, the post-leave processing of judicial review cases is relatively straightforward. Once leave has been granted, the applicant must serve notice on the respondent public body and then enter a request for a hearing of the full case. The respondent then normally has 56 days in which to file an affidavit and evidence against the application for judicial review. After this, the case will be listed for hearing either before a single judge or before a two, or exceptionally a three judge Divisional Court.[11] Judicial review cases are usually considered on the basis of (frequently very hefty) submissions on paper and oral arguments presented by the applicant's and respondent's legal

---

10 A grant of leave will only be struck out if the respondent can show that the leave decision was plainly wrong and that there is a 'clear knock out blow' to the applicant's case: Simon Brown J in *Secretary of State for the Home Department ex parte Sholola* [1992] COD 226.

11 Criminal matters are always considered by a full Divisional Court of two or, in rare cases, three judges.

representatives, without the presentation of oral evidence or cross-examination of witnesses. During the periods covered by our research it was open to either party to appeal against decisions of the Divisional Court in civil cases to the Court of Appeal either on law or the merits of the case[12] and also, with leave, to further appeal on a point of law to the House of Lords. In criminal cases the sole appeal beyond the Divisional Court lies to the House of Lords and then only if it is certified that the case raises a point of law of general public importance and leave to appeal is granted by the House of Lords.

The progress of applications

Diagram 6A provides a general picture of the way applications for judicial review filed in our study period progressed through the main phases of the procedure. It shows the number of applications at each of four main points of the process. The first bar shows the number of applications initially filed in the relevant year at the Crown Office. These are the figures that are usually referred to in discussions of the judicial review caseload. The second bar shows the number of applications that were dealt with at the leave stage, that is on which a decision to grant or refuse leave was made whether on the basis of a table or oral application or at a renewed hearing. The figures therefore do not include applications which might have been adjourned without a decision being made. The difference between these first two bars on the graph represents applications that were withdrawn after being filed at the Crown Office but before any leave decisions were made (pre-leave withdrawals).[13]

The third bar shows the number of applications that were eventually granted leave.[14] The grant/refusal rate at the leave stage can be calculated in either of two ways. The first, which has tended to be adopted in previous discussions of this issue, uses the total number of applications originally filed at the Crown Office as a base. The second takes account of the pre-leave withdrawals and calculates the

---

12 In 1993 a requirement was introduced to obtain leave to appeal in civil judicial review cases to the Court of Appeal. At present this requirement does not apply to immigration cases, but consideration is currently being given to a proposal to extend this requirement to these cases as well.

13 Withdrawals might have occurred after consideration of a leave application was adjourned.

14 The figures cited in Diagrams 6A, 6B and 6C for 'leave granted' are net figures, that is they take account of all decisions relating to leave, including those to set aside, or restore leave, or to strike out the case once leave had been granted. For details of the numbers of cases involving such decisions, see Chapter 7.

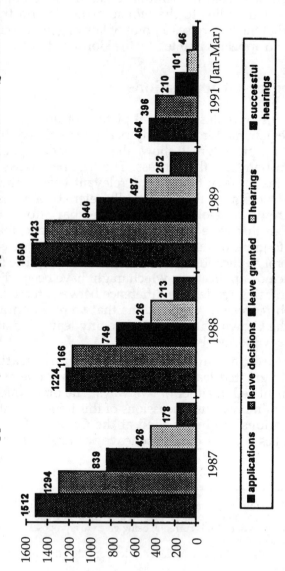

Diagram 6A

What Happened to Judicial Review Applications, 1987-1989 and 1st Quarter of 1991

* 1991 figures for hearings exclude two cases that were still 'live' in May 1995. Both were then before the European Court of Justice.

grant/refusal rate on the basis of only those applications which actually proceeded to a leave decision. Calculations made under the first method can be referred to as 'base grant/refusal rates' and those under the second method as 'actual grant/refusal' rates.

The fourth bar in the diagram shows the number of cases that went to a substantive hearing on their merits. The difference between this bar and the previous one indicates the number of cases that were withdrawn after leave had been granted without proceeding to a full hearing (post-leave withdrawals). The final bar shows the number of applications that were successful, in whole or in part, at the final hearing (taking account where possible of the result of appeals). Note that ultimate success/failure rates are normally calculated on the basis of the number of cases that are successful after a substantive hearing. In practice, however, this may not provide a true picture of how applicants fare in the process because many applications which do not reach a full hearing, especially those that are withdrawn after a grant of leave, may well involve at least an element of success for the applicant.

Diagrams 6B and 6C show similar information for immigration and homeless persons cases. As will emerge below, there are very substantial variations in the results of these different types of application at the various stages of the procedure.

Pre-leave withdrawals

The overall rate of pre-leave withdrawals ranged during our study period from a high of 14% for 1987 applications down to 5% for the 1988 cases and 8% for the 1989 cases. It is clear that the 1987 figure for pre-leave withdrawals is attributable to the high rate at which immigration applications brought in that year were withdrawn before a decision on leave (24%), and this may be related to the surge in asylum applications in that year (see Chapter 2). By contrast, only 6% of immigration applications made in 1988 were withdrawn at this pre-leave stage, but for 1989 and the first quarter of 1991 cases this figure rose again to 14% and 15% respectively.

Of homeless persons cases started in 1987, 10% were withdrawn before a decision on leave, but this fell to 5% for 1988 cases and rose again to 11% in 1989. Nearly 20% of homeless persons applications for the first quarter of 1991 were withdrawn at this pre-leave stage. The rate of pre-leave withdrawals in subject areas other than immigration and homelessness remained fairly low between 1987 and 1989, ranging between 4% and 7%, but rose to just over 10% in the first quarter of 1991.

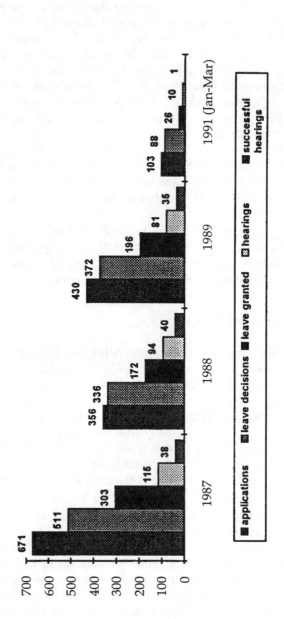

Diagram 6B

What Happened to Judicial Review Immigration Applications, 1987-1989 and 1st Quarter of 1991

Diagram 6C

What Happened to Judicial Review Homeless Applications, 1987-1989 and 1st Quarter of 1991

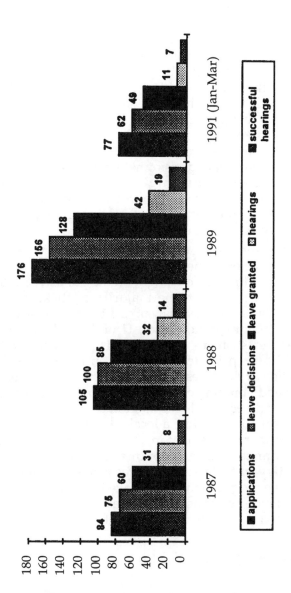

The statistics themselves do not indicate why applications for judicial review were withdrawn before even reaching the preliminary stage of the leave decision. One possible explanation already alluded to is that the tight time limits for applying for judicial review may stimulate premature and poorly prepared applications which, on further consideration by the applicants and their legal advisers, are later withdrawn. Such decisions may also be affected by a refusal of legal aid, although as we saw in the previous chapter evidence indicates that applications for leave are infrequently made in advance of a positive decision on legal aid. It is also possible that applications for leave stimulate respondents to review the issues at stake, leading to a more favourable decision which removes the need to continue with the challenge. This might occur, eg when consideration of an application for leave is adjourned so that the respondent can be asked to appear or present information, and rather than do so the respondent decides to settle the matter.

The more detailed information that we were able to collect on the substantive outcomes of applications made in the first quarter of 1991 enables us to shed some light on the pre-leave settlements arising from these cases. In fact, the majority of these pre-leave withdrawals resulted in at least partial success for the applicant. This was true in 10 of the 16 immigration cases, 11 of the 15 homeless persons cases, and 10 of the 14 other cases from this period where the application was withdrawn prior to a decision on leave. The following is a small selection of the types of case involved. In one a local housing authority decided to provide permanent accommodation once an application for leave had been filed and in another an authority made a fresh offer of more suitable housing; a local education authority agreed to include a speech therapy element in a statement of special educational needs in accordance with a recommendation of an appeal tribunal; the Secretary of State agreed to reconsider a Tamil's asylum application after the judge adjourned a leave hearing. These findings suggest that very few applications withdrawn at the pre-leave stage were ill-prepared or entirely without merit.

Leave decisions

It is, of course, the function of the leave stage to eliminate the weak and unmeritorious applications for judicial review. However, as we shall consider in later chapters, the criteria used by judges to decide leave applications are widely regarded as uncertain and this uncertainty appears to result in worrying inconsistency in judicial decision-making at the leave stage. As well as variations between judges there have been evident changes in judicial approaches over time as the courts appear to have increased the burden facing applicants (see Chapters 7 and 8). These are reflected in our data which tend to confirm the trend toward lower leave grant rates. During the period 1971-75 the base grant rate (that is, the proportion of all applications filed in which leave was granted) was approximately 66%[15] and during the early 1980s the average base grant rate was in the region of 73%.[16] This compares with rates ranging between 56% and 61% for applications made between 1987 and 1989, and as low as 46% for those in the first quarter of 1991. As we saw in Chapter 2, the official statistics show a leave grant rate of 37% in 1994. The actual grant rates (percentage of applications where a decision on leave was made and where leave was granted) in the study periods were 65% for 1987 cases, 64% for 1988, 66% for 1989, and 53% for the first quarter of 1991.

As we have observed earlier, one ought not to place too much reliance on generalised data. In this context there are, for example, very sharp variations in the success of applications involving different subject types at the leave stage. For immigration applications made in 1987 the actual grant rate was 60%, but this declined to just over 50% for 1988 and 1989 and still further for those brought in the first quarter of 1991, to only 30%. Put another way, between 30% and 40% of the original applications for judicial review in immigration in each of the full years 1987-1989 were disposed of by way of a refusal of leave, and this proportion reached 60% for the first quarter of 1991 immigration applications. The base grant rate for immigration cases fell to just 18% in 1994.[17]

This contrasts with the treatment of homeless persons cases at the leave stage where, despite the view of the House of Lords in *Puhlhoffer*,[18] the actual grant rate ranged between just under 80% and up to 85% during the periods covered by our research. In other words, only a very small proportion of less than 20% of all applications for judicial review in homelessness were eliminated by a refusal of leave.

Another way of looking at these figures is to ask what proportion of applications for judicial review of these different types survive the leave stage and join the queue awaiting a full hearing? Asking this question we found that of the applications begun in the 1987-89 period: between 45% and 50% of immigration applications, between

---

15 *Report on Remedies in Administrative Law* (1976) Law Com No 73, Cmnd 6407, para 37.

16 See Sunkin, 1987, p 453. This figure was based on known decisions in civil applications.

17 Data obtained from the Crown Office.

18 [1986] 1 All ER 467.

70% and 81% of the homeless person applications, and between 63% and 65% of applications in all other subject categories survived and joined the queue. The equivalent figures for the first quarter of 1991 were: immigration, about 25%; homeless persons, about 66%; all others, just under 50%.

Post-leave withdrawals

As we will see when we examine the time judicial review cases take, the longest delays occur between the grant of leave and the holding of a substantive hearing. In this time, a further portion of cases will be withdrawn. Again, different factors may lie behind the withdrawal of a judicial review application once leave has been granted. It may be, for example, that a grant of interim relief, stopping a decision adverse to the applicant from being implemented immediately, will be sufficient to satisfy the applicant's interests in the case. Also, if the leave decision was actually made on a purely *ex parte* basis, without the respondent having been represented, it will only be at the post-leave stage that the respondent's side of the case will be made known and be fully considered by the applicant's legal advisers. If their advice is that the application stands little chance of succeeding in light of the respondent's evidence, the applicant may decide to withdraw or be forced to do so by having legal aid taken away.[19]

On the other hand, there are a number of considerations which may lead respondents to settle the case at least partially in favour of the applicant after leave has been granted. The grant of leave may itself have attracted adverse publicity for the public body concerned, which can best be dissipated by an early settlement. The respondent may also consider that the grant of interim relief to the applicant makes the case less worthwhile or economical to pursue to a full hearing. For example, where a homelessness applicant is ordered to be allowed to remain in temporary accommodation at the respondent local authority's expense pending the outcome of the case, which may take many months, the authority may decide that it is more economical to offer cheaper permanent accommodation immediately.

Equally, the public body may consider that, on further review of the case and any comments made by the judge when granting leave, the applicant's case is justified or does not raise any important issues of

---

19 As shown in Chapter 5, a standard limitation placed on many grants of legal aid for judicial review proceedings is that, on receipt of the respondent's evidence, further counsel's opinion should be obtained on the merits of continuing with the case and the matter referred back to the Legal Aid Board for re-consideration.

principle worth pursuing to a full hearing. By the same token, the respondent may feel that the application does indeed threaten a key policy or procedure which it hopes to continue in general application, in which case a settlement of the particular applicant's case may forestall a broader declaration of illegality by the court. Finally, where the applicant is legally-aided, the respondent public authority is unlikely to be able to recover the costs of pursuing the case to a full hearing, even if successful, thereby rendering it more economical to settle the matter once the grant of leave has been made.

Whatever the reasons, our data show that a substantial proportion of judicial review applications are withdrawn following a favourable decision on leave. Just under half of all cases begun in 1987 and 1989 in which leave was granted were subsequently withdrawn without a full hearing, and this was true of 43% of the cases begun in 1988 in which leave was granted. Of cases begun in the first quarter of 1991 which were eventually granted leave, 51% had been withdrawn by May 1995 without a full hearing. Overall, of all applications started between 1987 and 1989, 27% and 29% were ultimately determined by being withdrawn after leave had been granted. The corresponding figure for the those application made in the first quarter of 1991 was 24%.

Withdrawal following a grant of leave was an especially significant feature in homeless persons cases. In fact, over the periods covered by our research, it was only in relation to the 1987 caseload that more of the homeless persons applications granted leave actually reached a full hearing than were withdrawn (31 homeless persons hearings compared to 29 homeless persons cases granted leave but withdrawn). Of the 1988 homeless persons cases granted leave, 62% were subsequently withdrawn without a full hearing; this proportion rose to over two-thirds in relation to 1989 cases and to 78% of cases in the first quarter of 1991. There was, of course, a high success rate for homelessness cases at the leave stage itself, with the result that withdrawals where leave had been granted were the dominant form of disposal of such applications after 1987, accounting for the outcome of about half of all homeless persons applications begun in 1988 and 1989 and in the first quarter of 1991.

Interestingly, despite the relatively low success rate in immigration cases at the leave stage, post-leave withdrawals were also a prominent feature in this area. Indeed, the number of immigration applications that were granted leave and subsequently withdrawn without a hearing exceeded the number reaching a hearing in three of the four periods covered by our study (1987, 1989 and the first quarter of 1991). By contrast, the proportion of non-immigration and non-homelessness cases that obtained leave and went on to a full hearing was about 60% between 1987 and 1989 and in the first quarter of 1991.

Substantive hearings

Case composition

The pattern of decisions on applications for judicial review at the leave stage together with the incidence of withdrawal before and after the grant of leave, has significant effects on the number and types of cases reaching a substantive hearing. The numbers are summarised in Table 6.1 below. Of cases commenced between 1987–1989 the proportions reaching a full hearing ranged between 28% and 35%, while only 22% of applications started in the first quarter of 1991 had completed a substantive hearing or were still waiting for one as at the end of May 1995.

<table>
<tr><td colspan="9" align="center">Table 6.1</td></tr>
<tr><td colspan="9" align="center">Judicial Review Applications by Type and Point of Disposal of Application, 1987-1989 and 1st quarter 1991</td></tr>
<tr><td></td><td colspan="2">Immigration</td><td colspan="2">Homeless</td><td colspan="2">Other</td><td colspan="2">Totals</td></tr>
<tr><td></td><td>No</td><td>%</td><td>No</td><td>%</td><td>No</td><td>%</td><td>No</td><td>%</td></tr>
<tr><td>1987 applications:</td><td></td><td></td><td></td><td></td><td></td><td></td><td></td><td></td></tr>
<tr><td>Withdrawals</td><td>348</td><td>51.9</td><td>37</td><td>44.0</td><td>245</td><td>32.4</td><td>631</td><td>41.7</td></tr>
<tr><td>Refusals of Leave</td><td>208</td><td>31.0</td><td>15</td><td>17.9</td><td>232</td><td>30.6</td><td>455</td><td>30.1</td></tr>
<tr><td>Substantive Hearings</td><td>115</td><td>17.1</td><td>31</td><td>36.9</td><td>280</td><td>37.0</td><td>426</td><td>28.2</td></tr>
<tr><td>1988 applications:</td><td></td><td></td><td></td><td></td><td></td><td></td><td></td><td></td></tr>
<tr><td>Withdrawals</td><td>98</td><td>27.5</td><td>58</td><td>55.2</td><td>226</td><td>29.6</td><td>382</td><td>31.2</td></tr>
<tr><td>Refusals of Leave</td><td>164</td><td>46.1</td><td>15</td><td>14.3</td><td>238</td><td>31.2</td><td>417</td><td>34.1</td></tr>
<tr><td>Substantive Hearings</td><td>94</td><td>26.4</td><td>32</td><td>30.5</td><td>299</td><td>39.2</td><td>425</td><td>34.7</td></tr>
<tr><td>1989 applications:</td><td></td><td></td><td></td><td></td><td></td><td></td><td></td><td></td></tr>
<tr><td>Withdrawals</td><td>173</td><td>40.2</td><td>106</td><td>60.2</td><td>301</td><td>31.9</td><td>580</td><td>37.4</td></tr>
<tr><td>Refusals of Leave</td><td>176</td><td>40.9</td><td>28</td><td>15.9</td><td>279</td><td>29.6</td><td>483</td><td>31.2</td></tr>
<tr><td>Substantive Hearings</td><td>81</td><td>18.8</td><td>42</td><td>23.9</td><td>364</td><td>38.6</td><td>487</td><td>31.4</td></tr>
<tr><td>1991 (Jan-Mar) applications:</td><td></td><td></td><td></td><td></td><td></td><td></td><td></td><td></td></tr>
<tr><td>Withdrawals</td><td>31</td><td>30.1</td><td>53</td><td>68.8</td><td>80</td><td>29.4</td><td>164</td><td>36.3</td></tr>
<tr><td>Refusals of Leave</td><td>62</td><td>60.2</td><td>13</td><td>16.9</td><td>112</td><td>41.2</td><td>187</td><td>41.4</td></tr>
<tr><td>Substantive Hearings (excluding Live Cases)</td><td>10</td><td>9.7</td><td>11</td><td>14.3</td><td>80</td><td>29.4</td><td>101</td><td>22.3</td></tr>
</table>

Although for different reasons, proportions of immigration and homeless person applications reaching a full hearing were both well below the average for the judicial review caseload as a whole. Of the 1987 immigration cases, in which as we have seen there were relatively high levels of pre-leave withdrawals and refusals of leave, only 17% eventually reached a substantive hearing. This rose to a quarter in relation to the 1988 immigration cases, but fell back to 19% for immigration applications brought in 1989. Immigration applications made in the first quarter of 1991 were subject to a very high refusal rate at the leave stage and, when combined with withdrawals, this meant that just under 10% of immigration cases begun in this period had reached a substantive hearing at the end of May 1995.

The proportions of homeless persons applications begun in 1987 and 1988 that eventually reached a full hearing were 37% and just over 30%. This declined to less than a quarter of cases started in 1989, and to a seventh of those commenced in the first quarter of 1991. This reduction in the proportion of homelessness cases reaching substantive hearings was primarily associated with the number of withdrawals, especially post-leave, rather than any rise in the rate of refusal of leave.

These findings on the proportions of different types of case reaching the substantive hearing stage have important implications for discussions about delays in the judicial review process. We will return to this issue below. At this stage the effect of leave decisions and the withdrawal rates on the composition of the judicial review caseload should be noted. There is a striking difference between the profile of applications for leave to seek judicial review, upon which the official statistics are based, and the profile of cases that eventually reach a final hearing. This difference is particularly notable in the latest two periods covered by our data (see Table 6.2).

While immigration accounted for over a quarter of all applications for judicial review made in 1989, immigration cases only made up a sixth of the substantive hearings that resulted from these applications. Similarly, 23% of applications made in the first quarter of 1991 concerned immigration, but this subject made up only 9% of cases from this period reaching a hearing. Equally, homeless persons cases, which accounted for 17% of applications begun in the first quarter of 1991, made up only 11% of cases from that period reaching a full hearing. By contrast, in both the 1989 and first quarter of 1991 caseloads, non-immigration and non-homelessness cases constituted some 60% of the original applications, but accounted for as much as 75% and 79% of hearings arising from the applications made in 1989 and the first quarter of 1991.

Table 6.2

Composition of Judicial Review Caseload at Application and Hearing Stages, 1987-1989 and 1st quarter of 1991

	Applications		Hearings	
	No	%	No	%
1987 Applications:				
Immigration	671	44.4	115	27.0
Homeless Persons	84	5.6	31	7.3
Other	575	50.1	280	65.7
1988 Applications:				
Immigration	356	29.1	94	22.1
Homeless Persons	105	8.6	32	7.5
Other	763	62.3	299	70.4
1989 Applications:				
Immigration	430	27.7	81	16.6
Homeless Persons	176	11.4	42	8.6
Other	944	60.9	364	74.7
1991 (Jan-Mar) Applications:				
Immigration	103	22.7	10	9.9
Homeless Persons	77	17.0	11	10.9
Other	274	60.4	80	79.2

* 1991 figures for other hearings exclude two 'live' cases before the European Court of Justice

Success/failure rates at substantive hearing

The overall pattern of results of substantive hearings for applications begun in 1987 to 1989 is shown in Table 6.3 As will be seen, only 41% of applications made in 1987 reaching a full hearing were fully or partially successful, as were just over half for cases from 1988 and 1989. The eventual success rate at full hearing for cases commenced during the first quarter of 1991 was 45%. However, there were again variations between subject areas. The success rate for applicants at final hearings in both immigration and homeless person cases was consistently below that for all other types of case. This discrepancy, however, progressively diminished between 1987 and 1989. On the other hand, the success rate for applicants in all other types of case varied only marginally, between 47% and 54% over the same periods.

Table 6.3

Outcome of Judicial Review Applications at Substantive Hearing by Subject, 1987-1989 and 1st Quarter of 1991

	Immigration		Homeless Persons		Other		Totals	
	No	%	No	%	No	%	No	%
1987								
Successful	38	33.0	8	25.8	132	47.1	178	41.8
Unsuccessful and other*	77	67.0	23	74.2	148	52.9	248	58.2
1988								
Successful	40	42.6	14	43.8	159	53.2	213	50.1
Unsuccessful and other*	54	57.4	18	56.2	140	46.8	212	49.9
1989								
Successful	35	43.2	19	45.2	198	54.4	252	51.7
Unsuccessful and other*	46	56.8	23	54.8	166	45.6	235	48.3
1991								
Successful	1	10.0	6	54.5	38	47.5	45	44.5
Unsuccessful and other*	9	90.0	5	45.5	42	52.5	56	55.4

* Other can be taken to include hearings where there was no order or where there was an agreement to withdraw by consent. In the case of 1991 data, however, it also excludes two cases before the European Court of Justice.

Delay in the processing of judicial review applications

Delay has been a persistent and recurring problem for the judicial review system. During the late 1970s it was taking on average two years for cases which had not been expedited to reach a substantive hearing.[20] The reforms of the early 1980s and particularly the increased use of single judges and the introduction of the written procedure for

---

20   *Hansard* Vol 975 HC Deb, 11 December 1979, col 427.

dealing with leave applications were introduced in an attempt to improve the efficiency of the process and reduce these delays. By the mid-1980s Sunkin reported a marked improvement with most applicants by then being able to expect their cases to be dealt with well within a year.[21] As the caseload continued to increase during the 1980s and early 1990s serious problems of delay returned. By the time our fieldwork was underway in 1992 delays were again reaching levels described by one High Court judge as a 'public scandal'.[22] The Lord Chief Justice went so far as to say that the situation amounted to 'a state of near crisis ...' and a 'national disgrace'.[23] The then Master of the Rolls, Lord Donaldson, echoed these concerns with equivalent force saying that the delays meant 'that we have no judicial review court' and that there was 'no effective administrative court in this country ...'[24] An infusion of additional judge time[25] helped to ease the crisis and by July 1994 waiting times for cases to be dealt with by a single judge in part B of the Crown Office List had been reduced from 23 months in April 1993 to 12 months.[26] At the time of writing, the delays are approximately nine months.[27]

In our study we looked at the incidence of delay in the context of three aspects of the procedure: the time taken to have an initial application for leave determined by either the written or oral procedures; the time taken to have renewed applications for leave determined; and the time taken to obtain a final hearing. Data were collected on these points in relation to applications made in 1987, 1988 and the first quarter of 1991, and the results are summarised in Table 6.4.[28] Although this information is now dated we believe it remains the most comprehensive publicly available data on the time it takes to have leave determined, the contrasts between oral and written procedures, and delays in having renewed applications for leave dealt with.

---

21 Sunkin, 1987, 461–2.

22 *Per* Popplewell J in *R v Wychavon DC and Secretary of State for the Environment* (1992) Lexis Co/429/90.

23 *HL Debates*, 22 October 1992, Vol 539 col 875, at 878.

24 *Ibid* at 883.

25 Law Commission Report No 226, *op cit*, para 2.21.

26 This list consists of cases which have not been expedited.

27 This is in accordance with the Crown Office's expectations, *ibid*, para 2.22 and Appendix C.

28 Insufficient relevant data was collected on 1989 cases to enable delays at various stages to be calculated.

Time taken to obtain an initial decision on leave

As will be seen, applications made through the oral leave procedure can be determined very quickly. Nearly half the applications initially filed for an oral hearing on leave in 1987 and 1988 were determined in 10 days or less, as compared with only about 30% of those processed through the table procedure. For applications filed in the first quarter of 1991, 43% of oral applications and 34% of table applications for leave were determined in 10 days or less.

Beyond this, the vast majority of table applications for leave were dealt with within 30 days. This was the case in 84% of such applications in 1987, 88% in 1988, and 79% in the first quarter of 1991. The oral procedure was nearly as efficient in the earlier two periods, with 78% of 1987 applications put through this procedure and 77% of those in 1988 being determined within 30 days. However, by 1991 delays in dealing with oral applications for leave had begun to increase noticeably, so that only 57% were dealt with within 30 days, and a quarter took more than 60 days to be determined.

Time taken to determine renewed applications for leave

The total time taken to determine renewed applications for leave (that is those refused leave on an initial table application but then renewed to an oral hearing on leave) is shown in Table 6.4b. It should be noted that the times shown are those from the date when the original application for judicial review was filed in the Crown Office until the renewed leave application was determined and not merely the additional time from the original table refusal to the hearing of the renewed application.

Again, the results were very similar for 1987 and 1988 cases that went to a renewal hearing on leave, with one-in-eight of the renewed applications being determined within 30 days and half of the rest being dealt with within 60 days. By contrast, renewed applications for leave took much longer to be decided in 1991, when only 14% were determined within 60 days and nearly half took more than 90 days.

Time taken to reach substantive hearing of cases

The deteriorating position as regards delay during the periods covered by the study is best illustrated by reference to the total time applications took from first being lodged in the Crown Office to reach a full substantive hearing, not including time taken for any subsequent appeals. In 1987, when there was a dramatic increase in applications for judicial review, a fifth of the cases that went to a full hearing were

Judicial Review in Perspective

Table 6.4

Time taken to Determine Judicial Review Applications, 1987-1988 and 1st quarter of 1991

a) Time taken – application to initial leave decision

Table applications:

	1987		1988		1991 (Jan—Mar)	
Days	No	%	No	%	No	%
0-10	150	30.4	192	28.9	71	33.5
11-20	168	34.0	253	38.1	63	29.7
21-30	97	19.6	136	20.5	33	15.6
31-60	55	11.1	69	10.4	30	14.2
61-90	14	2.8	6	9.0	6	2.8
90+	10	2.0	8	1.2	9	4.2

Oral applications:

	1987		1988		1991 (Jan—Mar)	
Days	No	%	No	%	No	%
0-10	284	49.1	243	48.1	78	43.3
11-20	102	17.6	84	16.6	19	10.6
21-30	65	11.2	62	12.3	6	3.3
31-60	84	14.5	89	17.6	32	17.8
61-90	19	3.3	16	3.2	34	18.9
90+	25	4.3	11	2.2	11	6.1

b) Time taken – application to renewed leave decision

	1987		1988		1991 (Jan—Mar)	
Days	No	%	No	%	No	%
0-30	32	12.9	34	12.2	4	5.6
31-40	32	12.9	32	11.0	8	11.3
41-50	54	21.8	60	21.5	–	–
51-60	44	17.7	44	15.8	2	2.8
61-90	47	19.0	66	23.7	23	32.4
91-120	25	10.1	21	7.5	21	29.6
120+	14	5.6	22	7.9	13	18.3

c) Time taken – application to substantive hearing

	1987		1988		1991 (Jan—Mar)	
Days	No	%	No	%	No	%
0-90	86	20.7	58	14.3	25	24.8
91-180	90	21.6	109	26.8	13	12.9
181-270	54	13.0	119	29.2	9	8.9
271-360	86	20.7	33	20.4	6	5.9
361-540	91	21.9	35	8.6	19	18.8
541-720	3	7.2	2	0.5	19	18.8
721-1000	6	1.4	1	0.3	5	5.0
1,001-1,500	-	-	-	-	5	5.0

* Figures for 1991 exclude two cases before the European Court of Justice which may eventually go to a full hearing.

determined within 90 days, but 30% took over 360 days to be heard. Of the 1988 applications going to a full hearing, only one-in-seven were determined within 90 days; but only 12% took over 360 days to be determined.

This contrasts sharply with the position of applications first lodged in the Crown Office in the first quarter of 1991. Although a quarter of these applications that went to a full hearing were completed within 90 days, just under half had not been determined within 360 days and 29% took more than 540 days to reach a full hearing. This may be compared with 1987 when over 90%, and 1988 when over 99%, of cases reached a final hearing in 540 days or less.

It is interesting to relate this apparently sharp deterioration in the time taken to process judicial review cases to the changes in the overall volume of applications. On our figures there was a 20% increase in the annual rate of initial applications for leave between 1987 and the first quarter of 1991,[29] and the rate of increase in the number of cases going to a full hearing between the periods was 17%. Yet, as we have seen these relatively small increases in caseload had a dramatic effect on waiting times, virtually doubling the proportion of cases taking more than a year to reach a substantive hearing. This suggests that delays in the judicial review system can build up very quickly and can be caused by comparatively small increases in case numbers. As with other aspects of the process this highlights the complexity of caseload management and underscores the need for empirical data on why delays occur. This is an important long term issue and past experience suggests that relatively minor procedural reforms can achieve benefits, but these tend not to have lasting effect. Perhaps most worrying is the tendency of reformers to try to shore up the system by strategies which make the procedure increasingly less accessible but with little long term advantage.

Summary and conclusions

Our findings on the progress of applications through the judicial review procedure and the different stages at which cases are concluded have significant implications in a number of areas. Legal commentary on judicial review tends to focus on reported decisions of cases at full hearing stage or subsequently in the Court of Appeal or House of Lords. Yet our research shows that it is only a minority of applications

---

29 Using the official statistics for 1991 as a whole [see Appendix 1] the increase in the number of applications between the two periods was 36%. This indicates that there was an accelerating rate of increase in the scale of applications later in 1991.

that reach a full hearing and that, in numerical terms at least, decisions taken at the leave stage and the processes of settlement and/or withdrawal before or after leave are far more important. This points to the need to pay much closer attention to the nature of the decision-making process at the leave stage and to the quality of such decisions, as well as to the reasons for withdrawal and the settlement process. We address some of these issues in the following chapters.

Our findings also have implications for debates on the growing judicial review caseload and the issue of delay. Most discussions of these points assume a direct relationship between the number and type of applications initially made for judicial review and delay during later stages of the process.

However, when the number of applications that withdraw are combined with the number refused leave it becomes clear that the majority of applications are not directly affected by these delays, nor do they necessarily contribute to the delays. This may be particularly significant in the context of the two areas of mass use of judicial review, immigration and homeless persons. It might be assumed from the number of applications for leave involving these areas that immigration and homeless persons cases play a significant part in contributing to delays. However, since very high proportions of cases in these two areas are either refused leave or are withdrawn it is arguable that they do not have a significant impact on overall delays. If this is correct, steps taken to divert immigration or homelessness cases from judicial review might not lead to a proportionate reduction in delays for cases in other fields.

On the other hand, it is possible that delays may increase the propensity of parties to settle, or lead to a situation in which the issues are more likely to go stale before they are heard. If so, steps to reduce delays at this later stage could be partially offset by reduced withdrawal rates as an increased number of applicants or respondents hold on for a full hearing.[30]

All of this points to the need for more detailed examination of the exact relationship between the incidence of delay and the demand for judicial review by different types of applicant, the processes of settlement or non-settlement of cases and the litigation strategies of the parties in judicial review.[31] More information is also required on the amount of judge and hearing time devoted to judicial review cases at different stages. Without this, it is difficult to predict how changes that

---

30 There is a view that recent reductions in delay have led to an increase in withdrawals, perhaps because the parties have been encouraged to settle by the prospect of a quick hearing.

might be made to curtail or manage the judicial review caseload will in fact influence the expedition of applications through the procedure.

The Law Commission's report indicated that judges and the Crown Office are taking an increasingly close interest in caseload management and this includes the setting of targets for the dispatch of judicial business, and the monitoring of case flows. Provided managerialism does not impinge upon the way judges consider the merits of individual cases (and there is some evidence that it might)[32] this is generally to be welcomed. The decision to produce an annual report to keep the state of the Crown Office List 'firmly in the public domain' will go some way to satisfy the call for '[a] clear and comprehensive report showing the way judicial review is working routinely available to Parliament and the public'.[33] The establishment of a User's Association is also to be welcomed, although it is to be hoped that the Association will include those able to represent the interests of applicants as well as respondents, the judiciary and court administrators; academics also have something to offer.

---

31   We are currently undertaking an Economic and Social Research Council funded project on the dynamics of judicial review litigation, one purpose of which is to study withdrawals and settlement in such cases.

32   Lord Donaldson MR in *R v Panel on Takeovers and Mergers, ex parte Guinness plc* [1990] 1 QB 146, at 177–8. M Sunkin, 'The Problematical State of Access to Judicial Review' in B Hadfield (ed) *Judicial Review: a Thematic Approach* (1995) Gill & Macmillan.

33   Sunkin, 1987 p 465.

Chapter 7

The Leave Procedure: General Policy and Practice

There has been a general trend over recent years toward higher rates of refusal of leave. There are, however, substantial variations in rates of grant of leave between different subject areas of judicial review. What factors lie behind these trends and what do they tell us about access to judicial review for different groups of applicants? The leave stage is an area of judicial review procedure in respect of which the Law Commission has put forward some of its most far-reaching proposals for change. How do these proposals relate to past policy and practice in relation to leave and to the empirical evidence on its operation?

As shown in Chapter 6, in the majority of judicial review cases the decision taken at the leave stage may be crucial, because either the applicant will be refused leave and the case not allowed to proceed further or, where leave is granted, the case will be subsequently settled and the application for judicial review withdrawn before it reaches a substantive hearing. This points to a need for much greater understanding both of the operation of the leave stage itself and of the processes influencing the parties in judicial review cases to reach settlements. The latter issue is beyond the scope of this report. In this chapter, however, we examine the general policy and practice together with the statistical evidence relating to the operation of the leave procedure. In the following chapter we focus particular attention on the role of judicial discretion and variations between judges in their decision-making at the leave stage.

The impact of leave procedures

Currently applicants for leave have a choice as to whether their applications are considered initially at an oral hearing in open court or on written submissions by way of a table application.[1] Where an initial table application is refused, applicants have a further opportunity to renew the application to an oral hearing before a different judge.

---

1   This position may change under the Law Commission's proposals (see below).

Initial applications for leave

The table procedure was an innovation introduced, along with the use of single judges, in 1980 as a way of improving the efficiency of the process.[2] Prior to these reforms it was thought to be important, in order to safeguard applicants, that leave decisions be given by three judges in open court, especially if leave was to be refused.[3] Now, instead, applicants who are refused leave under the table procedure have an automatic right to renew their application before a single judge in open court. The right to renew is designed to ensure that applicants have the opportunity for a public decision on whether they gain access to judicial review, albeit a public decision taken by one rather than three judges.

The written procedure is characterised by an absence of procedural formality and publicity. It tends to be used by applicants with limited funds or who require a speedy decision; where it is believed that the granting of leave will be a formality; and where points of law or the facts are thought to be clear. By contrast, the oral procedure is public and formal. It tends to be used where legal issues are thought to be complex or subtle; where applicants face a problem with delay or standing; where interim relief is also sought; and, where applicants wish to generate publicity for their cause.[4]

Throughout most of the 1980s a majority of applicants for leave to seek judicial review preferred to use the written procedure. The proportion of civil cases involving table applications ranged between 55% and 68% over the years 1981 to 1985.[5] During the periods covered by our research, the proportion of all applications, both civil and criminal, passing initially through the written leave procedure was between 53% and 58%, and the proportion of table application among civil cases alone ranged from 52% to 63%. These figures indicate a slight decline, as compared with the earlier period, in the popularity of the written procedure for applying for leave. This may have been because more applicants were seeking some form of interim relief at the time of applying for leave so that their applications had to be dealt with orally. Certainly, in homelessness cases, which constituted a major growth area in judicial review during the period studied, applications for interim relief in the form of injunctions to prevent evictions of

---

2   SI 1980 No 2000.

3   Law Commission Report No 73, *op cit*, para 40.

4   See Le Sueur and Sunkin, p 113. The Law Commission seemed to be critical of the use of the oral procedure in order to obtain publicity. Law Commission Report No 226, *op cit*, para 5.10.

5   Sunkin, 1987, pp 454–5.

applicants from temporary accommodation are regularly sought. This correlation seems to be supported by the finding that during the years in this study only between 31% and 43% of the applicants seeking judicial review in homeless persons cases initially used the written procedure to seek leave.

Another factor possibly influencing the declining popularity of the written procedure among applicants and their legal advisers could have been the perception that table applicants tend to be less successful, at least initially, in obtaining leave. From 1981 to 1985, the proportions of table applications refused leave in civil judicial review cases rose steadily from 33% to 47%, while the proportion of oral civil applications refused leave varied between 22% and 29% over the five year period.[6] The grant/refusal rates of applications made by way of the written and oral leave procedures during the periods covered by this study are shown in Table 7.1. The figures show that there has been a steady increase in the proportion of oral applications refused leave, from 30% in 1987 to only just under 40% in the first quarter of 1991. The rate of refusal of leave of table applications, although more variable over the same period, ranging from just under half to 57%, nevertheless, remained well above that for oral applications, by a margin of between 16% and 27%.

Table 7.1

Rates of Grant and Refusal of Leave to Seek Judicial Review by Table and Oral Procedures, 1987-1989 and 1st quarter of 1991

	Table Applications		Oral Applications	
	Granted %	Refused %	Granted %	Refused %
1987	42.7	57.3	69.7	30.3
1988	43.6	56.4	64.1	35.9
1989	51.3	48.7	67.6	32.4
1991 (Jan-Mar)	42.1	57.9	60.6	39.4

---

6   *Ibid.*

There is no straightforward explanation for the consistently higher refusal rate of table applications. It may be that the relative cheapness and speed of the written procedure encourages applicants with weak cases to 'have a go' or leads to table applications being less well prepared, for example by solicitors with limited experience of the procedure or litigants in person, than oral ones where (because of rules limiting rights of audience) a barrister is always involved. However, the high renewal rate from table applications refused leave and the relative success of such renewals in eventually obtaining leave (see below), may suggest that weak applications accounted for only a small proportion of those initially refused leave on the papers.

Another factor may be a tendency among judges to apply stricter criteria to table applications knowing that applicants currently have an unfettered right to renew the application to an oral hearing. This may mean, for example, that judges are not prepared to give applicants the benefit of the doubt on evidential issues raised in table applications in the expectation that fuller argument and consideration is possible at the renewed oral hearing. The absence of a clear obligation to provide reasons for refusing leave may also be a factor.[7] A further possibility is that applications are strengthened by oral argument even where applicants and their legal advisers view the issues as being relatively clear. It may be that rather than filtering out only hopeless applications, the written procedure initially excludes all but the relatively strong and well prepared cases, leaving others to be renewed to an oral hearing. Such explanations highlight the uncertainty of the criteria for granting leave and raise the possibility that the nature of the test facing applicants differs depending on the procedure being used.

As indicated, homeless persons cases tend more often to be taken through the oral procedure because they frequently include a request for interim relief, and homelessness applications also have a higher rate of grant of leave than those in other subject areas. This finding might underscore the benefits to applicants of using the oral route. However, we were conscious that this class of case might also skew the results producing an appearance that applicants in general fare better using the oral procedure. Whilst the figures are not produced here in detail, this matter was examined and we found that only a very small element of the differential in grant rates between the written and oral procedures could be attributed to the effect of homelessness applications.

---

7   The Law Commission recommended that brief reasons for refusing leave should always
     be given. Law Commission Report No 226, *op cit*, para 5.36.

Renewed applications for leave

The relatively high rates of refusal of table applications for leave highlights the importance of the unencumbered right to renew applications initially refused on the papers to an oral hearing. Between 1981 and 1985 the rates of renewal from refused table applications in civil cases ranged from just under one half to as high as 78% (in 1984); of these renewed applications between 45% and 60% were successful.[8] In the periods covered by this research (see Table 7.2), rates of renewal from refused table applications (both civil and criminal) ranged from just under 60% to 73% between 1987 and 1989, but declined to 52% in the first quarter of 1991. Similarly, the proportion of renewed table applications that were granted ranged between 40% and 48% between 1987 and 1989; a somewhat lower rate of success than in the early 1980s. However, the renewal grant rate in relation to the first quarter of 1991 applications was cut by nearly half, to just 25%. These figures again confirm the general trend toward higher rates of refusal of leave.

When renewal grants are taken into account (see Table 7.2), the overall proportion of applications initially put through the written procedure that were eventually granted leave increased: from 43% at the table application stage to 59% following renewals in 1987; from 44% to 60% in 1988; from 51% to 65% in 1989; and from 42% to 50% in the first quarter of 1991. The latter figure for each period can be compared with the overall proportion of applications initially put through the oral procedure that eventually obtained leave. The relevant figures were: 70% in 1987; 65% in 1988; 69% in 1989; and, 61% in the first quarter of 1991.[9] Thus, while the differential between grant rates of table and oral applications declined when renewals were taken into account, those who initially used the written procedure, nevertheless, continued to experience lower rates of success than those who used the oral procedure from the outset.

The Law Commission has recommended that applicants refused leave on the papers should retain their right to renew their applications to an oral hearing.[10] On the other hand, it has linked this recommendation with a separate proposal that the court should have the power to award costs against the applicant in the event of a renewed application for leave being unsuccessful, on the grounds that: 'this discipline should make the party's advisors reconsider the merits

---

8   Sunkin, 1987, p 456.

9   These figures include a small number of criminal applications initially refused leave at an oral hearing that were subsequently granted leave at a renewed oral hearing before the Divisional Court.

10 Law Commission Report No 226, *op cit*, para 5.12.

Table 7.2

**Renewed Applications for Leave from Table Refusals,
1987-1989 and 1st quarter of 1991**

	1987	1988	1989	1991 (Jan-Mar)
Table Applications:				
Granted	301	291	425	90
Refused	403	377	404	124
Table Applications				
Renewed	245	275	238	65
Renewal Rate	61%	73%	59%	52%
Renewed Table Applications:				
Granted	117	109	114	16
Renewal Grant Rate	48%	40%	48%	25%
% Applications Granted or Renewed Granted from initial				
Table Applications	*59%*	*60%*	*65 %*	*49%*
Oral Applications	*68%*	*64%*	*68%*	*61%*

carefully before deciding to renew an application.'[11] In other words, although the right to renew would be retained, it would no longer be unfettered; rather, those seeking to exercise it would run the risk of facing substantial financial penalties for doing so. The impact of such a change would in all probability be to reduce the renewal rate among those refused leave initially on the papers. When combined with the recommendation that applicants should normally be required to apply for leave through the written procedure, where refusal rates are higher, the overall effect would be to reduce access to judicial review in general.

There is a further stage of seeking leave in civil cases, namely the possibility of renewing an application again to the Court of Appeal. If

---

11   *Ibid*, para 10.3. The position as regard the award of costs on leave applications and renewals has been subject to differing judicial opinion, but the recent trend has been toward giving greater prominence to the court's powers to order costs on leave applications. For a discussion of these developments, see Chapter 5, n 10.

the Court of Appeal does not grant leave on a renewed application 'that is the end of the matter' and the House of Lords does not have a jurisdiction to consider appeals against refusals of renewed applications for leave.[12]

Although there is no formal restriction on the right to renew an application to the Court of Appeal, use of this facility is fairly infrequent; and, certainly in legally-aided cases a favourable opinion from counsel would normally be required before permission would be given for this step to be taken.[13] In 1987 there were 17 renewed applications for leave to the Court of Appeal from 258 applicants who would have been able to exercise this right (7%). In 1988 there were 20 Court of Appeal renewals from 293 eligible applicants (7%), and by 1989 there were just 13 out of 279 eligible cases (5%). During the first quarter of 1991, however, possibly as a reaction to the higher rates of refusal of leave evident in this period, no fewer than 20% of eligible applicants (20 out of 102) exercised their right to a further renewal to the Court of Appeal.

This increase in the frequency of Court of Appeal renewals was matched by a much higher rate of rejection of applications at this stage. In 1987, 13 out of 17 Court of Appeal renewals resulted in a grant of leave; and in 1988 14 out of 20 such renewals were successful. By contrast, in 1989 the Court of Appeal granted leave in only seven out of 13 instances; and by the first quarter of 1991 there was only one successful renewal to the Court of Appeal from 20 such applications. The Court of Appeal's decisions on leave are likely to have a significant influence on judicial attitudes throughout the process, and this shift towards a very low rate of success in Court of Appeal renewals perhaps reflects the more general policy change toward the imposition of more restrictive criteria for leave during this period (see below).

Respondents and applications for leave

Applications for leave to seek judicial review are normally expected to be heard *ex parte*, that is, without the respondent being present or making representations. There are opportunities, however, for respondents to intervene in the process. In some instances, such as

---

12 Law Commission Report No 226, *op cit*, para 9.3 and *Re Poh* [1983] 1 WLR 2.

13 Normally legal aid certificates covering applications for leave are limited to proceedings before the High Court. This means that no further permission is required to renew an application refused on paper to an oral hearing before a single judge in the High Court, but as a further renewal takes the matter into the Court of Appeal, an application must be made to amend the legal aid certificate before this can be done.

when applying for interim relief at the leave stage, the applicants may be required to serve notice on respondents thereby giving them the opportunity to attend the leave hearing and request to be heard. In other instances, judges may adjourn table or oral applications for leave precisely in order that the respondents may be notified and invited to make representations on the case. Specific encouragement to judges to adopt this procedure more frequently was given by the Court of Appeal in *R v Secretary of State for the Home Department, ex parte Doorga*.[14] Here Lord Donaldson MR placed leave applications into three categories: those showing *prima facie* grounds for judicial review, which should be granted leave on a 'quick look'; those which are clearly unarguable, where leave should be refused; and an intermediary category where there is no *prima facie* case but there is concern to know more about the matter. In this latter type of case, it was suggested that the proper procedure was to adjourn the application for leave to an *inter partes* hearing.

Our data do not enable us to determine how frequently respondents sought or were invited to intervene in initial decisions on the grant of leave. Previous research by Le Sueur and Sunkin showed that such *inter partes* hearings took place in 16% of leave applications covered by their study[15] Beyond this, respondents have a further opportunity, once leave has been granted, to apply for it to be set aside or for the application to be struck out.[16] Within our study period, there were 12 cases in 1987 where leave was set aside or the case struck out, but leave was subsequently restored in four of these cases. In 1988 there were 14 instances of leave being set aside or the case struck out, and leave was subsequently restored in six of these cases. In 1989, there were 19 cases where leave was set aside or the case struck out, and in only one of these was leave restored. Finally, in the first quarter of 1991 leave was set aside or the case struck out on five occasions and leave was restored only once.

The Law Commission has recommended that under the new procedure for 'preliminary consideration' of applications for judicial review judges should have the discretion to refer written applications submitted on an *ex parte* basis to respondents, along with a 'request for further information'.[17] Thus, while applicants in most cases would be restricted initially to a written application and have their right of renewal to an oral hearing made subject to a possible costs order

---

14   [1990] COD 109, 110.

15   See Le Sueur and Sunkin, p 118.

16   This may be done under RSC Order 32, r 6 or by virtue of the inherent discretion of the court, *Becker v Noel (Practice Note)* [1971] 1 WLR 803.

17   Law Commission Report No 226, *op cit*, paras 4.8–4.11.

against them (see below), respondents would be given a new opportunity to intervene in leave decisions (at relatively little cost to themselves) on paper. Indeed, the extra burden of costs in the proposed 'request for further information' procedure would fall mainly on applicants, who would be required to serve a complete set of papers relating to their applications on the respondents.[18]

Point of final determination of applications for leave

One way of assessing the relative significance of the table, oral, and renewed oral procedures for considering applications for leave is by examining the point at which the issue of leave is finally determined (see Table 7.3). The contribution made by the written procedure to the overall efficiency of the judicial review process is clear. Leave was finally determined on the basis of a table application alone in between a third and 40% of all cases. This obviously results in a not insubstantial saving in time and expense for judges, court officials and applicants alike, compared to the time and expense that would have been incurred had these applications been taken to oral hearings. While such hearings are normally expected to last no more than 20 minutes, empirical evidence suggests that only slightly over half were determined within this time limit.[19] If applications where leave was finally determined through the written procedure had gone to oral hearings lasting 20 minutes, something over 200 hours of additional court time would have been needed per annum. Against this must be weighed the duplication of judge and administrative time involved in dealing with renewed applications for leave. During the first quarter of 1991, for example, around a sixth of all applications for leave passed through the written procedure and were dealt with again at an oral hearing, after they had been renewed.

Resource questions, however, are not the only issues that need to be considered. The frequency of renewals from table refusals and their relatively high success rate raises questions about the consistency of judicial attitudes toward leave applications and throws doubt on the quality of the decisions taken on the basis of a quick perusal of written applications. In this context, particular concern should be focused on those cases where table applications are refused and applicants do not exercise their right to renew. Such cases accounted for nearly 15% of all leave applications determined in the first quarter of 1991, a slightly

---

18   At present, this is only required in most cases once leave has been granted.
19   Le Sueur and Sunkin, pp 115–16.

higher proportion than in the earlier periods covered by this study. It is
noteworthy that a fifth of the applicants in these cases (12 out of 59)
were litigants in person who may not have had any expert advice in
preparing their written application or on whether to renew their
applications orally.

Leave procedure and outcome of case

A final question to be considered in this part of the chapter is whether
there is any clear relationship between the type of procedure through

	1987		1988		1989		1991 (Jan-Mar)	
	No	%	No	%	No	%	No	%
Table Application only								
Granted	301	23.3	291	25.1	425	29.9	90	22.6
Refused and								
not renewed	158	12.3	102	8.8	166	11.7	59	14.8
		(35.6)		(33.9)		(41.6)		(37.4)
Oral Hearing								
Granted on -								
initial application	409	31.7	317	27.3	394	27.7	109	27.4
renewed application	122	9.4	114	9.8	125	8.8	16	4.0
Refused and								
not renewed	285	22.1	317	27.3	300	21.1	104	26.1
		(63.2)		(64.4)		(57.6)		(57.5)
Court of Appeal								
Granted	13	1.0	14	1.2	7	0.5	1	0.3
Refused or not								
proceeded with	4	0.3	6	0.5	6	0.4	19	48
		(1.3)		(1.7)		(0.9)		(5.1)

Table 7.3

**Point of Final Leave Decision of Applications for Judicial Review,
1987-1989 and 1st quarter of 1991**

*Figures in this table exclude a small number of cases where it was not ascer-
tained where leave was granted. Per cent figures relate to all leave decisions
where point of grant/refusal known.*

which leave is granted and the eventual outcome of the case.[20] Do ultimate success rates provide any indication as to whether or not the written procedure, with its low grant rates, is an effective filter of low quality applications? A low grant rate at the leave stage ought in theory to be reflected by a relatively high rate of success on final hearing. On the other hand, a low leave grant rate coupled with a low ultimate success rate might suggest that the initial stage was a poor filter of quality. Another assumption might be that applications obtaining leave through the oral procedure, or following renewals, would be comparatively more complex and contentious and therefore likely to lead to a higher rate of failure at the hearing stage. Testing out these hypotheses is made more complicated by the high rates of post-leave withdrawal of applications, as discussed in Chapter 6. High proportions of the more arguable cases might, for example, be settled and withdrawn because respondents recognise their strength.

Leave procedure and withdrawals

As will be seen in Table 7.4, when we traced the outcome of applications according to the type of procedure through which leave was granted, we found that applicants who obtained leave orally were somewhat more likely to withdraw their case prior to a final hearing than those granted leave on the papers. This was to be anticipated bearing in mind that applicants granted leave orally are more likely to seek some form of interim relief that may be sufficient to resolve their dispute with the respondent or otherwise to induce the respondent into a settlement. The differential in withdrawal rates is actually less than might have been expected.

Given that cases going to a renewed oral hearing on leave are more likely to be contested, it was probable that rates of post-leave withdrawal would have been lowest in this category of cases. This was so in 1987 and, to a considerably lesser extent, in 1988 as well. However, there was very little differential in withdrawal rates as between applications granted leave through the three different procedures in 1989.

Leave procedure and hearings

During 1987 applicants who had obtained leave on the papers alone were unsuccessful at the hearing stage more often than those granted

---

20 This question is further considered below in Chapter 8 in relation to variations between individual judges in their leave decisions.

leave after an oral hearing. Given the higher rate of failure of paper applications, this was the reverse of the pattern that may have been expected. During 1988 and 1989, however, the proportion of table grants that were unsuccessful at final hearings was somewhat lower than of those granted leave orally. Cases granted leave on a renewed application had, as anticipated, a higher rate of failure at final hearing in two out of the three periods covered. The exception was in 1989, when the pattern of results for cases obtaining leave at a renewed hearing was very similar to that for initial oral grants.

Applications granted leave following a renewal to the Court of Appeal have the lowest rate of success at final hearing. Although numbers are small, of those applications across the three years where leave had been granted by the Court of Appeal and there was a clear outcome at the final hearing, five were allowed and 17 were unsuccessful.

It is difficult to draw firm conclusions from these figures. If it were to be assumed that withdrawals are more likely to occur on the basis of respondents agreeing to settle in relatively strong cases,[21] it is perhaps surprising that there are not higher rates of failure among cases reaching a final hearing. This in turn may reflect the quality of leave decisions and suggest that at least some arguable cases are being unnecessarily dismissed on the basis of the limited information available to judges at this earlier stage. Such a proposition must be speculative, given that so little is known about the factors and reasons leading parties to judicial review to settle once leave has been granted. Nonetheless, there is certainly little evidence of very poor success rates at the final hearing stage such as might suggest that significant numbers of weak applications are being granted leave.

The leave criteria: changing context and policy

The factors which contribute to the trend toward higher rates of refusal of leave to apply for judicial review may be divided between contextual factors, external to the judicial review procedure itself, and those which arise directly from its operation, such as changing judicial policy toward the criteria for granting or refusing leave.

---

21 Contrary to this, it may be that comparatively weak cases are withdrawn after applicants see the respondent's arguments, even though leave has been obtained. Cases may also be withdrawn for reasons unrelated to their quality, such as costs or staleness.

Table 7.4

Outcome of Applications by Type of Procedure under which Leave Granted, 1987-1989

	1987		1988		1989	
	No	%	No	%	No	%
Table granted:						
Withdrawn*	138	45.9	121	41.6	198	46.6
Successful at hearing	72	23.9	104	35.7	140	32.9
Unsuccessful at hearing	91	30.2	62	21.3	83	19.5
Other	-	-	4	1.4	4	0.9
Oral granted:						
Withdrawn*	244	59.7	144	45.4	206	52.3
Successful at hearing	63	15.4	82	25.9	78	19.8
Unsuccessful at hearing	102	24.9	84	26.5	100	25.4
Other	-	-	7	2.2	10	2.5
Renewed granted:						
Withdrawn*	46	37.7	45	39.5	61	48.8
Successful at hearing	32	26.2	21	18.4	30	24.0
Unsuccessful at hearing	44	36.1	46	40.4	34	27.2
Other	-	-	2	1.8	-	-

* Includes small numbers of cases where leave set aside.

Contextual factors

Various suggestions have been made as to why the rate of failure at the leave stage has been increasing. One possibility is that, as the demand for judicial review has grown and legal representation of applicants has become more widely spread (see Chapter 4), the quality of applications has tended to decline. Lord Woolf, for example, has commented:

> Surely the figures indicate that more care should be exercised by practitioners to filter out unmeritorious applications before the leave stage.[22]

---

22   Lord Woolf, 'Judicial Review: a Possible Programme for Reform' 1992 *Public Law* 221, at 223.

If inexperience and lack of expertise among solicitors were major factors leading to the submission of badly prepared or weak applications and therefore to generally higher rates of refusal of leave, we might expect to find that applicants represented by solicitors' firms who are specialist or regular users of judicial review have significantly greater success in obtaining leave than those represented by firms making less frequent use of the procedure. In fact, we can find little evidence in our data to suggest that this is the case. Indeed, it is just as likely that poor preparation would be a feature of those fields in which judicial review is used very frequently and large numbers of cases are processed in a routine fashion by particular solicitors' firms. The two fields in which this applies are immigration and homelessness and, as we have seen in Chapter 5, while immigration applications tend to have a relatively low leave grant rate, those relating to homelessness have a high rate of success at the leave stage.

Of course, where an applicant for judicial review is supported by legal aid, the case will have passed through a preliminary vetting process by the legal aid authorities to determine whether there are reasonable grounds for taking the proceedings. Until the Court of Appeal decision in *ex parte Hughes* in 1992[23] it was assumed that the test of reasonableness to be applied to a legal aid application for judicial review was somewhat stricter than that of 'arguability' intended to be used by judges in making leave decisions. Even after the *Hughes* decision the legal aid merits test and the leave criteria are intended to be essentially the same.

As we saw in Chapter 5, many legal aid applications in this field are submitted by solicitors without a clear statement of the legal grounds on which it is intended to seek judicial review (although this may not prevent legal aid from being granted). A substantial proportion of grants of legal aid for judicial review are made, however, subject to counsel's opinion on the merits of the case, and generally in judicial review cases solicitors tend to rely heavily on barristers to prepare initial written applications and draft supporting materials. It may therefore be barristers who are primarily responsible for the quality of judicial review leave applications.

Whatever criticism might be levelled at legal advisers, there is evidence to indicate that those applicants who lack any legal representation at all fare worse at the leave stage. During the periods covered by our research, between 24% and 31% of litigants in person were eventually granted leave to proceed with their judicial review applications, as compared with between 46% and 61% of applicants in general. By contrast, both companies and other institutional applicants

---

23   See Chapter 5, n 19.

had high rates of grant of leave. Company applicants had a success rate in obtaining leave of between 77% and 86% and other non-individual applicant grant rates between 74% and 86% in the periods covered by our research. As discussed in Chapter 4, the proportion of litigants in person among judicial review applicants appears to have been growing, although they still constitute only a relatively small minority of all applicants.

If increased leave refusal rates seem unlikely to be attributable primarily to a lack of expertise in preparing or presenting applications, then the explanation for the growing failure rate at the leave stage might lie both in the nature of the law in specific fields and the use of 'anti-judicial review' devices in legislation and administrative decision-making which may be making it more difficult to challenge the actions of government. Central government, in particular, has been increasingly aware of the need to train its officials in the elements of fair decision-making, so as to improve the quality of decisions and to avoid the burden of costly, drawn out judicial review litigation.[24]

In general, the courts have resisted attempts to shield administrative decision-making from challenge by the use of specific 'ouster' clauses in legislation. Government has also sought to reduce its vulnerability to judicial review by adopting less direct techniques. These have included the delegation of wider discretionary powers to Ministers and others as well as the use of alternative mechanisms for administrative review and appeal. One example of the use of alternative remedies by government is the provision in the Education Act 1993 establishing a new regional tribunal to consider appeals against local authority decisions on the assessment of children's special educational needs, which has been a particular growth area in judicial review over recent years. Other examples are the provisions of the Immigration and Asylum Act 1993 giving new rights of appeal to those refused refugee status in this country and also creating a general right of appeal in immigration matters on a point of law from the Immigration Appeal Tribunal to the Court of Appeal. Although this latter Act does not appear to have stemmed the flow of immigration leave applications (see Chapter 2), it is notable that the most recent official statistics for 1994 show that only 18% of such applications were successful in obtaining leave.[25] This suggests that the legislation may have made it more difficult to obtain leave in this field.

---

24 See in particular the Cabinet Office's pamphlet, *The Judge Over Your Shoulder: Judicial Review of Administrative Decisions*, 2nd edn, 1994. For a comment on an earlier edition, see A Bradley (1987) *Public Law* 250. For a recent discussion, see Brigid Hadfield, 'Judge-proofing Reviewable Decisions – Should the Judges be Trusted with Review?' in Hadfield (ed) *Judicial Review: A Thematic Approach* (1995), Gill and Macmillan

25 Data obtained from the Crown Office.

In their survey of leave decisions over two short periods in 1988 and 1989, Le Sueur and Sunkin found that the second most frequently cited reason (after 'unarguability') for refusing leave was that judicial review was inappropriate, usually because there had been a failure to exhaust alternative remedies.[26] There were also additional cases where the application for judicial review was seen as premature, again in some instances because proceedings in other courts or tribunals were still continuing. The view that judicial review cannot be used where other remedies exist may become even more significant in light of the proliferation on new forms of internal administrative review and appeal under the current Government's Citizen's Charter initiative,[27] and the drive toward contracting out and privatisation of public services.

Judicial policy on leave

As well as the external factors which may be making it more difficult to obtain leave, it is necessary to consider how far judicial policy on granting or refusing leave may be affecting access to the procedure. The changing and uncertain nature of judicial policy and approach towards the leave requirement are now well known and documented.[28] The current leave criteria are inherently uncertain and this problem is exacerbated by the failure of the judiciary to adopt a uniform view on the purpose of the leave stage. As we shall see when we examine the decision-making records of the judges in the next chapter, during any single period there are considerable variations in the way the individual judges approach leave applications. There was also an undoubted change in what may be described as the general judicial policy toward leave during the 1980s.

Prior to the mid-1980s the dominant view was that leave should be used to filter out hopeless and unarguable applications. This view was sanctioned and reinforced by Lord Diplock who in the *IRC v National Federation of Self-Employed and Small Businesses Ltd* said that judges should grant leave if on a 'quick perusal' the application appeared

---

26   Le Sueur and Sunkin, pp 123–4.

27   In its discussion of the question of alternative remedies, the Law Commission recommended that only *legal* alternatives, that is those available before courts or tribunals or a statutory appeal to a minister, should be required to be exhausted before applying for judicial review. Although this may exclude informal or non-statutory administrative reviews, the position in relation to statutory reviews and complaint procedures as alternatives to judicial review remains somewhat ambiguous.

28   Le Sueur and Sunkin.

potentially arguable.[29] It was an approach that was reflected by the data. Reviewing grant/refusal rates during the mid-1980s Sunkin said that the grant rates 'may be thought to indicate that 'hopelessness' has been the primary reason for failure to obtain leave'.[30]

Dominant judicial policy began to change as the flow of applications for leave increased and this change culminated in the stricter approach taken in *ex parte Swati*[31] and *Puhlhoffer*.[32] Here the Court of Appeal and House of Lords rejected the earlier liberal attitude and called upon judges to look for actual, rather than potential, arguability.[33] Indeed, in some circumstances arguability itself became insufficient and judges were warned only to grant leave if applications were exceptional in some way.[34] In these cases the judges appeared to be driven by three concerns. One was to maintain the efficiency of the judicial review process by ensuring that unmeritorious applications did not clog the waiting lists. Another was to offer protection to hard-pressed public bodies. The third was to protect aspects of the administrative process from undue judicial interference.

This change in policy encouraged judges to become generally more cautious in granting leave. The result was that the leave requirement became a significantly more demanding obstacle to applicants than was originally envisaged by the Law Commission when recommending its retention in the mid-1970s.[35]

Judicial managerialism

One particular issue raised by the shift in judicial policy is whether it is legitimate for judges, in determining applications for leave, to have regard to the perceived pressures on the overall caseload and to the delays in applications reaching a final hearing. As noted by Le Sueur and Sunkin, this 'is currently one of the most sensitive issues surrounding the leave process' and one on which a clear division of judicial opinion emerged during the early 1990s.[36] On the one hand, Lord Donaldson, who had previously commended the accessibility of

---

29 [1982] AC 617, 644.
30 Sunkin, 1987, p 453.
31 [1986] 1 All ER 717.
32 [1986] 1 All ER 467.
33 The distinction was set out again in the case of *ex parte Hughes*, Chapter 5, n 10.
34 See *R v Harrow Council, ex parte D* [1990] Fam LR, 133, 138.
35 Law Commission Report No 73, *op cit*.
36 Le Sueur and Sunkin, p 125.

judicial review to the individual citizen[37] subsequently argued that the
public interest in the speedy administration of justice necessitates some
limitation being placed on the number of applications granted leave.[38]
On the other hand, Sir Konrad Schiemann reflected a more traditional
view when he argued that applications should be considered on their
individual merits without regard to considerations of administrative
convenience or demands on scarce judicial resources.[39]

For its part, the Law Commission appears to have endorsed a more
managerial approach to leave, noting that:

> a filtering requirement can be a tool for the efficient management of
> the caseload and that there have been calls for greater judicial
> management of cases at an early stage in other areas of civil
> procedure. It is possible that future developments in civil
> procedure will lessen the contrast between the initial stages of an
> application for judicial review and the initial stages of other
> proceedings.[40]

As noted in Chapter 6, the Law Commission has recommended
that applications for 'preliminary consideration' should initially be
determined without an oral hearing, unless the application either
includes a claim for immediate interim relief or it is decided on the
basis of written submissions that 'a hearing is desirable in the interests
of justice'. Indeed, under the Law Commission's proposals, not only
judges but also Crown Office administrators would be given formal
powers to decide when leave applications are to be submitted to an
oral hearing under the latter criteria.[41] The use of the Crown Office in
taking this important decision would represent a small but significant
step away from the principle that access to judicial review is a judicial
rather than an administrative matter.[42]

New criteria for leave?

The Law Commission has stated its intention not to depart 'from the
existing grounds for the refusal to grant leave to apply for judicial

---

37 *Parr v Wyre BC* [1982] HLR 71, 80.

38 *R v Panel on Takeovers and Mergers, ex parte Guinness plc* [1990] QB 146, 177–8.

39 Sir K Schiemann, *'Locus Standi'* (1990) *Public Law* 342.

40 Law Commission Report No 226, *op cit*, para 5.6. The Law Commission appears here to
have been referring to the review of the civil courts being carried out under Lord Woolf,
whose subsequent report *Access to Justice – Interim Report to the Lord Chancellor on the Civil
Justice System in England and Wales*, Lord Chancellor's Department, 1995, recommended
greater responsibility for the courts and judges in the management of cases and a
partnership between judges and court administrators to ensure the effective use of
resources.

review'.[43] However, its proposal for statutory formulation of these grounds, and in particular its suggestion that 'unless an application discloses *a serious issue* which ought to be determined it should not be allowed to proceed to a substantive hearing'[44] may be taken as confirmation of the higher threshold that applicants are now required to meet in order to obtain leave and arguably opens the way for even stricter judicial interpretation of the leave criteria in future.

The desire to have the leave criteria spelt out more clearly is laudable. Unfortunately the proposed 'serious issue to be tried' test appears to increase the potential burden facing applicants and to add a new dimension of uncertainty. Although the arguability test has been criticised,[45] it does have the virtue of focusing on the specific merits of the application.[46] The 'serious issue to be tried' test is potentially a very different and more uncertain animal. The key problem lies in the word 'serious'. Is seriousness to be determined only by reference to the merits of the application, or is it to be assessed in the light of wider public interest considerations, including managerial concerns? Might an application which is serious in its own right be considered less than serious when compared with other applications, or if judges regard its consideration to be an inefficient use of judge time?

Summary and conclusions

The leave stage plays a significant role in the determination of a majority of judicial review applications, yet it remains one of the most procedurally complex and controversial aspects of the process. Our data indicate that the written procedure, despite supposedly being quicker, cheaper and more convenient, has suffered declining popularity among applicants. Part of the explanation for this may be the consistent evidence that table applications are less successful, at least initially, in obtaining leave than those that proceed immediately to an oral hearing. Despite its declining popularity, the efficiency of the written procedure has been maintained; over a third of all leave applications were determined on the papers alone and during the first quarter of 1991, 15% of all applications were refused leave on the papers and not renewed to an oral hearing.

---

41 Law Commission Report No 226, *op cit* paras 5.9–5.11.
42 See further, M Sunkin, 'The Problematic State of Access to Judicial Review' in B Hadfield (ed) *op cit*, esp pp 24–25.
43 Law Commission Report No 226, *op cit*, para 5.14.
44 *Ibid*, para 5.15 (emphasis added).
45 Le Sueur and Sunkin.
46 M Sunkin, 'The Problematic State of Access to Judicial Review', *op cit*, pp 25–6.

The danger inherent in the current procedure is that good applications may be summarily refused access to the courts. Where this occurs, it causes injustice and it also has broader societal implications. It means, for example, that governmental illegality may go unchallenged, that standards of public administration may not be maintained, and that legal principle may not develop.[47] For these reasons it is vital that the filter operates, and is seen to operate, fairly and consistently.

Unfortunately, the quality of leave decisions is open to question. As we have seen, as well as the lower rate of success amongst table applications, there is also a relatively high rate of renewal from table refusals. Prior to 1991, between 40% and 50% of these renewed applications were granted leave at this 'second bite', and a clear majority of these were later settled and/or withdrawn, or were successful at the final hearing. In fact, of all applications for judicial review that were successful at the final hearing in the three complete years covered by our research, 10% in 1987, 18% in 1988, and 12% in 1989 were only granted leave at a renewed oral hearing. They would not have reached this stage but for the persistence of the applicant and his or her legal advisers in the face of an initial refusal on the papers.

The risk that good applications may be rejected at the leave stage is probably highest where information that is central to the case is not available to the applicant or the judge.[48] It also exists where applications are poorly prepared. The problem is likely to be most acute under the written procedure where judges currently have minimal opportunity to elicit material from applicants. The Law Commission's proposal for judges to have a discretion to send a 'request for further information' to respondents and for the applicant to be given an opportunity to make written representations on any response, may help to ensure that more relevant information is made available for the determination of table applications. However, the effectiveness of any such procedure will depend on how frequently judges exercise their discretion to use it,[49] and there is also a danger that it will lead to a drawn out 'paper chase' between the court and the

---

47 Le Sueur and Sunkin, p 105.

48 *R v Norfolk CC ex parte M* [1989] QB 619 is a notorious example of a case in which critical information was unavailable until the substantive hearing.

49 In contrast with the present situation where effectiveness of leave procedures is at least partly dependent on applicants exercising their right to renew from table applications. This point will be discussed further in Chapter 8. Also, see the estimate of one judge below, cited by the Law Commission, that information from respondents is needed in order to decide leave applications in only one-third of cases.

parties and cancel out some of the advantages in speed and cheapness for which the table application procedure was first created.

It must also be doubted whether applicants will regard this type of procedure as a satisfactory substitute for their present, unencumbered right to renew applications to a full oral hearing. The sharp rise in refusal rates for renewed applications (and the complete reversal in previously high success rates of further renewed applications to the Court of Appeal) may already have given a signal to applicants, their legal advisers and, indeed, to judges that renewals from initial refusals of leave are not to be encouraged. This message will certainly be reinforced if, as the Law Commission proposes, applicants are to face the penalty of costs orders against them for unsuccessfully pursuing the right of renewal.

Our data indicate that these recommendations could lead to improvements in the efficiency of the judicial review procedure by saving judge and court time, albeit at the cost of potentially restricting access to judicial review. Another factor that needs to be considered here is the role of leave in triggering settlement of disputes between public authorities and those adversely affected by their decisions. It might be considered that restricting access will help to minimise situations where, following a grant of leave, an application is left undecided for a long period, with all the uncertainty this entails for the public body concerned, other persons indirectly affected by the decision or policy under challenge, and the applicant. The evidence indicates, however, that the grant of leave is often followed by the settlement and/or withdrawal of the application, so that a substantial number of grants of leave do not, in practice, lead to extended periods of delay and uncertainty. In this context, a policy to restrict access to judicial review through leave decisions may not only be denying individuals the right to a judicial determination of their disputes with public bodies; it could also be depriving them of the specific benefits to be derived from much earlier settlement of their disputes.

Settlement after the grant of leave can be a strategic device used by respondents to avoid wider issues relating to the legality of their decisions and policies being raised and determined at full hearings. To this extent it may be questioned whether the process of post-leave settlement ought to be encouraged. But this does not point to a policy of a more restrictive interpretation of the criteria for granting leave, nor to the need for procedural devices which enable respondents greater opportunity to intervene at the leave stage in order to attempt to deliver a 'knock-out blow' to applicants. Such devices, if introduced, would be likely to have the detrimental effect of encouraging even more respondents to hold out at least until the leave decision before giving serious consideration to the possibility of settlement.

In any event, proposals aimed at tightening the leave requirement appear to be premised on an assumption that significant numbers of entirely unmeritorious applications for judicial review are currently 'slipping through' the leave filter. Nothing in our data relating to the success/failure of applications at the final hearing stage lends support to this proposition. In fact, the opposite is more likely to be the case: the current uncertainties and procedural complexities surrounding leave decisions are probably resulting in meritorious applications being prematurely rejected.

The more appropriate policy response, in light of our data, would be to adopt measures to promote even earlier settlement of disputes, before applications for leave are considered. To some extent, the provision of alternative mechanisms for internal review and administrative appeal of decisions (see above) may be a means of doing this, although one which is itself problematic in terms of its effect on access to judicial review and the creation of additional inconvenience and delay for the aggrieved party if the alternative remedies prove ineffective.

In our view, the creation of procedural requirements designed to encourage a greater exchange of information at the pre-leave stage deserve further consideration. Since the period covered by our research, judicial authority has established that applicants will normally be expected to have written a 'letter before action' to the respondent prior to applying for leave to seek judicial review,[50] but this will not necessarily place any pressure on respondents to react other than defensively or to engage in serious internal reviews of decisions being challenged.

Proposals were made to the Law Commission for a pre-litigation questionnaire, modelled on that available to plaintiffs in race and sex discrimination cases, to enable judicial review applicants to obtain more information from respondents on the background and justification of their decisions in advance of making a formal application to the court for leave. Under this procedure, it would be open to the court to draw adverse inference from a respondent's failure to reply adequately to the questionnaire when deciding on leave. It was argued not only that this might encourage earlier settlement, reduce the need for formal litigation, and thereby save public time and money, but that it would also alleviate the problems

---

50   *R v Horsham District Council ex parte Wenman* (1993) *The Times* 12 October.

judges currently face at the leave stage in terms of the lack of information on which properly to assess the arguability of applications for judicial review.[51]

The Law Commission unfortunately rejected this proposal on the grounds that 'in many cases information from the respondent is not needed in order to decide whether or not to allow the matter to proceed to a substantive hearing' and that it would therefore 'place an unnecessary burden on the respondent in the majority of cases'. As evidence for this conclusion, the Law Commission cited the view of just one judge that information from respondents was required in only a third of cases.[52] It also appears to have ignored the indirect benefits that a pre-litigation questionnaire might bring (other than in providing information for judicial consideration of leave) in promoting better standards of public decision-making and encouraging earlier reviews and settlements of potential judicial reviews. In this way, a pre-litigation questionnaire might be more effective in addressing the interests of judicial 'managerialism', which are becoming increasingly explicit in relation not only to judicial review but also in other areas of civil litigation,[53] than by importing such concerns into decisions on leave itself. Indeed, to paraphrase an earlier quotation from the Law Commission's report,[54] there have been calls for greater use of alternative dispute resolution and encouragement of early conciliation between disputing parties in other areas of civil litigation, and there seems little reason that judicial review should be exempt from such reforms.

The need for clarity in the criteria for leave is all the more important in the light of the data, examined in detail in the next chapter, revealing very wide variations in the success and failure of applications considered by individual judges. In its attempt to add clarity and consistency to the criteria for leave, however, the Law Commission appears to have recommended replacing an imperfect arguability test – which at least is based on sound principle – by an even more uncertain test. If the Law Commission was mainly concerned with filtering hopeless application and did not intend to increase the burden nor to add uncertainty, several alternative formulations of the criteria seem better suited to achieve its objects. As

---

51 Law Commission Report No 226, *op cit*, para 4.8.

52 *Ibid*. As we have seen, in opting instead for the post-application 'request for further information' procedure, the Law Commission choose instead to place the additional burdens on applicants.

53 See Lord Woolf's Interim Report, *op cit*.

54 See p 152 above.

well as recommending a criteria of 'hopelessness' or 'arguability' it
could have simply dropped the word 'serious' from its formulation, so
that applicants would be required to show that there is an 'issue to be
tried'.[55]

---

55 A source of the Law Commission's new test appears to have been the Le Sueur and
    Sunkin article. (See Richard Gordon QC 'The Law Commission and Judicial Review:
    Managing the tensions between case management and public interest challenges' (1995)
    Public Law 11.) In that article, however, the authors proposed a package of reforms
    designed to entrench a presumption in favour of access to judicial review. This package
    provided, *inter alia*, that leave should be granted, *unless* there were *no* serious issues to be
    tried: the burden was not intended to be upon the applicant. It seems that the Law
    Commission may have taken one part of this package and inverted it so that what was
    originally a presumption in favour of leave becomes an obstacle which the applicant will
    have to surmount.

Chapter 8

Leave and the Role and Impact of Judicial Discretion

As we have seen in previous chapters, the chance of success in obtaining leave to seek judicial review can vary depending on the type of applicant (represented or unrepresented; institutional or individual) and the subject area of applications. Moreover, as well as a general shift in judicial policy toward tightening the criteria for granting leave, there are also differences between judges as to what factors should be taken into account on leave and, in particular, what role managerial concerns over the size of the judicial review caseload and the extent of delay should have in such decisions. These policy shifts and differences emphasise the scope for the exercise of individual judicial discretion at this crucial step in the judicial review process.

In this chapter we examine the role of judicial discretion at the leave stage and attempt to gauge its impact on the eventual outcome of judicial review applications. When we first published our preliminary findings on this issue,[1] they tended to confirm impressionistic and anecdotal evidence of very wide differences in the approaches of individual judges and in the patterns of their leave decisions. As the Law Commission noted of the consultations leading up to their 1994 report:

> ... there were very strong complaints about inconsistency as between different judges in relation to the way in which they exercised their discretion, particularly on granting leave. The general effect of the evidence, from all sides, was that the present arrangements were too much of a lottery, and that more should be done to ensure a greater consistency of approach as between different judges.[2]

Indeed, the Law Commission reported that 'inconsistency in decisions on leave applications was the single issue which, apart from delay, had caused the most concern to our respondents' and that our earlier findings 'had merely confirmed many respondents' own experiences on inconsistencies as between different judges ...'.[3]

---

1   These appeared in the first edition of *Judicial Review in Perspective, op cit*, and are reproduced below. The findings presented here are based on considerable data analysis, in particular they cover the effects of judicial variations in leave grant rates on the eventual outcome of judicial review applications.

2   Law Commission Report No 226, *op cit*, Appendix C, para 1.2.

3   *Ibid*, Appendix C, para 8.4.

The scope that differences in judicial policy on leave provides for variations in decision-making tends to be reinforced by the way in which the hearing of judicial review applications is organised. As we shall see, the vast majority of leave decisions are taken by individual judges sitting on their own. Moreover, in an attempt to address concerns over delay in processing judicial review applications, the number of judges assigned to hear such cases has been increased over the past few years, with both additional High Court judges being included on the list nominated to hear Crown Office cases on a regular basis and some types of judicial review applications being routinely heard before part-time Deputy High Court judges (see Chapter 6). Reacting to the fear that this will lead to greater inconsistency, the Law Commission has recommended that a smaller cadre of judges should be picked to handle all the 'preliminary consideration' applications[4] on paper as the main method for achieving 'greater consistency and predictability'.[5] As we shall see, it is not clear that a smaller group of judges, each handling larger numbers of leave applications, will necessarily reduce inconsistencies between them.

The Law Commission also believed that the policy of using a smaller cadre of judges to consider paper applications for leave would potentially eliminate 'unnecessary oral hearings'.[6] As was seen in Chapter 7, a considerable proportion of applications initially refused leave on the papers have tended in the past to be renewed to an oral hearing, frequently with a good deal of success. As our analysis confirmed, there are wide variations between judges in their leave grant rates; this raises the question as to how far the current ability of applicants to renew applications operates as a check on judicial discretion and serves to even out differences between individual judges. In other words, does the renewal process help to make the process of obtaining leave less of a lottery than it might otherwise be?

There is a further, perhaps more basic issue to be considered, namely, how should we interpret variations in judicial approach at the leave stage? Common sense might suggest that those applicants who come before judges who tend to be relatively generous in granting leave will have a greater chance of eventually succeeding in their applications for judicial review. Is this true? There is, after all, the alternative possibility, that the judges who are more liberal in their approach to granting leave only succeed in letting more applications through this preliminary filter that will ultimately be refused judicial

---

4   That is, leave applications as they are presently known.
5   Law Commission Report No 226, *op cit*, Appendix C, para 9.1.
6   *Ibid*.

review on their merits when they are finally determined. If this were the case, the judges associated with lower leave grant rates, rather than possibly denying applicants access to justice, might be said to be acting in their favour by saving them the time and expense of pursuing their applications unsuccessfully to a full hearing. This leads to a further issue: are some judges more accurate in their assessment of the potential arguability of cases than others? We examine this by looking at how applications granted leave by different types of judge fare at later stages of the judicial review process.

Patterns of judicial sittings

The Law Commission's proposals to utilise a smaller cadre of judges on the consideration of leave applications would actually extend a policy first developed in the 1970s. Indeed, the establishment of a specialised cadre of judges with particular expertise in administrative law matters was a central feature of the reforms of the judicial review procedure at that time. It was hoped that over time the judges nominated by the Lord Chief Justice to handle the Crown Office list would both develop their experience of administrative law and establish a consistent body of legal principle that would form the core of a new public law. Initially there were nine nominated judges, although at the time the cases included in our research sample were being considered this had been increased to 18.[7] This growth in the numbers of judges inevitably means that judicial review should no longer be seen as being the exclusive preserve of a small number of specialist judges, but what other effects has it had on the operation of the procedure?

Two issues, in particular, are important in this context. One is the question of expertise and the other is concerned with consistency in the law and its administration. It is the latter that primarily concerns us in this chapter. It has never been clear, however, in what senses the nominated judges were expected to be expert in administrative law, for there seems no obvious reason why a larger group of judges should be any less expert than a smaller group. In fact, it might be argued that no small group of judges could be expected to develop specific expertise in all the areas of public administration potentially open to challenge by way of judicial review, and also that expertise may be enhanced by more frequent use of judges from other divisions of the High Court

---

7   The number of nominated judges was further increased to 22 in 1994 and to 23 in 1995. At the same time, the frequency of their sittings on Crown Office cases was also increased. See Chapter 5.

specialising in such areas as family or revenue law, to sit on judicial review cases in these fields.[8]

The nominated judges do not sit exclusively on judicial review or Crown Office matters: they are part of a wider pool of Queen's Bench Division judges who, for a considerable part of their time, are assigned to hear general criminal and civil High Court business. In fact, the nominated judges will sit hearing Crown Office list cases for periods of only three or four weeks at a time. Sitting on Crown Office list cases is said to impose an intensive burden on individual judges, the work being described as 'deeply interesting but onerous' and as 'physically and intellectually demanding'.[9] For these reasons, the Law Commission has doubted the feasibility of requiring nominated judges to sit on judicial review cases (at least as single judges) for more than three or four weeks at a time. On the other hand, since the period covered by our research, policy has shifted to enable the nominated judges to undertake three or four week stretches on Crown Office cases more frequently and to reduce the extent to which they are required to do other work. This has meant that nominated judges now usually spend between nine and 10 weeks each year sitting as a single judge on Crown Office cases. At the time of our research, it was not unknown for nominated judges to be available to act in this capacity for only one three week period in a whole year.

Data from our research on judges' sittings relate to the handling of cases first initiated in three periods (1987, 1988 and the first quarter of 1991). Decision-making on these cases extended over much longer periods, and for applications lodged in the first quarter of 1991 our data on sittings cover all those taking place up to the end of 1992. In the whole period, 1987 to 1992, a total of 32 judges were included on the list of nominated Crown Office judges at one time or another. However, a total of 70 judges were involved at some stage in decisions on cases begun in 1987, 78 judges on cases started in 1988, and 75 judges (up to December 1992) in cases initiated in the first quarter of 1991. As these figures indicate, many more judges beyond the listed nominated judges, were involved in at least some aspects of decision-making on judicial review cases during these periods. These other judges will include formerly nominated judges who may periodically sit hearing Crown Office list matters at first instance; other High Court

8   For the Law Commission's comments on this practice, see Law Commission Report No 226, *op cit*, Appendix C, paras 3.1–3.2, where it is suggested that there was little support for extending it beyond the current use of Family Division judges to hear judicial reviews involving family law matters and Chancery judges to sit on those relating to revenue matters.

9   *Ibid*, Appendix C, paras 2.2 and 8.11.

judges hearing occasional judicial reviews, especially in the vacations; judges sitting on appeals from the Divisional Court in judicial review cases; and judges brought in to hear judicial reviews where their specialist knowledge is thought appropriate.

Table 8.1 shows the frequency of sittings by individual judges in respect of applications made during 1987, 1988 and the first quarter of 1991. For these purposes, a 'sitting' is taken to include any procedural step where a judge's name appears in the Crown Office records on the case. Where judges have sat as part of a two or a three judge bench, each judge will have been credited with one 'sitting'. Sittings have been grouped into those involving the 32 judges whose names were on the nominated list at any time between 1987 and 1992 (even though they may not have been a nominated judge at the time of a particular sitting) and those by other judges who were not on the nominated list during this period.

As will be seen, work on judicial review cases is by no means evenly distributed among the nominated judges. The nominated judges were responsible for 80% of the sittings on 1987 applications, 85% of those in respect of 1988 applications, and 71% of those started in the first quarter of 1991. There were, however, three nominated

Table 8.1

Number of Sittings by Individual Judges in respect of Judicial Review Applications 1987-1988 and 1st quarter of 1991

No of Sittings	1987 Applications		1988 Applications		1991 Applications (Jan-Mar)	
	Nominated Judges	Other	Nominated Judges	Other	Nominated Judges	Other
200 or more	1	-	1	-	-	-
150 - 199	2	-	1	-	-	-
100 - 149	6	1	6	-	-	-
75 - 99	4	1	3	-	-	-
50 - 74	2	-	5	1	3	1
25 - 49	2	4	4	3	5	-
10 - 24	2	5	3	5	10	2
Less than 10	6	33	4	42	10	44
TOTAL	25	45	27	51	28	47

judges (Judge D, L and B)[10] who each sat 150 or more times in relation to 1987 cases, thereby accounting for 23% of all sittings on 1987 cases. There were a further seven judges (six nominated and one former nominated) who sat between 100 and 149 times on 1987 cases, and this group handled a further 37% of all such sittings. There were just two nominated judges (Judges O and K) who sat 150 or more times on 1988 cases, and these two judges together accounted for no less than 19% of all sittings in relation to 1988 cases. A further six nominated judges sat between 100 and 149 times on 1988 cases and handled an additional 31% of all sittings. Finally, three nominated judges (Judges S, O and L) together dealt with 25% of sittings held by the end of 1992 in relation to the first quarter of 1991 cases.[11]

Table 8.2 shows the number of one, two and three judge sittings in respect of judicial review applications. Table applications for leave are almost exclusively determined by a single judge, but 11% of initial oral leave applications and 23% of renewed leave applications were heard before two or (much more rarely) three judges. The use of more than one judge to hear oral leave applications declined sharply in 1988 and the first quarter of 1991 cases with less than 2% going before two or three judge courts. On the other hand, 17% of renewed leave applications arising from 1988 applications and 30% of those relating to 1991 applications were heard before more than one judge. The overall picture, however, is one in which leave is largely determined by judges sitting on their own. This was also the case for 64% of the substantive hearings arising from 1987 applications and 60% of those in relation to 1988 applications; of the hearings held by the end of 1992 on applications lodged in the first quarter of 1991, just under half were before single judges.

Patterns of individual judges' decisions

The above data indicate that in the vast majority of cases, judicial decision-making within this jurisdiction is exercised by judges sitting on their own. This is especially so in respect of the leave stage. What effect does individual judicial discretion have on the consistency of

---

10 As will be seen, we have decided to refer to individual judges throughout this chapter by a letter code rather than by name.

11 The fourth 'judge' shown in Table 8.1 as dealing with 50 or more sittings in respect of 1991 applications was a High Court Master, largely presiding over withdrawals by consent. The Law Commission has produced more recent data on the concentration of decision-making on paper applications for leave among particular judges. In the second half of 1993 four judges handled more than half of such table applications and another four judges a further quarter, and in the first seven months of 1994 eight judges handled 70% of such applications. Law Commission Report No 226, *op cit*, Appendix C, para 8.4.

Table 8.2

Number of Judges Sitting to Determine Applications for Judicial Review by Type of Hearing, 1987-1988 and 1st quarter of 1991

	1987 Judges			1988 Judges			1991 Judges (Jan-Mar)		
	1	2	3	1	2	3	1	2	3
LEAVE DECISIONS									
Table Applications:									
Number	729	4*	-	673	3*	-	222	-	-
%	99.5	0.5	-	99.6	0.4	-	100.0	-	-
Oral Applications:									
Number	567	68	3	491	6	1	199	3	-
%	88.9	10.7	0.5	98.6	1.2	0.6	98.5	1.5	-
Renewals:									
Number	181	50	3	234	48	1	49	21	-
%	77.4	21.4	1.3	82.7	17.0	0.4	70.0	30.0	-
All Leave Decisions:									
Number	*1,477*	*122*	*6*	*1,398*	*57*	*2*	*470*	*24*	*-*
%	*92.0*	*7.6*	*0.4*	*96.0*	*3.9*	*0.1*	*95.1*	*4.9*	*-*
SUBSTANTIVE HEARINGS									
Number	264	142	6	252	162	4	25	26	-
%	64.1	34.5	1.5	60.3	38.8	1.0	49.0	51.0	-

* *These are cases in which two judges' names were listed on the card index in the Crown Office from which data were taken.*

decision-making? To attempt to answer this question, we analysed of the records of those judges most frequently involved in leave decisions on applications filed during three of our four sample periods (1987, 1988 and the first quarter of 1991).[12]

---

12 Unlike the above data on patterns of judicial sittings, all remaining data in this Chapter have been up-dated to incorporate decisions on first quarter of 1991 cases taken up to May 1995.

Initial leave decisions

The analysis presented here is based on three separate samples of
those judges who were responsible for the vast majority of the initial
leave decisions[13] taken by single judges. The aim here is to exclude
those judges involved in only small numbers of leave decisions in any
one period. The sample for 1987 cases includes 15 judges who were
together responsible for 86% of initial leave decisions on these
applications (including those where the identity of the judge making
the initial leave decision could not be determined). The 1988 sample of
17 judges and the first quarter of 1991 sample of 14 judges each were
responsible for 91% of initial leave decisions during the relevant
periods.

We have focused our analysis upon figures that exclude individual
judges' decisions on renewed applications for leave for a number of
reasons: first, because there may be a case for arguing that by their
nature renewed applications differ from initial applications in that they
may be more contentious; second, because their inclusion would
involve a degree of double counting that might exaggerate refusal
rates; and third, because these factors might produce misleading
results, particularly for those judges who handled higher proportions
of renewals than others. It should be noted, however, that when
calculations of leave grant rates for individual judges included their
renewal decisions, in all but a very few cases the results differed from
those based only on initial table and oral applications by at most two
or three percentage points.[14] We go on below to consider the overall
effect of renewals in smoothing out variations between individual
judges' decisions on initial leave applications.

There is no indication in the data that individual judges, especially
those handling large numbers of cases, specialise in particular subject
areas and for our purpose we have assumed that each judge in the
sample carried a random distribution of subjects. We have, however,
screened these data for 'block bookings' of numerous similar
applications that might have skewed the results and these are pointed
out where appropriate. It should be added that our working
assumption is that, by and large, applications for leave are randomly
distributed amongst the judges and that it is therefore unlikely that
particular judges will have a substantially larger number of weaker
applications to consider than others. As well as providing the largest

13 Initial leave decisions include both table and oral applications but not renewals.
14 The figures are shown in square brackets in Table 6.3, p 89 of the first edition of *Judicial
    Review in Perspective, op cit.*

and most reliable sample of decisions, the pool of judges upon which we have focussed is also likely to include the most experienced judges.

Overall, there were 24 separate judges included in the three samples, and these have been identified by a letter code (Judges A – Y). Of the 24 judges, five (Judges C, J, K, L and O) appear in all three sample periods as among those dealing with substantial numbers of leave decisions; six (Judges A, B, F, H, I and N) appear in the samples relating to 1987 and 1988 applications; six (Judges P, Q, R, S, T and U) in the samples relating to 1988 and the first quarter of 1991 applications; four (Judges D, E, G and M) in the 1987 sample only; and three (Judges W, X and Y) in the first quarter of 1991 sample only.[15]

Table 8.3 shows the full list of judges, the number of initial leave decisions each took during the relevant periods, and the percentage of these applications that were granted as a result of these initial decisions. The first point to be noted is that there were very wide variations in leave grant rates as between individual judges in each of the samples. In the 1987 sample, the difference between Judge A at the top of the list and Judge O at the bottom was no less than 64 percentage points; in 1988 the difference between Judge P and (again) Judge O was 33 percentage points; and in 1991 the gap between Judge P and Judge X was 43 percentage points. It is worth noting that, since these data were first published in 1993, the Crown Office has begun to keep its own records on leave grant rates for individual judges, and data from these were published by the Law Commission in 1994. These show separate grant rates for table and oral applications considered over the first seven months of 1994. Taking account of only those judges dealing with more than 30 applications of the particular type in this period, the variation between the 'top' and 'bottom' judge on each list covered 48 percentage points for table applications and 35 percentage points for oral applications.[16]

Given the differences of judicial opinion and uncertainties surrounding the criteria for leave, some variation in the pattern of individual judges' decisions at this stage in the judicial review process would have been expected. But the sheer scale of the variation revealed by the above figures is surprising and worrying. It has already been noted that our samples, based as they are on the judges who sit on judicial review matters most frequently, are likely to have contained the most experienced judges in this field. More importantly,

---

15 The fact that a judge's name does not appear in a particular sample does not indicate that he did no judicial review work on the relevant cases but only that his sittings on initial leave applications were not frequent enough in the period to be included.

16 Law Commission Report No 226, *op cit*, Annex 1. For a comment on these figures, see para 5.13.

Table 8.3

Grant Rates of Selected Judges on Initial Applications for Leave to Seek Judicial Review, 1987-1988 and 1st Quarter of 1991

1987 Applications

Judge and Judge Group		No of Initial Leave Applications considered	% Granted
High	Judge A	44	82
High	Judge B	67	69
High	Judge C	44	61
High	Judge D	138	60
Medium	Judge E	69	58
Medium	Judge F	47	57
Medium	Judge G	79	57
Medium	Judge H	29	52
Medium	Judge I	46	50
Medium	Judge J	68	49
Medium	Judge K	91	48
Medium	Judge L	99	46
Low	Judge M	105	41
Low	Judge N	67	37
Low	Judge O	81	21

1988 Applications

Judge and Judge Group		No of Initial Leave Applications considered	% Granted
High	Judge P	31	68
High	Judge Q	70	67
High	Judge R	39	67
High	Judge A	29	66
High	Judge J	74	66
High	Judge B	43	65
High	Judge C	59	64
High	Judge L	59	63
Medium	Judge K	118	55
Medium	Judge S	55	55
Medium	Judge T	67	54
Medium	Judge H	38	53
Medium	Judge U	53	49
Medium	Judge I	39	46
Low	Judge N	69	42
Low	Judge F	28	39
Low	Judge O	180	25

1991 Applications

Judge and Judge Group		No of Initial Leave Applications considered	% Granted
High	Judge P	9	78
High	Judge Q	23	65
High	Judge C	32	63
Medium	Judge J	14	57
Medium	Judge K	9	56
Medium	Judge W	28	54
Medium	Judge T	12	50
Medium	Judge L	47	47
Medium	Judge Y	11	46
Low	Judge R	9	44
Low	Judge S	53	42
Low	Judge U	27	41
Low	Judge O	51	37
Low	Judge X	20	35

the data show that judges who handled very large numbers of initial leave applications in each of the periods appeared at various points on the spectrum between those with high and those with low leave grant rates. Thus, in 1987 Judge D, who handled 138 initial leave applications, granted 60% of them, while Judge M handled 105 applications and granted only 41%. In 1988, Judge K granted 55% of the 118 initial leave applications he considered, while Judge O granted only 25% of his 180 initial leave applications. This may indicate that concentrating larger numbers of initial leave applications in the hands of fewer judges, as the Law Commission has proposed, may not result in greater consistency in decisions.

For the purposes of further analysis, it is useful to place individual judges into groups according to their initial leave grant rates in each of the three periods covered by our research. Judges who have been included in the 'high' group are those who had initial leave grant rates of 60% or above in the relevant year; those in the 'medium' group had initial leave grant rates of between 45% and 59%; and those in the 'low' group had initial leave grant rates below 45%. These groupings are also shown in Table 8.3. Thus, in 1987 the 'high' group consisted of four judges (A–D), the 'medium group of eight judges (E–L), and the 'low' group of three judges (M–O). In 1988 the sample divides into eight judges in the 'high' group (P, Q, R, A, J, B, C and L), six judges in the 'medium' group (K, S, T, H, U and I), and three in the 'low' group (N, F and O). The 'high' group in 1991 consisted of three judges (P, Q and C), the 'medium' group of six judges (J, K, W, T, L and Y), and the 'low' group of five judges (R, S, U, O and X).

Another notable feature of these data is that, while there were very wide variations in grant rates between judges, the individual judges seem remarkably consistent in their approach toward leave decisions from year to year. Of the five judges who appear in all three of our samples for 1987, 1988 and the first quarter of 1991, Judge C was in the 'high' group band across all three periods, Judge K was consistently in the 'medium' group, Judge O was always in the 'low' group, and Judges J and L moved between the 'high' and 'medium' groups. Similarly, of the 12 judges appearing in two out of the three samples, five were in the 'high' group in both years (A, B, C, P and Q), three were in the 'medium' group in both years (H, I and T), and one was in the 'low' group in both years (N). Looked at another way, there were only two of the total of 24 judges included in the analysis (F and R) whose ranking varied, from one year to another, between the 'high' and 'low' groups.

This pattern of consistency in each individual judge's leave grant rates has important implications for the operation of the procedure. On the one hand, it may indicate that the variations *between* judges in respect of leave decisions are due to some (as yet undetected) systemic factors in the way in which cases are allocated within the Crown Office list to particular judges. A more likely explanation, in light of current evidence, is that the attitudes and approaches that each judge brings to bear on his decisions on leave have a important effect on the overall pattern of results at this stage.

Two factors which have been shown (see Chapters 6 and 7) to influence grant/refusal rates at the leave stage are the type of procedure used (table or oral applications) and the subject matter of the application. The above data relates to all initial leave decisions by particular judges, whether through the written or oral procedures. Because table applications tend to be less successful than oral applications, it is possible that the results will be skewed by some judges being allocated a higher proportion of table applications than others. To check on this, we analysed the records of judges by distinguishing between table and oral applications. As expected, grant rates were generally lower for table applications than for oral applications, but similar variations were found between the rates for individual judges to those outlined above. Most importantly, the same judges tended to have 'high' and 'low' grant rates under both the written and oral procedures.

Initial leave decisions by subject

The main subject area of applications likely to have a major impact on the overall pattern of leave decisions on 1987 and 1988 applications was immigration; this area accounted for 37% of 1987 cases taken through the leave stage and 29% of those in 1988.[17] As noted in Chapter 6, immigration cases generally had a lower level of success in obtaining leave than other types of application. Table 8.4 shows how the initial leave grant rates of those sample judges in 1987 and 1988 who handled significant numbers of immigration applications were affected by their decisions in this one major subject area. Judges are listed here in descending order of their general grant rates for all initial leave decisions.

The first two columns of the table show that grant rates for initial leave decisions by individual judges on immigration applications were lower than their general rates (as shown in the final column of the table). In fact, there were only three judges out of the 13 listed from the

---

17   These figures exclude those where the application was withdrawn prior to a decision being taken on leave.

1987 sample that were actually more generous in granting leave in immigration cases than in other types of application, and this included one judge (A) whose record in this respect was greatly affected by one 'block booking' of 23 immigration cases where leave was granted. In 1989 there were four judges (P, L, K and T) from those listed that were more generous in respect of immigration applications. By contrast, some judges were considerably less generous in their approach to immigration leave decisions than other types of case. In this respect, one might particularly note Judges G and O in 1987; and Judges C, I, N and O in 1988.

Overall, variations between the grant rates of individual judges on immigration applications were as wide as they were in the general samples. In 1987 the gap in immigration leave decisions between the grant rate of Judge B (63%) and Judge O (4%) spanned 59 percentage points. In 1988 the equivalent range was between Judge P, with a 77% grant rate in immigration cases, and again Judge O with a grant rate of 11%, a difference of 66 percentage points.

The wide differential between individual judges in their overall leave decision-making in these years was clearly not a function of their treatment of immigration applications, as the single largest subject group in those years. As shown in the third and fourth columns of Table 8.4, even when immigration cases are excluded, there remain very large differences in individual judges' leave grants rates for other types of applications. In the 1987 sample, these differences ranged from a 77% non-immigration leave grant rate for Judge G down to a 30% rate for Judge O, a span of 47 percentage points; in 1988 the range was from a 78% non-immigration leave grant rate for Judge A down to a 31% rate for Judge O, a span of 47 percentage points. In fact, the general effect of excluding immigration decisions was to make those judges in the 'high' group (again, with the exception of Judge A) somewhat more generous in their leave grant rates. On the other hand, the judges in the 'low' group also had marginally higher grant rates once immigration cases were discounted, although they were still considerably out-of-line with their judicial colleagues.

The number of applications in the first quarter of 1991 was not large enough to enable any meaningful conclusions to be drawn from a breakdown of individual judges' leave decisions into particular subject areas. Equally, the number of homelessness cases in 1987 and 1988 (when such applications accounted for just 6% and 9% of leave decisions respectively) was too small, when dispersed across the various individual judges, to have a significant impact on their overall leave grant rates. We nevertheless examined the pattern of leave decisions in both housing and criminal applications and found that

Table 8.4

Grant Rates by Selected Judges on Initial Applications for Leave to Seek Judicial Review in Immigration and Other Matters, 1987 and 1988

	Immigration		Non-immigration		% Grant – All Initial Leave
	No of Decisions	% Grant	No of Decisions	% Grant	
1987 Applications					
Judge A*	31	84	13	38	82
Judge B	19	63	48	71	69
Judge C	12	42	32	69	61
Judge D	46	54	92	63	60
Judge E	19	53	50	60	58
Judge F	20	60	27	56	57
Judge G	32	27	47	77	57
Judge H	7	43	22	55	52
Judge I	16	56	30	47	49
Judge J	21	48	47	49	49
Judge K	29	31	62	56	48
Judge L	51	23	48	48	46
Judge M	37	27	68	49	41
Judge N	22	18	45	47	37
Judge O	27	4	54	30	21
1988 Applications					
Judge P	13	77	18	61	68
Judge Q	14	50	56	71	67
Judge R	15	67	24	67	67
Judge A	6	17	23	78	66
Judge J	26	54	48	73	66
Judge B	16	63	27	67	65
Judge C	18	39	41	76	64
Judge L	22	73	37	57	63
Judge K	37	57	81	54	55
Judge S	11	46	44	57	55
Judge T	21	57	46	52	54
Judge H	10	40	28	57	53
Judge U	13	38	40	53	49
Judge I	10	20	21	55	46
Judge N	13	15	56	50	42
Judge F	10	30	18	44	39
Judge O	54	11	126	31	25

* Includes one 'block' of 23 immigration cases where leave granted.

there were similar very wide differentials between the grant rates of individual judges in these areas as well.

This examination raised the question whether judges were consistent in their approach across subject areas. To begin to address this, we looked at the records of those judges who appeared in our samples in more than one year, with a view to comparing their grant/refusal rates in immigration, homelessness and crime. The relevant data are presented in a simplified form in Table 8.5. This is based on a system of placing judges on a ranking scale according to the following formula: 1 for a grant rate of 60% or more; 2 for a rate of 50-59%; 3 for a rate of 40-49%; 4 for a rate of 30-39%; and 5 for a rate of less than 30%. The table shows the rankings allocated to individual judges (where they dealt with sufficient cases in the relevant sample periods), both in terms of their decisions on general applications and on those in immigration, housing, and crime. As has already been noted, there is a high level of consistency in individual judges' general leave grant rates from year to year, and this is especially so in the case of those judges at the 'high' and 'low' ends of the spectrum.

Turning to the specific subject areas, judges displayed the greatest consistency, one year to the next and within their overall leave grant rates, in the field of housing. Individual judges' leave decision-making in the fields of immigration and crime appears to have been somewhat more variable, however, with only three of the relevant judges (B, H and O) having the same score both for 1987 and 1988 in immigration and only two (J and N) the same scores in crime. These two areas also produced some examples of differences between judges' general records and their scores in particular areas of work. For example, Judges A and C had generally generous records in their treatment of leave applications, but they nevertheless both scored 4 or 5 on the 1987 criminal applications and 1988 immigration applications that they handled. On the other hand, Judge O had a consistently low grant rate across the various sample periods and subject areas, save that he scored a 1 in his treatment of 1988 criminal applications. Although the general picture of individual judges varying widely in their approaches to leave decisions is confirmed, these data do provide a warning against the adoption of stereotypical views of judges, with their treatment of criminal applications perhaps being the most unpredictable.

The impact of renewals on leave differentials

If applicants are refused leave at first instance they have at least one opportunity to renew their applications. This means that the very wide differentials between individual judges in their initial leave grant rates

	General Caseload 1987 1988 1991 (Jan-Mar)			Housing 1987 1988		Immigration 1987 1988		Criminal 1987 1988	
Judge A	1	1	-	1	1	1	5	4	1
Judge C	1	1	1	1	1	1	4	5	2
Judge B	1	1	-	1	2	1	1	1	2
Judge Q	-	1	1	-	-	-	-	-	-
Judge P	-	1	1	-	-	-	-	-	-
Judge R	-	1	3	-	-	-	-	-	-
Judge H	2	2	-	1	1	3	3	2	5
Judge T	-	2	2	2	4	2	5	5	2
Judge J	3	1	2	1	1	3	2	1	1
Judge L	3	1	3	1	1	3	1	5	2
Judge K	3	2	2	1	1	4	2	2	1
Judge I	2	3	-	-	-	-	-	-	-
Judge S	-	2	3	-	-	-	-	-	-
Judge F	2	4	-	-	-	-	-	-	-
Judge U	-	3	3	-	-	-	-	-	-
Judge N	4	3	-	4	5	1	5	1	1
Judge O	5	5	4	4	5	5	5	5	1

Table 8.5

Grant Rate Scores of Individual Judges on Initial Applications for Leave to Seek Judicial Review by Selected Subject Areas, 1987 and 1988

may not have as dramatic an effect on overall access to judicial review as might be assumed. In this section we address the question of how applicants' chances of eventually obtaining leave, either on the initial decision or as the result of a renewal, are influenced by having their applications initially considered by a judge in the 'high', 'medium' or 'low' groups. Put another way, how far does the availability of the right to renew an application to another judge provide a safeguard for applicants against inconsistent judicial decisions at the initial stage?

On renewal it is intended that an application for leave should be considered *de novo*, without reference to the fact that it has been refused previously by a different judge. It might be expected, therefore, that the process of renewal would have the effect of levelling out inconsistencies between judges in their initial leave decisions. Applications initially going before judges with relatively high grant rates would not lead to many renewals, while those going before judges with relatively low grant rates would more frequently be renewed and, as a result of their fresh consideration by a different judge, be granted leave on renewal often enough to remove at least some of the differential between judges in the overall granting of leave.

It must be borne in mind here that respondents do not have a similar right of appeal against, or to challenge, the grant of leave. The opportunities that respondents do have, once leave has been granted, to apply to have it set aside or struck out are designed to be much more restrictive than those of applicants to renew an application. This is relevant in considering the effect of renewals in levelling out differentials between judges in their initial decisions on leave, since it could be argued that if judges with high leave grant rates are being overly generous, this could only be compensated for by giving respondents similar rights to demand reconsideration of leave grants as applicants have to renew. To accord respondents such rights, however, would transform the leave procedure from a preliminary *ex parte* process into something approaching a summary *inter partes* consideration of the merits of the case.[18]

In order to examine some of the above questions, we have grouped the applications in our sample according to the group of the judge to which the case was assigned at the stage of the initial leave decision. We have then traced through these applications to determine their outcomes at later stages of the process (eg once having taken account of renewed applications for leave or following a substantive hearing), regardless of the identity of the judge making the decision at these subsequent stages. The analysis therefore does not show how the judges in the 'high', 'medium' or 'low' groups decided cases that came before them at later stages beyond the initial leave decision; it shows how the cases they initially considered for leave eventually fared in the overall process of judicial review.

The results of this analysis taken up to the stage of renewed applications for leave are shown in Diagram 8A. These indicate that the renewal process, although having some effect in reducing differentials between judges in terms of applicants' overall prospects of obtaining leave, is not sufficient in itself to eliminate such differentials. Thus, for each of the three samples relating to 1987, 1988 and first quarter of 1991 cases, 66% of cases considered by the 'high' group of

---

18 For a discussion of these issues, see Law Commission Consultation Paper No 126, *op cit*, pp 32-6. In their final report, the Law Commission proposed to retain and, indeed, to reinforce the *ex parte* nature of the leave process, by recommending that all applications normally be considered first on their papers. However, they also suggested that, where judges considered it necessary to do so, respondents should be requested to provide further information in writing to the court. These proposals are discussed in Chapters 6 and 7.

judges were granted leave on their initial applications. The initial leave grant rate for the 'medium' group of judges ranged between 53% and 50%, and that for the 'low' group of judges between 31% and 39%. In the 1987 sample, a further 8% of the applications initially considered by the 'high' group of judges were granted leave by other judges following renewals, with the result that a total of 74% of the applications first considered by this group eventually received leave (that is, 66% on the initial leave decision and 8% on renewals from initial refusals). This compares with a total of 62% of cases initially considered by the 'medium' group of judges that eventually received leave (52% on the initial leave decision and 10% on renewals) and 54% for cases first considered by the 'low' group of judges (34% on the initial leave decision and 20% on renewals). As shown in Diagram 8A, a very similar pattern was evident in decisions on 1988 applications first considered by the 'high', 'medium' and 'low' group of judges. In the first quarter of 1991 cases, however, there was clear evidence of the declining effectiveness of the renewal process for applicants, with only an additional 2% of applications initially considered by the 'high' and 'medium' group of judges and 6% of those first handled by the 'low' group of judges being granted leave on renewals.

The effect of the renewal process in correcting for variations between judges in their leave grant rates can be gauged by examining the percentage differentials between the three groups following the initial decision on leave and after renewals have been taken into account. The gap between the 'high' group of judges and the 'low' group of judges in their initial leave grant rates spanned 32 percentage points in 1987 (66% minus 34%), 35 percentage points in 1988, and 27 percentage points in the first quarter of 1991. Once the effect of renewals is added in, the differential in the proportion of 1987 cases initially considered by the 'high' and 'low' groups of judges that eventually obtained leave was reduced to 20 percentage points (74% minus 54%), compared with 32% on the basis of initial leave decisions alone. In other words, the renewal process eliminated about one-third of the leave grant differential between these two groups of judges in this year. For 1988 cases the differential between the 'high' and 'low' groups of judges, of 35 percentage points following initial leave decisions, was reduced by almost half, to 19 percentage points, once renewals were taken into account. The differential between these two groups of judges in the first quarter of 1991 was reduced only by four percentage points, however, from a gap of 27 percentage points on the basis of initial leave decisions to 23 percentage points following renewals. This again reflects the overall decline during this period in the proportion of applicants successfully obtaining leave on the basis of renewals.

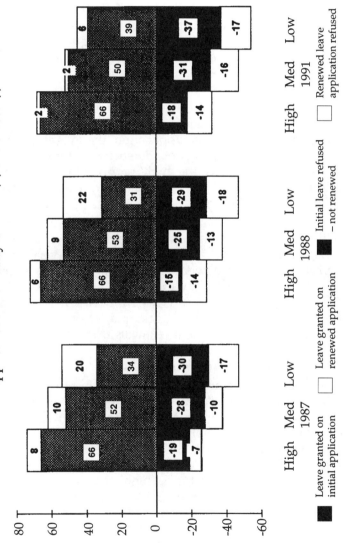

Diagram 8A

Applications for Judicial Review, 1987-1988 and 1st Quarter of 1991 by Group of Judge Making Initial Leave Decision and Percentage of Applications Eventually Granted (+) or Refused (-) Leave

If the renewal process did not even out differentials between the 'high' and 'low' groups of judges to a great extent, could it be said at least to have brought the leave grant rate of cases first considered by the 'low' group of judges up to a level similar to that for the 'medium' judges? In the 1987 cases, a differential between these two groups of 18 percentage points in their respective initial leave grant rates was reduced to just eight percentage points as a result of renewals, and in the 1988 cases the reduction in the differential was from 22 percentage points at the initial leave stage down to just nine percentage points following renewals. Again, for the first quarter of 1991 cases, the renewal process had a somewhat lesser impact, reducing an initial leave differential between the 'medium' and 'low' groups of judges of 11 percentage points down to seven percentage points.

Even when successful renewals arising from cases first considered by the 'low' group of judges are added to those cases in which they granted leave on the initial application, the overall proportion of their cases granted leave in each of the study periods was still below the *initial* leave grant rate for the 'high' group of judges. In the first quarter of 1991 it was also still below the *initial* leave grant rate of the 'medium' group of judges.

In seeking an explanation for the limited impact of renewals in levelling out differentials between judges in their leave grant rates, it can be observed from Table 8.6 that there was very little variation in the proportions of renewed applications for leave arising from 1987 cases initially considered by the 'high', 'medium' and 'low' groups of judges that were successful (varying between 50% and 53% for the three groups). In the 1988 and first quarter of 1991 samples, however, there was a clear pattern that renewals from the 'low' group of judges tended to be more successful (55% granted in 1988 and 27% in 1991) than those from the other two groups.

An important factor behind the persisting differential between the 'high', 'medium' and 'low' groups of judges in the proportions of initial applications they considered that eventually obtained leave appears to have been a reluctance on the part of applicants to exercise their rights of renewal. In 1987 cases, the renewal rate from the 'low' group of judges, at 55% of applications initially refused leave, was somewhat higher than from the 'high' and 'medium' groups of judges (44% and 42% respectively). For 1988 cases, however, the renewal rate from applications initially refused by the 'high' group of judges, at 56%, was nearly the same as that from the 'low' group of judges (58%) and above that for the 'medium' group (47%). Similarly, in the first quarter of 1991, the renewal rate from the 'high' group of judges (46%) was above that for the other two groups (37% and 38%).

Table 8.6

Initial Leave Applications for Judicial Review, 1987-1988 and 1st Quarter of 1991 by Group of Judge Considering Application, Grant and Refusal Rates, Renewal Rates and Percentage of Renewed Applications Granted

Application Year	1987			1988			1991 (January - March)		
Judge Group	High	Medium	Low	High	Medium	Low	High	Medium	Low
No. of Initial Leave Applications	293	528	253	404	370	277	64	121	160
% Granted	66	52	34	66	53	31	66	50	39
% Refused	34	48	66	34	47	69	34	50	61
% Refused Applications Renewed	44	42	55	56	47	58	46	37	38
% Renewed Applications Granted	54	50	53	29	43	55	10	14	27

As a result, in the 1987 and 1988 samples around 30% of applications initially considered by the 'low' group of judges were refused leave *and not renewed*, and in the first quarter of 1991 this proportion rose to 38%. These figures do not indicate that applicants appear to abuse their rights of renewal. Rather, they imply that an initial refusal of leave, even from judges who might be considered generally to have a less generous attitude toward the granting of leave, may act as a deterrent to applicants considering pursuing their cases further through the renewal process.

In summary, the unfettered right which applicants for judicial review currently have to renew their applications for leave appears, at least in the periods covered by this research, to have had only a limited impact in levelling out differentials between judges in their initial leave grant rates. On the other hand, the renewal process did reduce some initial inconsistencies. If the right of renewal is further restricted, for example, by the risk of costs orders against applicants who are unsuccessful in their renewed applications being made more explicit, its effect in reducing levels of judicial inconsistency in leave decisions is likely to be further watered down and the widespread perception of access to judicial review through the leave procedure being a lottery will be reinforced.

Leave differentials and the final outcome of cases

We now turn to consider what effect differences between judges in their initial leave grant rates has on the eventual results of applications for judicial review. We again trace through the results of cases divided into groups depending on the type of judge ('high', 'medium' and 'low') that first considered the application for leave. Our analysis is based on four different outcomes that can arise from an application for judicial review. First, an application can end with a refusal of leave, either because an initial decision not to grant leave goes unrenewed or because the renewed application is itself refused. Second, an applicant may be granted leave and subsequently withdraw the application, either because of a settlement of the dispute with the respondent public body or for other reasons.[19] Third, an application once granted leave may be successful at the substantive hearing or, fourth, it may be dismissed.[20] Diagrams 8B–8E show the percentages of applications in our three sample periods, divided between the groups of judges who

---

19   The different reasons why applications may be withdrawn following a grant of leave are
     discussed in Chapter 6.

20   The analysis here takes account of the results of substantive hearings in the Divisional
     Court but not of subsequent appeals to the Court of Appeal or the House of Lords.

dealt with them at the stage of the initial leave decision, which eventually reached each of these four types of outcome.

Leave refused

Diagram 8B shows the proportions of applications initially considered for leave by each of the judge groups which resulted in leave being refused, either because a refusal of leave by the initial judge was not renewed or because the application was renewed and refused again. In fact, the data shown here are the obverse to those discussed above in respect of the granting of leave to applications initially considered by the 'high', 'medium' and 'low' groups of judges. It is confirmed that applicants whose cases are considered initially by judges in the 'low' group had a greater chance of being denied leave, even after account is taken of renewals.

Withdrawals

As discussed in Chapter 6, there is considerable evidence that the granting of leave can act as a stimulant toward settlement of judicial review cases. Of course, without further investigation of the reasons why judicial review applications are withdrawn following a grant of leave, it cannot be said that all or even most of these cases end in settlements in favour of applicants, although our data do provide some indications that this is often the case.[21] It is therefore interesting to observe from Diagram 8C that, apart from the lower proportions of cases they originally considered that eventually obtained leave, the main difference between the 'low' group and other judges is that smaller proportions of cases initially assigned to them resulted in post-leave withdrawals or otherwise in no substantive hearing being held. Of the 1987 applications originally considered by the 'low' group of judges, 19% were eventually granted leave but did not reach a substantive hearing, as compared with 40% of those initially handled by the 'high' group of judges and 28% of those dealt with by the 'medium' group of judges. There was a similar pattern in respect of 1988 cases, where 18% of those first considered by the 'low' group of judges did not reach a substantive hearing after being granted leave, as compared with 33% of those initially assigned to the 'high' group and 29% of those initially dealt with by the 'medium' group. As regards the first quarter of 1991 applications, there was a higher overall level of

---

21   There will also be a few cases in which leave will be set aside or struck out and therefore do not result in a substantive hearing.

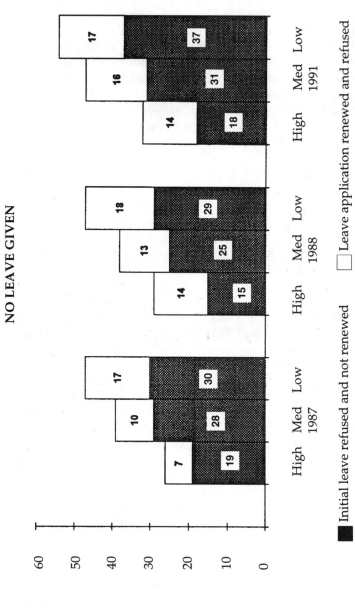

Diagram 8B

Applications to Seek Leave for Judicial Review 1987-1988 and 1st Quarter of 1991 by Group of Judge Making Initial Leave Decision and Percentage of Applications Resulting in

NO LEAVE GIVEN

■ Initial leave refused and not renewed   □ Leave application renewed and refused

Diagram 8C

Applications to Seek Leave for Judicial Review 1987-1988 and 1st Quarter of 1991 by Group of Judge Making Initial Leave Decision and Percentage of Applications Resulting in

NO HEARING

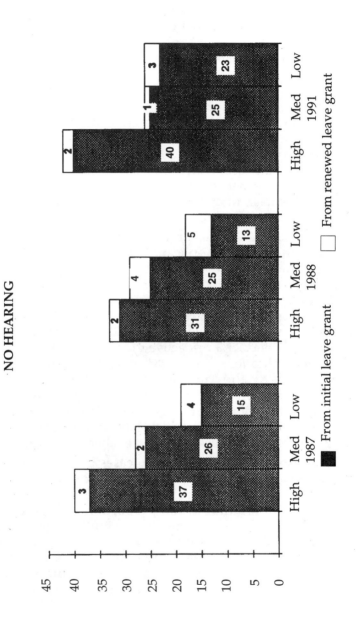

post-leave withdrawals, and this was particularly evident in cases first considered by the 'high' group of judges, 42% of which obtained leave but did not reach a substantive hearing. This compares to 26% of cases originally assigned both to the 'medium' and 'low' groups of judges.

Applications dismissed

It might be thought that judges who tend to be relatively generous in granting leave will produce higher proportions of cases in which applications for judicial review are eventually dismissed on their merits at substantive hearings. The proposition behind this hypothesis is that such judges are not applying the leave criteria strictly enough to weed out all the cases which are likely to prove unmeritorious and that therefore their generosity in granting leave may actually be working to the disadvantage of applicants by giving them scope to pursue their cases unsuccessfully through to a substantive hearing.

Table 8.7 shows the proportions of cases in which leave was granted on an initial application by the 'high', 'medium' and 'low' groups that resulted either in no substantive hearing or in the application either being allowed or dismissed. A higher proportion of the 1987 applications granted leave on an initial application by the 'medium' group of judges were eventually dismissed (31%) than of those that had obtained leave from either the 'high' or 'low' group of judges (27% and 25% respectively). A similar pattern was evident in the 1988 applications, where 28% of cases granted leave on an initial application by the 'medium' group of judges ended up being dismissed, as compared to 22% for the 'high' group and 17% for the 'low' group. Only in the first quarter of 1991 cases did the proportion of dismissals arising from initial leave grants from the 'high' group of judges marginally exceed that for the other two judge groups.

The above data relate only to cases granted leave on the initial application. As shown in Diagram 8D, once cases granted leave on a renewed application are added in, there is only a small and inconsistent variation in the proportions of applications initially considered by the 'high', 'medium', and 'low' groups of judges that were eventually dismissed at a substantive hearing. In both the 1987 and 1988 samples, however, more than half of the applications that were originally considered by the 'low' group of judges and were eventually dismissed at a substantive hearing had been granted leave following a renewal to another judge.

Table 8.7

Initial Leave Applications for Judicial Review, 1987-1988 and 1st Quarter of 1991 by Group of Judge Considering Application and Outcome of Case Where Leave Granted on Initial Application

Application Year	1987			1988			1991 (January - March)		
Judge Group	High	Medium	Low	High	Medium	Low	High	Medium	Low
No of Initial Leave Applications	293	528	253	404	370	277	64	121	160
No. Granted on Initial Application	192	273	85	265	195	86	42	61	63
% Resulting in									
Successful at Full Hearing	17	19	30	31	24	41	14	31	19
Dismissed at Full Hearing	27	31	25	22	28	17	24	20	22
No Hearing	57	52	45	47	48	42	62	49	59

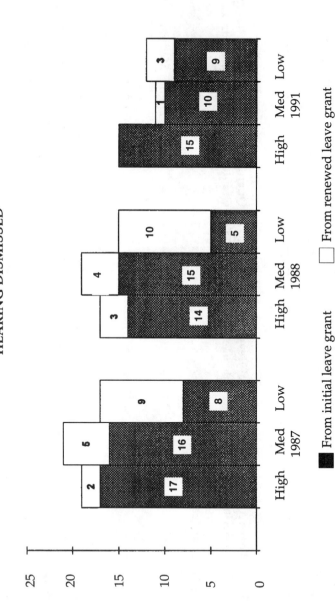

Diagram 8D

Applications to Seek Leave for Judicial Review 1987-1988 and 1st Quarter of 1991 by Group of Judge Making Initial Leave Decision and Percentage of Applications Resulting in

HEARING DISMISSED

Applications successful at full hearing

Much of the concern expressed to the Law Commission over inconsistencies between judges in their decisions on leave probably stemmed from a perception that applicants whose cases are assigned initially to judges with low leave grant rates thereby have much less chance of eventually having a day in court and obtaining a favourable outcome. Our data suggest, however, that this popular view may not be accurate. As shown in Diagram 8E, 16% of applicants in 1987 whose cases were initially considered for leave by the 'low' group of judges eventually obtained a favourable judgment, as compared to only 13% of those whose leave applications were first considered by both the 'high' and 'medium' group of judges. In 1988, 19% of the applications first considered by the 'low' group of judges were eventually successful at full hearing, as compared with 22% of those on which the initial leave decision was taken by one of the 'high' group of judges and 15% of those initially assigned to the 'medium' group. It was only in the first quarter of 1991 sample that popular expectation was borne out, with just 8% of the applications first considered for leave by the 'low' group of judges eventually obtaining a favourable judgment. This compared with 11% of applications initially dealt with by the 'high' group and 17% of those originally dealt with by the 'medium' group of judges.

Summary and conclusions

Judicial review is a procedure that allows very considerable scope for individual judges to exercise their discretion. The discretionary nature of the process stems both from the 'open textured' nature of the legal doctrine and from the way in which the procedure is organised. As we have seen, although the criteria for leave have generally become tighter over recent years, they are still open to differing interpretations by individual judges sitting on their own. The growth in the caseload has probably widened the scope for discretion still further, especially as it has necessitated the assignment of more judges to sit regularly hearing judicial review applications.[22]

In order to counteract the tendency toward greater degrees of inconsistency that growth in the caseload has entailed, the Law

---

22 Considerable concern was expressed to the Law Commission that any further dispersion of judicial review cases to a wider group of judges or decentralisation of the procedure to courts outside London would lead to a decline both in the quality and the consistency of decision-making in this field. See Law Commission Report No 226, *op cit*, Appendix C.

Diagram 8E

Applications to Seek Leave for Judicial Review 1987-1988 and 1st Quarter of 1991 by Group of Judge Making Initial Leave Decision and Percentage of Applications Resulting in

HEARING ALLOWED

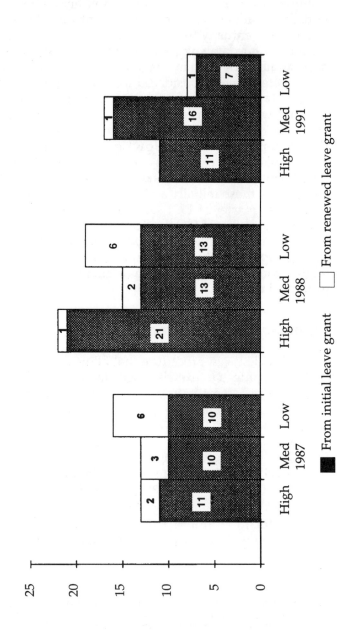

Commission placed a good deal of emphasis on the idea of a relatively small 'cadre' of administrative law judges to whom the bulk of cases would be assigned, at least for the initial consideration of leave on the basis of written submissions. Our data do not indicate, however, that assigning larger numbers of cases to fewer judges will necessarily result in greater consistency in decision-making; judges who undertook very considerable numbers of cases were found at both the high and low ends of the scale of leave grant rates. Nor does the evidence support the proposition that as judges gain more experience of judicial review, their views on how to exercise their discretion tend to converge. Indeed, one of the most interesting findings to emerge from our data, other than very wide variations between judges in their leave grant rates, is that individual judges were each remarkably consistent from one year to the next in their positioning in the leave grant rankings. As we have indicated, this may suggest that differences between judges in their leave decisions are less a factor of regularity and experience than of attitude and approach to the substantive issues involved in such decisions.

As well as recommending the use of a smaller cadre of judges at the leave stage, the Law Commission has put forward proposals to codify the criteria for granting leave and also proposed that written reasons should accompany every refusal of leave. In the previous chapter we were critical of the 'serious issue' test on the grounds that it appears to add a new dimension of uncertainty. The Law Commission seems also to be recommending that some of the procedural checks on inconsistency in decision-making at the leave stage should be weakened. Our data confirm that renewals are important in levelling out at least some of the initial and very wide variations between judges in their rates of granting leave. During the periods covered by our research, the effectiveness of the renewal process in reducing the effects of inconsistencies in judicial decision-making might have been greater had it not been for the apparent reluctance of applicants, turned down once for leave, to renew their applications again; and this reluctance can only be exacerbated if they are to face greater risks of costs orders against them on unsuccessful renewals in the future.

Despite the effect of renewals, it remained the case that applicants whose cases were assigned (apparently on a random basis) initially to one of the judges who had a less generous approach to granting leave were much less likely in the end to obtain leave or be able to pursue their applications beyond this preliminary stage. Paradoxically, however, these applicants appeared to have roughly the same likelihood of their cases reaching a substantive hearing and either obtaining a favourable judgment or having their application dismissed, as those whose cases were considered at the initial leave stage by other judges. Of course, applicants whose cases went first to the 'low' group of judges were more often required to go to the trouble of renewing their leave applications before being allowed to proceed, but there is no indication from our data that this tended to prejudice their cases at the substantive hearing stage.

The apparent contradiction between the above findings – that applicants whose cases were initially considered by the 'low' group of judges having less overall chance of obtaining leave to proceed to a full hearing but no less of a chance of actually reaching such a hearing – is explained by withdrawals. In other words, applications that were considered initially for leave by judges in the 'high' or 'medium' groups had a greater propensity to be withdrawn following the grant of leave or otherwise not to reach a full hearing on their merits. It is possible, of course, that the judges in these groups were more inclined to grant leave to weak cases which subsequently had to be withdrawn, although it has to be said that there was no evidence to support the conclusion that they were being soft in applying the leave criteria in terms of their cases having less overall success at the substantive hearing stage. Another possibility is that the process of an application being refused leave once and then obtaining it on a renewal may itself encourage the parties, especially respondents, to contest the matter through to a full hearing, rather than considering an early settlement.

Many of these questions will only be resolved through further research, looking in particular at the process of settlement in judicial review litigation. Our findings on the extent of the variations between individual judges in their initial leave decisions may have confirmed widely held perceptions among users of judicial review of the process being a lottery. In some respects, that impression is reinforced by the further analysis presented here, covering the impact of variations in leave decisions on the eventual outcome of judicial review applications. There is no simple equation to be drawn between varying degrees of success or failure that applicants might receive before different judges and the ultimate outcome of their applications. In part, the unpredictability of the judicial review process, even beyond the leave stage, is due to further opportunities afforded to applicants to renew their applications, but it is also likely to have a great deal to do with the fact that judicial review litigation is itself only one element in a wider and even more complex process of negotiation and political bargaining between the parties.

Chapter 9

General Conclusions

The primary aim of this report has been to provide an up-to-date, factual overview of the present operation of the judicial review procedure in England and Wales and of related aspects of legal aid. This edition of the report is published at a crucial juncture in the development of both judicial review and legal aid. The Law Commission has completed the major enquiry into judicial review it initiated in 1991 and published a report containing a wide range of proposals for the further reform of the procedure.[1] The Government's Green Paper on legal aid[2] also heralds a period of fundamental reform in this field which may have profound effects on the availability of legal advice and representation to those seeking to challenge government decisions by way of judicial review. Finally, Lord Woolf has now published interim proposals for general reform of civil procedure which may have implications both for the way in which judicial review operates and the more activist and managerial role that judges are expected to perform in all forms of civil adjudication.[3]

Legal practitioners are often sceptical about the value of the type of empirical analysis presented here, claiming that 'statistics don't tell the whole story' and are subject to various limitations,[4] not least that they may not reflect the most recent, practical working of the procedure under examination.[5] The provision and analysis of empirical data are a

---

1   Law Commission Report No 226, *op cit*.

2   *Legal Aid – Targeting Need, op cit*.

3   *Access to Justice, op cit*.

4   In this respect, the comments of Lord Justice Simon Brown to a conference held on Law Commission Report No 226 at the University of Warwick on 3 December 1994 may be instructive. He was remarking on statistics contained in Annex 1 of the Law Commission Report relating to inconsistencies between individual judges in grants of leave (see Chapter 8 for further details). He queried: 'How reliable ... are the bare statistics ... One cannot say for sure but I suspect that they give, quite innocently I hasten to say, a somewhat misleading impression of disparities between individual judges. Not only do individual cases vary greatly, but there are quite different categories of work and one judge may deal with larger numbers of one category than others ... Or a judge may be sent a large group of cases raising identical or almost identical points and his decisions with regard to these may well distort the overall picture of his rate of grant.' In fact, as noted in Chapter 8, our data indicate that inconsistencies between judges in grants of leave tend to persist across different subject areas and are not explained by 'block bookings' of cases of particular types.

5   Although data from our research date back to 1991 and earlier, more recent official statistics cited through this report tend to indicate that most of the trends identified have continued since then, with the one major exception of the considerable improvements made in reducing delays in completing substantive hearings of applications for judicial review.

necessary first step, however, to understanding how the system is actually operating, identifying pressure points, and evaluating the potential for effective reform. A particular value of our data is that they highlight the need to see judicial review as an overall process. This broader perspective is sometimes unavailable to practitioners and judges who naturally tend to focus on aspects of the system with which they come into regular contact. As we have seen, representation in judicial review by solicitors is very fragmented, with only a few firms undertaking sizeable numbers of cases within particular specialist fields, whilst most others only become involved in the procedure occasionally. It is also unlikely that many solicitors will regularly represent both applicants and respondents. This is probably less true of barristers, but they may lack direct knowledge of many of the pre-court aspects of the process, such as obtaining legal aid.[6] The data on judicial sittings indicates that judges' experience of the procedure also varies a great deal, even among those on the nominated list of Crown Office judges.

This is not to say that practitioners and judges are reluctant to cite statistics when putting forward views on judicial review. In this respect one of the 'facts' about judicial review most frequently referred to is that the procedure has been subject to an 'explosion' in its use over the past decade, which in turn tends to be taken as evidence of its growing importance, but is also linked to procedural problems such as delay in the processing of cases. The trouble with such statistics is not so much that they are incorrect as over-simplified. As a result, misleading impressions and inferences as well as wrong policy conclusions may be drawn from them. Our research indicates that the reality of judicial review is far more complex, and that the policy solutions to periodic 'crises' in the procedure may well lie in very different directions to those which are often proposed.

All the evidence suggests that any 'explosion' in the use of judicial review has been limited to two fields of activity in particular, immigration and homelessness. Given the fundamental character of the rights at stake in both of these areas and the very large numbers of persons affected annually by adverse decisions by the government bodies concerned, it is arguable that even the present number of several hundred judicial review applications each year relating respectively to immigration or homelessness represents a low level of use. Certainly in both fields there are very heavy concentrations of applicants in London, where the judicial review procedure is itself

---

6 Most legal textbooks on judicial review, many of them written by barristers, are confined to the formal court processes. For an exception to this, see The Public Law Project, *An Applicant's Guide to Judicial Review* (1995) London: Sweet & Maxwell.

centralised, and this may indicate an under-utilisation of the procedure in these fields in other parts of the country. No doubt, the provision of alternative rights of independent appeal for those denied accommodation under homelessness legislation, as has been proposed by the Law Commission,[7] could lessen the pressures on judicial review. The lesson from immigration, however, is that the relationship between the creation of statutory appeals and levels of demand for judicial review is complex and may depend on whether alternative appeal rights are accessible[8] and perceived to be administered in an independent and robust manner. The alternative course of weakening the substantive rights of the homeless to public accommodation, as canvassed in the Government's recent White Paper on housing[9] may also prove ineffective in reducing demand for judicial review and could just as well increase it as pressure groups and the growing numbers of specialist legal practitioners in this field attempt to use the courts to challenge aspects of any new legislation.

In other fields the problem with judicial review is certainly not one of over-use. Growth in the number of applications other than in immigration, homelessness and crime has been relatively modest during the past decade. The limited use of judicial review is demonstrated not only by the relatively small overall number of applications outside of these 'core' areas. It is also shown in the limited extent to which judicial review has penetrated into the practices of solicitors in private practice and into law centres, and in the infrequent appearance of pressure groups directly as applicants. It is further indicated by the surprisingly low rates of use of judicial review to challenge the actions of most central government departments. Outside the fields of immigration and housing, it is used far more readily against local authorities than central government. Although these are early days, our data reveal little evidence that the drive toward privatisation and contracting out of public services has resulted in any significant increase in the use of judicial review against either the new executive agencies or private organisations performing public functions.

There are lessons to be drawn here about the constitutional significance of judicial review. Judicial review is often depicted as a weapon in the hands of the citizen to be used against the over-mighty powers of central government, and it has certainly performed this role

---

7   Law Commission Report No 226, *op cit*, para 2.26.

8   In this respect the lack of availability of legal aid for representation before administrative tribunals may be a critical limitation on the effectiveness of any alternative remedy.

9   *Our Future Homes – Opportunity, Choice, Responsibility*, London: HMSO, 1995.

in a number of recent, high profile cases.[10] Our data suggest, however, that over the past decade it has been used more often as a weapon to further limit the autonomy of local government rather than as a constraint on the power of the central state. Moreover, we have yet to see whether judicial review will become a remedy for those seeking to challenge or regulate the powers of the new generation of non-departmental public bodies.

The limited use of judicial review in many areas in which it is potentially available suggests that access to the procedure is a greater problem than is usually assumed. The evidence on representation shows that judicial review and the use of the courts to challenge the actions of government has yet to become a standard element in the culture and practices of most solicitors or other legal services outlets. This in turn may be a factor in explaining the apparently wide variations in the use of the procedure from one part of the country to another. It seems unlikely that future legal aid reforms involving a switch from case-by-case funding to a system of bulk contracts with smaller numbers of solicitors' firms offering legally-aided services, will encourage wider public or geographical access to judicial review.

There is a remarkably similar pattern in demand for legal aid for potential judicial reviews, both in the limited spread of subject matters and in geographical concentrations of applicants, as are apparent in the data on applications for leave to seek judicial review made to court. On the other hand, the volume of applications made for legal aid is much greater than the number of cases actually reaching the courts. This again suggests that present levels of use of judicial review in the 'core' subjects, such as immigration and homelessness, represent only the 'tip of the iceberg' of potential litigation.

Although legal aid may not in general act as a significant barrier to access to judicial review, the evidence indicates very wide variations in decision-making under the legal aid merits test between different subjects and parts of the country. The criteria for granting legal aid, certainly in terms of the individualised basis on which they have traditionally been applied by the legal aid authorities, also appear to be at variance with the purposes of judicial review as a supervisory jurisdiction operating in the wider public interest. This would appear to adversely affect access to the procedure for certain types of applicant and case. These would include potential judicial reviews

---

10 Most notably, the ruling that Government overseas aid payments to the Pergau Dam project in Malaysia were unlawful in *R v Secretary of State for Foreign Affairs, ex parte World Development Movement Ltd* [1995] 1 All ER 611, and that the introduction of a new non-statutory compensation scheme for victims of crime was an abuse of Parliament in *R v Secretary of State for the Home Department, ex parte Fire Brigades Union* [1995] 2 All ER 244.

seeking to protect primarily procedural rights or with only small sums at stake and those involving the interests of much wider groups than the particular applicants. The Law Commission has endorsed the principle that it should be possible for the legal aid authorities to have regard to the public, and not just the individual interest in a potential judicial review when deciding whether it is reasonable to provide legal aid. It is unclear, however, how this recommendation would fit in with the proposals set out in the legal aid Green Paper to reform the legal aid merits test and possibly to delegate its application to individual solicitors providing services under bulk contracts.[11]

The current cost rules and the substantial financial risks they generate for unsuccessful applicants who are not legally-aided undoubtedly act as a major deterrent to many potential users. This problem affects pressure groups as much as it does individuals. It would therefore be unrealistic to see the recent trend toward the liberalisation of rules of standing in judicial review, and the Law Commission's proposals for institutionalising this in new rules,[12] as sufficient in themselves to ensure that judicial reviews involving a wider public interest reach court. Indeed, it may be that without changes in the way legal aid is determined in such cases, more liberal rules of standing will have little effect in opening up access to the procedure in public interest cases.

Another possibility considered by the Law Commission would be to alter the current cost rules so that once leave (or 'preliminary consideration') had been granted and the case had thereby been endorsed by the court as raising a matter of public interest, the applicant would no longer be faced with the risk of having to pay the respondent's costs if unsuccessful in the substantive application.[13] The Law Commission did not adopt this as a recommendation in its final report, however, preferring the less radical proposal that judges should have the discretion to award costs in public interest cases out of central funds.[14] Because such awards would be discretionary and be made only at the end of cases, they would be unlikely to reduce the disincentive toward starting judicial reviews that results from the current costs rules. Also, the Law Commission itself has endorsed the use of the risk of paying the respondent's costs in order to discourage applicants from renewing leave applications refused on paper to an oral hearing.

---

11 *Legal Aid – Targeting Need, op cit*, para 7.7–7.9.
12 Law Commission Report No 226 *op cit*, paras 5.16–5.22.
13 Law Commission Consultation Paper No 126, *op cit*, paras 11.1–11.14.
14 Law Commission Report No 226, *op cit*, para 10.6.

This latter proposal is an aspect of what we have termed the 'managerialism' that underpins many of the Law Commission's recommendations, not least in respect of the leave procedure. In fact, the concern to manage and to exercise judicial control over the size of the caseload has been a (mostly) unstated factor in the trend toward stricter application of the leave criteria, and higher rates of refusal of leave, for a number of years. It has also been evident in shifts in the judicial interpretation of the leave criteria and changes in administrative procedure, such as the progressive move away from the requirement that all leave applications had to be considered in open court toward paper applications becoming the norm. What is perhaps new about the Law Commission's proposals is both the explicit acknowledgement of the use of leave as a tool of caseload management and the recognition that administrators in the Crown Office, as well as judges, may have a role to play in assigning cases to particular procedural routes. This raises important issues concerned with whether access to the courts is to be determined on the basis of legal principle or as a matter of administration.[15]

It is clear from the data that leave (unlike legal aid in the generality of cases) is a significant filter and one which it is becoming increasingly difficult for applicants to pass through. Furthermore, the evidence also indicates that there is a substantial risk that potentially arguable applications are being prematurely rejected. Our research does not enable us to assess directly the quality of individual leave decisions. The statistical evidence we have presented does suggest, however, that the leave test is not producing consistent results, whether between various types of applicant, subject matter or different time periods, or in relation to the decisions of different judges. This is especially so when leave applications are considered only on the papers, as will become standard procedure if and when the Law Commission's proposals are implemented.[16]

The present checks and balances built into the system, in particular the unfettered right of applicants to renew applications for leave, have had an important role in protecting applicants from the vagaries of leave decision-making, although they have not eliminated completely the discrepancies in leave grant rates. The effectiveness of renewals as a corrective to uncertainties in the application of the leave criteria is likely to diminish if applicants are deterred from renewing leave applications by the fear of incurring a costs penalty. Nor will the more explicit statement in the rules of the criteria for granting leave or the

---

15   These issues are further discussed in Sunkin, 'The Problematic State of Access to Judicial Review', *op cit*.

16   Law Commission Report No 226, *op cit*, para 5.11.

provision of reasons for its refusal in individual cases, as again recommended by the Law Commission, necessarily counter-balance the likely decline in the effectiveness of renewals. These measures are to be welcomed in themselves, although the Law Commission's formulation of the leave criteria and, in particular, its suggestion that applicants show that there is a 'serious issue' to be tried, runs the risk of contributing to a further uncertainty and to a potential tightening of the test which applicants have to pass in order to gain access to judicial review.

There are two more general criticisms that can be made of the Law Commission's proposals on leave. First, in seeking to make the procedure more certain and at the same time a more effective tool of judicial management of the system, the Law Commission has risked tipping the balance too much in favour of respondents. The proposals for respondents to make written representations on leave applications under a 'request for further information' could, if widely used by judges, lead to a form of *inter partes* summary judgment, without compensating advantages for applicants in the provision of better and fuller discovery from respondents. Yet, all the available evidence suggests that the present procedures already operate as a disincentive to public authorities to review their decisions at an early stage with a view to reaching settlements with prospective applicants for judicial review. This problem will be exacerbated if the criteria for leave are tightened or respondents are allowed additional procedural opportunities to intervene and to openly contest the granting of leave. Equally, any transfer of judicial review out of the High Court and into a possibly less authoritative (and cheaper) jurisdiction, as has been proposed for homelessness cases, might reduce the current incentives on both applicants and respondents to settle, even after the grant of leave, and therefore be counter-productive.

The second criticism of the Law Commission's proposals on leave is that they adopt too narrow a perspective, concentrating too much on the effects of the procedure on subsequent stages of judicial review, and giving insufficient attention to the inter-relationship between leave and the wider litigation strategies and processes of settlement between the parties to judicial review. Our research indicates that very substantial number of withdrawals of judicial review applications take place before a leave decision has been obtained and even more so after it has been granted. Such withdrawals are as important as refusals of leave in regulating the flow of cases through the system and reducing the overall workload of the courts in conducting full substantive hearings. This raises the question of whether current procedures are doing enough to encourage early settlement of disputes before judicial review litigation is embarked upon. Research in other fields[17] has shown that processes of settlement entail very complex inter-relationships between the litigation strategies of the parties and the rules and procedures involved in the particular area of law. We clearly need to know a great deal more about how settlements are achieved in the various fields of judicial review. This is especially relevant in respect of homelessness applications, since this is the subject area where the rate of settlement is most significant at present.

We have suggested that reforms should be focused on the pre-leave aspects of the judicial review procedure, and in particular on providing applicants with improved rights to information from respondents on which to base their applications in the first instance (or, alternatively, to reach a settlement without the necessity even of applying for leave). In our submission, this would be a more open and possibly a more effective means of addressing the current problems of judicial review than other proposals for restricting access through the leave filter. It could also have the effect of reducing legal aid costs on judicial review applications, so many of which end in withdrawals and/or settlements but only after several hundred and even thousands of pounds have been spent on preparing the full application and obtaining leave. This would in turn contribute to the objective, set out in the legal aid Green Paper, to 'provide the most effective and economical solutions to problems in the interests of the client and the tax payer'.[18]

We have noted above how the constitutional image of judicial review, as a means of protecting the citizen from the over-mighty power of the central government, may be at variance with the reality of its role. There is, however, a further paradox in the public image and perception of judicial review. It is seen, on the one hand, as upholding the rule of law against arbitrary state action, yet at the same time the procedure itself is widely perceived as operating in a highly arbitrary and inconsistent manner. The Law Commission has now confirmed our own findings, reported earlier, of very wide discrepancies in the leave grant rates of individual judges; and the further data contained in this report show that such inconsistency extends back into processes of legal aid decision-making. The fact that we can find no direct correlation between the low rate at which some judges grant leave on initial applications and the final outcome of cases, while in some senses offering reassurance to applicants, nevertheless lends further credence to the notion of judicial review being a lottery.

---

17 See H Genn *Hard Bargaining: Out of Court Settlement in Personal Injury Actions* (1987) Oxford: Clarendon Press.

18 *Legal Aid – Targeting Need, op cit,* para 4.2.

For some commentators, inconsistency in judicial review decisions is considered either not to be problematic or an inevitable consequence of judicial independence. Lord Justice Simon Brown, in commenting on the Law Commission's statistics on variations in leave decisions between judges, has stated that:

> Perhaps in the public law field above all others ... some significant degree of disparity is to be expected. Why? Because in what is in any event a somewhat imprecise area of substantive jurisprudence, one is deciding essentially a question of arguability. How can one begin to define the point at which an uncompromising argument becomes in truth unarguable? What to one judge will seem unconvincing but arguable to another will seem simply hopeless. No doubt it depends principally on how knowledgable, confident and decisive the individual judge may be. But there can never be uniformity in the distribution of these qualities.[19]

Our research certainly calls into question how far the system for nominated judges contributes to consistency in the development of this area of the law. The range of difference between judges, at least so far as their decisions on leave are concerned, is already very wide, and it may be that the use of a larger pool of High Court judges, whether in London or on circuit, to hear judicial review cases would further exacerbate this problem. On the other hand, it might contribute to a more efficient disposal of judicial review business, without adding significantly to current levels of inconsistency or necessitating other damaging restrictions on public access to the procedure.

The difficulty with dismissing inconsistency as inevitable is that judicial review is not merely 'a somewhat imprecise area of substantive jurisprudence' but one which deals with questions of great political sensitivity and constitutional significance, as well as affecting the vital interests of citizens. To allow a public perception of inconsistency and arbitrariness in decision-making to persist therefore leaves the procedures and the judges who operate it open to charges of political bias, whether as being over-protective of public authorities or 'anti-government'. If notions of judicial political bias gain ground, this could eventually threaten the very jurisdiction and jurisprudence that the judges have crafted from the common law to enable them to exercise supervision over the legality of government action. Any such threat would be detrimental to the individual citizens and to the notion of democracy under the rule of law. For this reason alone, the Law Commission was surely right to point to need for greater

---

19 Speech to Public Law Project – University of Warwick Conference on the Future of Judicial Review, 3 December 1994.

consistency in decision-making as one of the key challenges facing reformers in this field. Although our research does not itself indicate easy solutions to this problem, hopefully it will serve to inform further debate and help to avoid unintended and damaging consequences of ill-considered changes, whether to judicial review procedures or in related areas such as legal aid.

Appendix 1

Judicial Review – Official Statistics

Table A

Applications for Leave Received, Allowed and Refused / Not Proceeded With, 1981-1994

	Total Applications Received			Allowed		Refused/Not Proceeded With	
	No	% increase from previous year	from 1981	No	%	No	%
1981	533	-	-	376	71	157	29
1982	685	29	29	468	68	217	32
1983	850	24	59	621	69	229	25
1984	915	8	72	701	77	214	23
1985	1169	28	119	787	67	382	33
1986	1189	2	123	627	54	528	46
1987	1529	29	186	767	59	532	41
1988	1229	-20	131	695	55	578	45
1989	1580	29	196	905	59	645	41
1990	2129	35	299	902	52	823	48
1991	2089	-2	292	923	50	929	50
1992	2439	17	358	1123	47	1268	53
1993	2886	18	441	1049	47	1204	53
1994	3208	11	502	1260	37	2129	63

Source: Civil Judicial Statistics (1981-85), Judicial Statistics (1986-94) and Crown Office

Table B

Substantive Hearings Allowed and Dismissed and Cases Withdrawn, 1981-1994

	Total Applications Determined	Allowed	Dismissed	% Successful	Cases Withdrawn
1981	271	119	152	44	n/a
1982	298	148	150	50	n/a
1983	311	162	149	52	n/a
1984	380	187	197	48	n/a
1985	501	211	290	42	n/a
1986	404	178	226	44	n/a
1987	506	216	290	43	n/a
1988	409	177	232	43	293
1989	387	187	200	48	179
1990	448	282	166	63	88
1991	636	434	202	68	168
1992	504	262	242	52	366
1993	488	236	252	48	421
1994	747	441	306	59	724

Source: Civil Judicial Statistics (1981-85), Judicial Statistics (1986-94) and Crown Office

Table C

Applications for Leave in Selected Subject Areas and Proportion of Total Leave Applications, 1987-1994

	Immigration		Crime		Homeless	
	No	% of all leave applications	No	% of all leave applications	No	% of all leave applications
1987	697	44	194	13	n/a	n/a
1988	329	29	142	12	n/a	n/a
1989	419	27	256	16	n/a	n/a
1990	569	27	620	29	n/a	n/a
1991	506	24	314	15	n/a	n/a
1992	544	22	334	14	n/a	n/a
1993	668	23	472	16	447	15
1994	935	29	321	10	447	14

Appendix 2

Crown Office Data Sources and Definitions

Data selection, origins and quality

Given that our principal aim was to provide a comprehensive body of empirical information on the current use of judicial review (with special emphasis upon changes in the pattern of use over recent years), there was only one source for the information required: the Crown Office in London. The Crown Office lies at the heart of what, in administrative terms at least, is a remarkably centralised procedure. Not only must all applications for judicial review in England and Wales be lodged there, but this is also the place where the records are maintained, updated and, once a case is completed, stored indefinitely.

At the Crown Office we had access to 'raw' rather than 'pre-digested' information. Our first source was the so-called 'Blue Book' – basically an annual register of all applications (including judicial reviews) lodged with the Crown Office. As applications are lodged the date is recorded and they are assigned a number according to the order and year in which they arrive (eg all 1987 applications would be noted along the following lines, 1/87, 2/87 ... 1150/87, etc). Also listed are the names of the litigants, representatives and judges together with the date and result of any judgment or withdrawals. Amongst other things, it is this source which helped us establish the size of our universe.

Our second source of information was the 'card index' compiled by and for the use of Crown Office lawyers. It was neither as comprehensive nor as up to date as the 'Blue Book', but for those cases which it did cover a summary of the substance of each was provided.

Finally, and most importantly of all, there were the case files themselves. All files may be divided into two types: 'live' (ie current) and 'dead' (ie closed) cases. The essential difference between them is that the former files have not been stripped of bulky submissions which, for reasons of storage and convenience of handling, is what happens to closed cases after a certain period of time. As far as the collection of information for the database was concerned, detailed submissions were regarded as being beyond the scope of the project. Instead, collection of material from the files was confined to the following case variables:

(1) case number;

(2) date of inception;

(3) subject matter;

(4) type of applicant;

(5) type of respondent;

(6) name of legal representative (if not represented in person);

(7) judge at each stage of a case's progress;

(8) nature of outcome at each stage;

(9) corresponding date at each stage.

The present project built upon computer records of all judicial review applications between 1987 and 1989 previously compiled by Sunkin and his research assistant. These records were checked, updated and re-categorised. Given financial and time constraints it was not possible to bring the computer records up to date for the whole of the subsequent period. Instead, a compromise was reached whereby it was decided to select a period (in this case the first quarter of 1991) which on the one hand, would provide us with as up to date an insight into the present situation without at the same time making it so up to date as to render virtually all cases live and therefore of limited value.

Operational definitions

If initial data selection proved a relatively simple task, then our choice of operational definitions proved anything but that. Certain categories such as case number, dates, legal representatives and judges were both self-evident and self-defining. Other categories in particular: subject matter, respondent and (albeit to a much lesser extent) applicant, were far from self-defining. In other words, they were not mutually exclusive categories with readily identifiable borders and possessing specific values. A subject, for example, may possess multiple identities and therefore defy simple categorisation. Putting it into any one single category, as we eventually had to do, necessarily entails stripping it of other competing subject properties and in this sense should be regarded as a matter of judgment. What we had to do then was to try and avoid arbitrariness in our selections. One way of preserving case specifics was to note the secondary characteristics of each. These secondary characteristics would later prove useful in identifying why there was a rise or fall in a broad subject area or, where that level had remained constant from one year to the next, whether there had been a substantial change in the nature of its composition. Similarly, when it came to respondents and applicants we had to develop a series of categorisations capable of embracing the diversity of the material whilst at the same time providing a meaningful structure through which it could be understood.

Subject definition

The process by which we arrived at our subject definitions was essentially evolutionary. Instead of imposing a series of definitions we asked ourselves 'what was the central subject (rather than legal) issue that gave rise to this case in the first place?'. Although much of the time part of the answer was relatively simple and fell into what eventually became one of our main categories (eg immigration, housing, criminal matters, etc), at the same time we recorded secondary or even tertiary characteristics. Thus, to give a specific example, not only is there a category for immigration, but in some of the immigration cases it can be seen that the application was made by a Tamil and that he or she was seeking asylum. This sort of case is relatively simple to categorise. Other cases are more complex because they are either difficult to categorise or they straddle categories. Is a case that concerns water quality a public health, environmental or pollution issue? The answer is debatable. At a certain stage in the research, we had developed two categories, one concerning the police and another concerning matters of discipline. We later came across a case that arose from a police disciplinary hearing. Into which of the categories should we put this case? Eventually we opted to put it under the discipline category (with the secondary characteristic as police) because we felt that this constituted its central core.

Respondent definition

The process by which we arrived at our respondent definitions was more conceptual in character than our subject definitions. Not only did we ask the question 'what is the name of the respondent organisation?', to which the answer was quite specific, but we also asked a more functional question 'what kind or organisation is it?' These two questions were directly reflected in our coding which was not composed of primary or secondary characteristics (as with the subjects), but instead was divided into two distinct parts: (a) the type of organisation; and (b) its name.

Dealing with the latter point first, there were literally hundreds of named respondents in any one year even though certain individual respondents (like the Home Office) appeared on hundreds of occasions and even though we subsumed many of the individual respondents under generic rather than specific names (eg a local authority in Wales is coded in exactly the same manner as a local authority in England). Strictly speaking, of course, it means that on occasions there is an element of functionality in our names category.

The relative simplicity of this exercise was in sharp contrast to the process of categorising our organisations according to the type of function they exercised. We asked ourselves a number of interrelated questions: What does the organisation do? What is the source of its power? What kind of power does it exercise? In whose name does it exercise that power? To whom is it accountable? The difficulty in answering these questions is illustrated by the fact that they are quite closely related (although clearly not identical) to a question that is constantly addressed by the courts themselves and over which there remains much debate, namely: what makes this organisation open to judicial review? It is only by answering some or all of the above questions that the judiciary can decide whether an organisation is reviewable or not.

We came to the conclusion that four broad types of power were being exercised: (a) governmental (whether central or local), (b) judicial, (c) public, and (d) non-governmental.

In many respects this said as much about who or what we thought was exercising the power as the kind of power itself. Indeed, that was translated into the five respondent categories we eventually chose, ie:

(1) central government;

(2) local government;

(3) non-departmental public bodies;

(4) non-governmental organisations; and

(5) courts and tribunals.

In no way can or should these categories be regarded as mutually exclusive. We soon recognised that these organisations formed part of a public-private continuum. At one end of the scale were public organisations, the most formal expressions of which were central and local government entities, as well as the judiciary. At the other extreme were private limited companies and groups like the Jockey Club. In between, however, there were a myriad of other organisations with characteristics that frequently overlapped. Below we set out our five categories.

Central government

We understood such organisations or individuals to exercise powers usually conferred on them by Act of Parliament and to be accountable for their actions in Parliament. This includes all central government departments and Ministers of the Crown. Less obvious are certain recently created regulatory groups like the Director General of Gas Supply and the Director General of Telecommunications otherwise known as Ofgas and Oftel respectively. Also included in our list were prison governors since they are directly answerable to the Home Secretary. Given moves towards the creation of so-called executive agencies, certain groups were dropped from this category and moved to another during the course of this research, eg the Director General of Ordnance Survey.

Local government

These are organisations or individuals which exercise powers conferred on them by Act of Parliament but which carry out executive (ie policy making and implementation) functions on a regional or local rather than national basis and, in a large number of instances, receive a significant proportion of their funding through local taxation. The most obvious examples of these are local government authorities such as county and borough councils as well as local education authorities. Other groups covered by our survey include the London Fire and Civil Defence Authority (which used to receive its funds from the GLC but which now receives a portion of funds from the Home Office (on the civil defence side) and a portion from local government (on the fire side)) and the Inner London Education Authority as it then was.

Non-departmental public bodies (NDPBs)

These organisations are notoriously difficult to define (the very term NDPB begins with a negative suggesting what these bodies are not rather than what they actually are). Amongst these institutions are non-ministerial departments, management boards and executive agencies which carry out a range of administrative, executive and regulatory functions conferred on them by central government. In the last analysis it is this which renders them (to varying degrees) answerable to a Minister who in turn is answerable to Parliament.

The sorts of bodies which we encountered and in our view clearly fall within this category are: the Certification Officer for Trade Unions; the Drug Licensing Authority; Legal Aid Area Committees as currently operating under the Legal Aid Board; the Monopolies and Mergers Commission; the residuary bodies created in the aftermath of recent changes in local government; the British Broadcasting Corporation and nationalised industries such as the British Railways Board and (at the time of our study) the Electricity Board.

Non-governmental organisations (NGOs)

NGOs enjoy an advantage over NDPBs in that they lie at the end of the public-private spectrum instead of the middle. Essentially what we are talking about when we use the term NGOs are privately constituted organisations – be they companies, professional, trade and voluntary associations, or charities – that may or may not make a profit. In formal terms at least, they are primarily answerable to their members rather than to Ministers or Parliament, although we do recognise that the tentacles of government – be they through contracts, market regulation, fiscal intervention, the legislative process, etc – may exercise a highly significant if not determinant role over them. The symbiotic relationship of private limited companies in the defence sector provide perhaps the most powerful illustration of this fact; but even such supposedly autonomous organisations as charities (a large number of whose activities are already underwritten by central and local government) may find themselves stepping into the breach as the welfare state is contracted. Naturally, it was into the NGO category that we placed recently privatised organisations like British Gas and what later became known as British Airports Authority plc.

Courts and tribunals

Essentially we understood these bodies primarily to exercise judicial functions. They included county, Crown, juvenile, Central Criminal and magistrates' courts; bodies like the Immigration Appeal Tribunal, Social Security Appeal Tribunal, Ministry of Defence Appeal Tribunal, Mental Health Commissioners, VAT Tribunal, Employment Appeal Tribunal and Industrial Tribunal. All these bodies are charged with interpreting the meaning of statutes and regulations and of adjudicating in a manner that is binding on all the parties.

Applicant definition

Our applicant categories were defined in exactly the same way as our respondent definitions ie: (1) central government; (2) local government; (3) non-departmental public bodies; (4) non-governmental organisations; and (5) courts and tribunals but with the difference that we added a sixth category, that of individual applicants. As we would expect with a procedure like judicial review, individuals turned out to be by far the largest single group of applicants.

The judicial review database

A cross section of the information which was entered into the database is shown below. There are 10 columns which, reading from left to right, list: (1) case number; (2) date of inception; (3) subject matter; (4) type of applicant; (5) type of respondent; (6) name of legal representative (if not represented in person); (7) the case number (the repetition of which is necessary in order to locate items of information which are contained on more than one line); (8) nature of the outcome at each stage; (9) corresponding date at each stage; and (10), the judge at each stage of a case's progress. Although based on actual examples from the database, the names have been changed here in order to protect the identities of individuals involved.

If we take case A/87 as an example of the kind of information that is available we can see that this application was lodged on 2 January 1987; that the subject matter 'i-at' was an immigration case concerning a Tamil seeking asylum; that the applicant concerned 'i' was an individual; that the respondent 'cg-h' was central government in the form of the Home Office; that the applicant was represented by the firm of Singh and Co; (now move to the second table and follow the row corresponding to case number A/87) under the column entitled 'action' we have the code 'adj' that tell us that this case was adjourned; the date was 13 November 1989, and the judge 'bs'. If one now looks at case number C/87, particularly in the second table, it will be seen that three sets of case numbers, dates and judges appear. This simply reflects the fact that this case went through three important stages: on 20 January 1987 it was refused at the table stage by judge 'pcm'; on 12 February 1987 leave was granted on renewal by judge 'q' whilst on 20 October 1987 at a full hearing of the substantive motion presided over by judge 'n' the application for judicial review was dismissed.

1 Cn	2 Date	3 Subject	4 Applicant	5 Respondent	6 Represented
A/87	2 Jan 1987	i-at	i	ch-h	Singh
B/87	5 Jan 1987	l	i	lg-cc	Henry Jones
C/87	5 Jan 1987	h-hp	i	lg-la	John Smith

7 Cn	8 Action	9 Date	10 Judge
A/87	adj	13 Nov 1989	bs
B/87	tr	5 Jan 1987	pcm
C/87	h-d	20 Oct 1987	n
C/87	rg	12 Feb 1987	q
C/87	tr	20 Jan 1987	pcm

Appendix 3

Sampling and Collection of Legal Aid Data

At the outset of the study in 1991, there was no information even on the number of legal aid applications received or granted by the Legal Aid Board relating to prospective judicial review cases. Nor was there any mechanism available by which judicial review legal aid applications could be readily identified from the general body of all civil legal aid application. As the Legal Aid Board was then processing 450,000 civil legal aid applications each year, over half of which related to non-matrimonial proceedings, and it was anticipated that only a very small proportion of these would involve judicial review proceedings, this lack of basic data constituted a major methodological challenge to the research.

To overcome this problem, it was arranged through the Head Office of the Legal Aid Board in London for a list of current applications relating to judicial review cases to be routinely collected by officers in each of the 13 Area offices beginning in May 1991. The aim was that, when research fieldwork began in early 1992, there would be available lists of all relevant applications extending back over at least a six month period. However, once in the field it became apparent that the reliability of the lists compiled by the Area offices was extremely variable.[1] On the other hand, it also emerged that all judicial review legal aid applications were assigned to a sub-category of cases bearing a distinct reference number. Although not all applications with this reference number related to judicial review – they also included, eg those relating to High Court bail and habeas corpus proceedings – the fact that judicial review cases were coded in this way opened up the possibility of an alternative means of identifying relevant cases.

Arrangements were therefore made for the computing staff at the Legal Aid Head Office to run off special lists of applications in the relevant case category from a new computer system which had been installed at each Area office during 1991. These lists covered varying periods depending on the point when the new computer system became operational in each area. This new information was then

1   In making this comment no criticism of the Legal Aid Board or its Area Office staff is intended. The task of compiling the lists usually fell to be completed by the officers directly responsible for determining the applications, and from our own observations it was clear that these staff were frequently operating under very considerable pressure, not least in dealing with requests for emergency legal aid. We are, in fact, extremely grateful to all the staff of the Legal Aid Board who assisted us in this research.

combined with the lists previously compiled manually by Area office staff to obtain as complete a catalogue of applications potentially involving judicial review proceedings as possible. The files relating to these applications were then traced and checked to see if in fact they did involve judicial review cases, and arrangements were made to have relevant data extracted on an anonymous basis. Overall, it is estimated that the research involved the tracing of well over 2,000 files under these procedures, although not all of these related to judicial review proceedings or involved the collection of full data.

In the end, data were obtained from applications spanning a period from May 1991 up to the end of March 1992. After a review of the different lists of applications available to us, however, it became clear that it was only in the period October to December 1991 that we could be reasonably confident of having identified most of the cases relevant to our research. Outside this three month period it was clear that the lists were incomplete and could not therefore be relied upon to produce a complete or even a representative sample of legal aid judicial review applications. It was therefore decided to concentrate our resources on tracing and obtaining full data on as many of the relevant applications in the October to December 1991 period as possible. After several repeat visits to the different Area offices up to the end of 1992, a total of 905 legal aid applications relating to judicial review proceedings in this three month period were traced, although at the end of the research there were still a further 44 applications that could not be located. Of course, not all of these 44 cases would have related to judicial review proceedings. At the same time, because of the vagaries of the Legal Aid Board's then recently installed computer system, it is not possible to claim with complete confidence that every relevant application even in the October to December 1991 period was identified on the lists made available to us. All we can say is that our sample in this period was as comprehensive as could be obtained at the relevant time or (we suspect) subsequently.

In addition to the sample of 905 applications in the October to December 1991 period, full data were also collected on a further 625 legal aid applications relating to judicial review proceedings drawn from the periods prior to October 1991 (362 cases) and after the end of December 1991 (263 cases). In fact, many more judicial review cases falling outside the October to December 1991 period were successfully traced. Once a decision had been made to concentrate resources on this period, however, only limited data were obtained on other cases, especially where a grant of legal aid had been made. On the other hand, where legal aid was refused in cases falling outside the October to December 1991 period, full details of the reasons for such refusals were recorded. This information will be used in subsequent reports purely to illustrate qualitative aspects of the legal aid decision-making process, but the statistical findings contained in this report are all based on the sample of 905 applications drawn from the final three months of 1991.

Index